Forging
New Freedoms

William G. Ross

Forging
New Freedoms

Nativism, Education,
and the Constitution,
1917–1927

University of Nebraska Press
Lincoln and London

Publication of this book
was made possible by a grant
from the Andrew W. Mellon Foundation.

Library of Congress Cataloging-in-Publication Data
Ross. William G., 1954–
Forging new freedoms: nativism, education, and the
Constitution, 1917–1927 / William G. Ross.
p.   cm.
Includes bibliographical references and index.
ISBN 0-8032-3900-9 (acid-free paper)
1. Education, Bilingual—Law and legislation—
United States—History.   2. Language and languages—
Study and teaching—Law and legislation—United States—
History.   3. Native language and education—United
States—History.   I. Title.
KF4204.R67   1994
344.73′07917—dc20
[347.3047917]
93-44308   CIP

Contents

Illustrations

Acknowledgments

It is a pleasure to acknowledge some of the many persons who helped with the production of this book. Two deserve special mention. Dean Parham H. Williams, Jr., of the Cumberland School of Law of Samford University provided indispensable financial assistance in the form of summer research grants and travel stipends. His unfailing encouragement also was much appreciated. David Langum, my friend and colleague, offered invaluable advice about the book's research, writing, and production. David read the manuscript in one of its final stages and made helpful comments.

The book greatly benefited from the comments of the readers, Paul L. Murphy of the University of Minnesota and Frederick C. Luebke of the University of Nebraska. Professor Murphy wisely suggested that the manuscript would be improved by some major cutting, and Professor Luebke offered useful suggestions based on his extensive knowledge of German-American history.

Special thanks are also due to Cumberland students C. Scott Johnson and Jane Majors Hauth for their diligence in checking the accuracy of citations. I also appreciate the assistance of various Cumberland students, especially Jeffrey C. Foster, and the encouragement of my friend and colleague, Robert A. Riegert.

I also appreciate the encouragement of John R. Wunder of the University of Nebraska, who suggested that I write a book on the *Meyer* case after I published an article about *Meyer* in the *University of Cincinnati Law Review*. Thanks are also due to John W. Johnson of the University of Northern Iowa and Stephen H. Wasby of the State University of New York at Albany, who offered critiques of a paper on *Meyer* that I delivered at the 1991 symposium on Law and the Great Plains at the University of Nebraska.

I appreciate the efforts of several archivists. Roy Ledbetter, reference and research assistant at the Concordia Historical Institute in Clayton, Missouri, made the Theodore Graebner Papers and other collections available for my review, helped to obtain several of the photographs that are used in this book, and provided other useful advice and assistance during my visit to the institute. Anthony Zito, archivist of the Catholic University of America, enabled me to review the National Catholic Welfare Conference archives and other collections during my visit to Catholic University. Marsha Trimble of the University of Virginia Law Library's Special Collections likewise was very helpful during my inspection of the James C. McReynolds Papers. I also appreciate the assistance of Paul J. Eisloeffel, Betty Louden, and other librarians at the Nebraska State Historical Association, as well as the librarians at the Manuscript Division in Washington, D.C., and at the Oregon Historical Society. And I am grateful for the dedication of Cumberland librarians Professor Laurel Rebecca Clapp and Edward L. Craig, Jr.

Raymond Parpart and Clarence Heiden kindly met with me to share their personal memories of the *Meyer* case. I am grateful to the Rev. James Craver of the Zion Lutheran Church in Hampton, Nebraska, who arranged this meeting. I also thank the Rev. Hubert W. Riedel of the St. John Lutheran Church in Garfield Heights, Ohio, and the Rev. Edward Anderson of the St. John Lutheran Church in Denver, Iowa, who provided information about the Ohio and Iowa language cases, respectively. Special appreciation also is due to Martha Rahe, a member of Pastor Riedel's congregation, who made available the diary of her father, who served on the congregation's school board at the time of the Ohio language case. The Rev. Ferdinand Reith, archivist of the Nebraska District of the Lutheran Church—Missouri Synod, also provided useful documents. And I am indebted to Werner Bornemann von Loeben of Heidelberg, Germany, for unraveling the handwriting of the German-language records of the Zion Lutheran Church.

Finally, I wish to thank W. Hubert Plummer, who supported my research for my *University of Cincinnati Law Review* article concerning the historical background of the *Meyer* case when I was an attorney in his office at Oppenheimer Wolff & Donnelly in New York.

Introduction

The spire of the Zion Lutheran Church rises ninety-eight feet above the prairie amid wheat fields four miles northeast of Hampton, Nebraska. The spire and the resolute white frame edifice it crowns are incongruous sights in an area where vast expanses of farmland are broken by no other landmarks than an occasional barn, toolshed, or farmhouse. Far from being an alien intruder, however, the church is no less endemic to the prairie than are the crops, for the seeds of both were brought to Nebraska by German immigrants and planted in a soil in which they flourished. For more than a century, the Zion Church has served as the spiritual, cultural, and social center of a thriving German-American community. The three hundred souls who worship at Zion today are linked by modern transportation and communication to a wider world, but the Germans who originally settled in this region of southeastern Nebraska had little beyond the church to connect them to civilization. For them, the church provided both a vital reminder of their European heritage and a portal to their future as Americans. Zion was at once the lost homeland over which they wept and the promised land to which they had come. Like the turreted synagogues of Manhattan's pushcart district, the onion-domed Orthodox sanctuaries of the Pennsylvania coal fields, and the Roman Catholic churches that towered above the slaughterhouses of Chicago—like immigrant houses of worship everywhere—Zion provided a respite from the harsh exigencies of daily toil and a familiar setting in which immigrants could escape from the strangeness of a new land. From the large pipe organ came exquisite German hymns, the only instrumental music that most immigrants were likely to hear apart from an occasional mouth harp and the fiddle at a barn dance. The church's walnut beams, vaulted ceilings, canopied pulpit, carved stone altar, and intricate reredos were the highest forms of art that many of Zion's parishioners ever would see. And here the immigrants could educate their children, introducing them to the ways of the New World while transmitting the culture of the Fatherland.

The parishioners of Zion established a parochial school almost immediately after they formed their congregation in 1873. Within a dozen years, they had hired a permanent, full-time teacher and had erected a separate building for the school. Two years later they built a residence for the teacher, a house as large and as solid as the parsonage. Instruction was conducted in German during the first decades. But although German continued to be the exclusive or principal language of many Zion communicants until well into the twentieth century, and English was not the primary language in Zion's church services until the middle 1940s, all subjects at the Zion school were taught in English by the early twentieth century.[1] After switching to English, however, the school began to teach the German language to students who had not learned it at home, in order that the young people could maintain a link with the culture of their forebears, communicate with members of the community who spoke only German, and participate in German-language worship services.

During the early twentieth century, Zion was the nucleus of a vibrant and prosperous German-American community. In 1915, attendance at Zion's school had grown so large that the congregation erected a second school building and hired a second teacher.[2] Two years later, however, this community, like German enclaves everywhere in the United States, received a shock from which it never fully recovered. America's declaration of war against Germany suddenly transformed Zion's parishioners from objects of respect into targets of suspicion among their non-German neighbors. Public hostility toward German culture shook the hope of Zion's leaders that the community could remain authentically German even while it became fully American, and the war hastened the process of assimilation. The size and strength of Hampton's German community, however, made it more resistant to change than weaker communities. When state officials urged churches to conduct all services in English, Pastor C. F. Brommer temporarily held one service each Sunday in English but defiantly retained a German service.[3] Under pressure from Nebraska authorities, Zion's schools temporarily suspended instruction in German in January 1918.[4] When a Nebraska law enacted shortly after the war prohibited the teaching of foreign languages in all schools, Zion abandoned its German lessons. But when the state supreme court interpreted the statute to permit the teaching of German during recess periods (an interpretation that clearly was at odds with the language and intent of the statute), Zion immediately extended its recess period by half an hour each day and began to teach German during the additional time.[5] The lingering anti-German sentiments that the statute reflected were mirrored in continuing hostility against Zion's German-American community. Soon after Zion's two schools resumed the teaching of German, vandals ransacked the North School, blasting out the windows with shotguns and ripping up all German-language books except the Bible.[6] Meanwhile, opponents of German-language instruction made plans for enactment of another statute to prohibit the teaching of German at any time and called for enforcement of the existing statute against schools that had attempted to avoid its terms by altering recess hours.

On May 25, 1920, Frank E. Edgerton, the Hamilton County attorney, arrived at Zion's South School during the recess period and entered its classroom without knocking. The teacher, Robert T. Meyer, never had met Edgerton but knew who he was and why he had come. His abrupt arrival startled Meyer, although the county school superintendent had visited Meyer's class during a German lesson the previous week. When Edgerton entered the classroom, the dozen students of the fifth grade class stood in front of Meyer's desk, reading from a book of German-language Bible stories while the rest of the fifty students sat in their seats, reading silently from English-language books.[7] Meyer, a forty-two-year-old father of six, knew that county officials wanted to encourage him to desist from teaching German, but he also knew that they wished to maintain cordial relations with the German-American community and that they would not unnecessarily harass him. "I had my choice," Meyer later explained to his attorney. "I knew that, if I changed into English language, he would say nothing. If I went on in German, he would . . . arrest me. I told myself that I must not flinch. And I did not flinch. I went on in German."[8] The teacher at the North School was not so brave. When he learned that Edgerton was planning to visit his German class, he warned his students during recess that they would have no German lesson that day and later conducted a class in English during Edgerton's visit.[9]

When Edgerton entered Meyer's classroom, "there was a real hush," Raymond Parpart, one of the fifth-grade students, recalled seventy years later. "We were wondering what was going on. We could tell by the look on

Teacher Meyer's face that something pretty serious was happening." Like many of the other students, Raymond had first learned German at home. He had spoken only German until he was five years old, but his family used mostly English by 1920, and he and his classmates spoke only English among themselves at school. Edgerton asked eleven-year-old Raymond to read from his book of Bible stories and then to explain in English what he had read. When Raymond had finished reading a few lines, Edgerton took the book away to use it as evidence against Meyer. It was never returned. Edgerton turned to Meyer, and the two men had a long, whispered conversation in which Meyer admitted that he taught German each day from one o'clock until one-thirty by orders of Zion's school board. Meyer then resumed the lesson in German. Edgerton listened for a while and departed.[10]

When asked later why he had chosen to provoke prosecution by continuing the lesson in German, Meyer explained, "It was my duty. I am not a pastor . . . but I have the same duty to uphold my religion. Teaching the children the religion of their fathers in the language of their fathers is part of that religion."[11] Pastor Brommer and the congregation of Zion stood behind Meyer's defiance of the statute.[12] Although Meyer was not arrested, he was indicted for teaching German in violation of the Siman Act, the Nebraska statute forbidding the teaching of foreign languages. On June 29, 1920, a local court found Meyer guilty and fined him twenty-five dollars,[13] the equivalent of his monthly salary.[14] The Missouri Synod, with which Zion was affiliated, advised Meyer to pay the fine, and a dozen men in the community offered to pay it for him. But Meyer declared, "I shall not pay the fine. It is not a matter of money. This is a question of principle. If I go to jail for doing what I know to be right, I go to jail. I shall not compromise with what I know is not right."[15] Raymond's father posted bond to keep Meyer out of jail after he refused to pay the fine.[16] Meyer appealed his conviction to the district court. Covered with robes to keep warm, Meyer, Raymond Parpart, and Brommer, rode eleven miles through the snow in a carriage shortly before Thanksgiving to testify before the court in Aurora.[17] During the hearing, Brommer testified that "the ultimate and only object we had in view in teaching German" was to enable children to worship at home and at church with their German-speaking parents.[18] Brommer's explanation was unavailing, and the court upheld the conviction and the fine.

Meyer, Brommer, and the Zion congregation decided to appeal the conviction to the state supreme court. Meyer engaged the services of Arthur F. Mullen, a prominent Omaha lawyer and active Roman Catholic layman, who recognized that the Nebraska statute was part of a broader assault on parochial education. At the same time that Nebraska and nearly two dozen other states were enacting laws to restrict instruction in foreign languages, campaigns were under way in several states to require all elementary school children to attend public schools. The enactment of a compulsory public education law in Oregon in 1922 demonstrated that foes of nonpublic education had the power to destroy parochial schools in states in which Roman Catholics and Lutherans were numerically weak. The growing assault on nonpublic schools alarmed civil libertarians everywhere because it represented a spirit of intolerance and bigotry that increasingly pervaded postwar America. If the states were permitted to snuff out private and parochial schools, there seemed no end to the power of the state to persecute ethnic and religious minorities and to enact legislation that intruded on the most intimate aspects of the lives of American citizens.

Although the Nebraska Supreme Court upheld Meyer's conviction, the United States Supreme Court in 1923 declared that the law under which Meyer had been prosecuted violated the due process clause of the Fourteenth Amendment of the U.S. Constitution because it deprived language teachers and parents of liberty without due process of law. The Court reasoned that the statute exceeded the scope of the state's police power because the state had failed to demonstrate any need for the prohibition on foreign-language instruction. Although the Court did not need to say any more in order to overturn Meyer's conviction, its opinion also articulated a broad vision of personal freedom. The Constitution, the Court said, protects an array of liberties, including the right to marry, to bring up children, and to worship God according to one's conscience. This was the first time that the Court had declared that the federal Constitution protects civil liberties against infringements by states involving matters other than racial discrimination and the enactment of economic regulations.

The decision in *Meyer* was the basis for *Pierce v. Society of Sisters,* the 1925 ruling in which the Court saved Oregon's parochial schools from virtual extinction by invalidating an Oregon law that required all elementary school children to attend public schools. Two years later, *Meyer* and *Pierce* served as the principal precedents for *Farrington v. Tokushige,* in which the Court completed its trilogy of parochial school decisions by nullifying restrictions on Asian-language schools in Hawaii. Together these decisions spelled the death of what had been a growing movement to destroy parochial and private elementary education. *Meyer* also presaged the process by which the

Court later incorporated into state law most of the specific liberties that are guaranteed by the Bill of Rights. *Meyer* therefore inaugurated a new era of judicial activism, extending to the present day, in which the Supreme Court has jealously and often zealously protected civil liberties from intrusions by state legislatures.

This book explores the evolution of the statutes that were struck down in the *Meyer, Pierce,* and *Farrington* decisions. It explains how a complicated melange of war hysteria, fear of anarchy and Bolshevism, postwar anomie, nativism, pietism, populism, and progressivism contributed to the enactment of those laws. It also studies the legal arguments that were presented by proponents and opponents of the statutes and analyzes the reasoning and enduring significance of the decisions in which the Supreme Court struck down those laws.

1 The Origins of the School Controversies

The educational controversies that arose during and shortly after the First World War had complex antecedents. The intensity of those conflicts reflected a widespread recognition that a nation's destiny is largely forged in its schools. Elementary education occupies a singular position in the American psyche. The Framers of the Constitution understood that an educated public was essential to the survival of democracy. The schools would provide the learning that was required for self-government and would inculcate the respect for republican virtues that was necessary to create a national identity transcending social class, geography, and ethnicity.[1] Just as universal education has been essential for democracy, democracy has been essential for universal education, since the equality of opportunity that is the essence of the American creed requires that all children receive a basic education.

Foreigners who visited the Republic during the nineteenth century expressed admiration for the prevalence of literacy among the common people and marveled at the vast sums of money spent on public education.[2] During the twentieth century, when increasingly large numbers of citizens received a college education, Americans continued to invest considerable interest and resources in their elementary and secondary schools. The growing fear that these schools are in some respects inferior to those of the world's other industrial nations recently has kindled an intense and far-reaching national debate about school reform that reflects the widespread appreciation of the importance of childhood education.

The relationship between democracy and education is particularly close in America because public education traditionally is managed by the most local units of government in which ordinary citizens have a strong voice. In a highly litigious nation, it is not surprising that education has inspired many legal battles. Some of the most important judicial decisions of the past several decades have involved elementary education. And the direct manner in which the daily lives of ordinary Americans have been touched by those decisions has given them a public visibility that other significant rulings often have lacked. It is telling that perhaps the most famous case of the twentieth century is *Brown v. Board of Education,* in which the United States Supreme Court declared that the Constitution prohibited the racial segregation of public elementary schools.[3] Although the Court incrementally had paved the way for *Brown* in significant earlier decisions involving higher education and would later hand down other important decisions requiring desegregation of other institutions, *Brown* ignited more controversy and inspired more resistance than did any other desegregation ruling. Both proponents and opponents of the decision recognized that integration of children in schools would transform racial attitudes in America, since the integration of elementary and secondary schools would expose children to the ideal of racial equality during their most formative years.

Less than a decade after *Brown,* the Court once again struck profound chords in the American people when it ruled that the Constitution prohibited public prayer and the reading of the Bible for devotional purposes in the public schools.[4] Few decisions of the Supreme Court have received more attention from ordinary Americans or have triggered more intense and widespread outbursts of hostility toward the Court. During the 1970s, the controversy over court-ordered busing of elementary and high school children in order to achieve racial integration shattered the tranquility of many neighborhoods and shifted the focus of racial tension from the South to the North.

Most children since the earliest days of the Republic have attended public schools, but a significant number have received instruction in private institutions. Although private schools have ameliorated tax burdens, they often have encountered widespread hostility from Americans who have feared that they foster elitism or fail to inculcate American ideals. And many Americans also have looked with disfavor and suspicion on parochial schools that have been formed to help preserve minority ethnic and religious traditions. The very word "parochial" suggests isolation from the mainstream of society. Although the word is derived from the Latin *parochia,* meaning "parish," and a parochial school literally is one that is operated by a parish, the word "parochial" has secondary definitions of "provincial" or "narrow." For many Americans, the parochialism of a church-operated school has corresponded more to this secondary meaning than to its literal definition. In a land in which the Anglo-Saxon majority traditionally has expected minorities to assimilate to the dominant cultural norms, the parochial school has seemed to threaten the fragile unity of a highly heterogeneous population.

The earliest settlers in Anglo-America brought to the New World a well-established tradition of elementary education, since schools had flourished in England for centuries. A high proportion of the early colonists were literate, and they wanted their children to have at least a basic education. Protestant New Englanders particularly emphasized education, for literacy was essential to an understanding of the Bible. But all colonists recognized that education was necessary for the transmission and maintenance of European culture in the wilderness of the New World. A Massachusetts colonist in 1663 explained that settlers needed "to use utmost care and diligence to keep up learning and all helps to education among us, lest degeneracy, barbarism, ignorance and irreligion do by degrees break in upon us."[5] This sentiment would be echoed by countless other immigrants through the centuries, down to the present time.

Although churches sponsored most education during the very first years of settlement, public authorities throughout the colonies began to support education at an early stage in the nation's development.[6] The early schools were highly varied in their sponsorship and support,[7] but the so-called public schools of the colonial and early national periods usually were jointly financed and managed by churches and the state.[8]

The birth of the Republic provided a major impetus for the development of public schools, because Americans of the late eighteenth and early nineteenth centuries were keenly aware that democracy was a fragile experiment that was dependent on an educated citizenry. The erosion of class differences during the early nineteenth century also encouraged the development of public schools by creating an ideology of equality of opportunity.[9] Westward expansion further favored the growth of public schools, since many Americans perceived that a common system of schooling could ameliorate the centrifugal tendencies of frontier society.[10] As Oscar Handlin has pointed out, the public "schools were thus to be a force for cohesion in a nation characterized by heterogeneity."[11] Although public education remained primarily the concern of local governments, the federal government facilitated the growth of a common school system in the West by granting public lands for the endowment of schools and writing public education provisions into the enabling acts for new states.[12]

By the 1830s, the Industrial Revolution had infused the common school movement with urgency, as capitalists recognized that the discipline instilled in the public schools would help to create and sustain a reliable work force.[13] The leaders of the common school movement attempted to inculcate a matrix of economic, social, and moral ideals that were best exemplified by the bromides found in *McGuffey's Reader*. Hard work, self-discipline, thrift, self-reliance, and obedience to reasonable authority were among the principal tenets of this ideology, which was closely related to the values of the Calvinistic Protestantism espoused by the majority of Americans, particularly the elites who founded and maintained the schools. As Carl Kaestle has explained, "the homilies of native Protestant belief became both the justification and the message of common schools."[14] The movement for common schools therefore became an integral element of the religious revivalism that swept through the nation during the early nineteenth century, since schools were seen as agents of the self-regeneration that sectarian Protestants viewed as necessary for salvation.[15]

Members of other religious faiths and ethnic groups embraced many of the values that animated the common school movement but often differed in their interpretation and application of those ideals. While most ethnic Americans were diligent workers, for example, many did not regard poverty as evidence of moral deficiency or adhere to the rigid rhythms of labor that were demanded by an industrializing society. Similarly, few of the immigrants viewed the use of alcohol as a sin, or participation in sport on Sunday as a desecration of the Sabbath. As we shall see, the religious, cultural, and class characteristics of the immigrants increasingly came into conflict with the often smug and ethnocentric Anglo-Americans who controlled the public schools. This conflict provided a major impetus for the development of nonpublic schools by various immigrant groups, as did the desire of many immigrants to provide an environment that would transmit their cultural values and distinctive religious beliefs.

Since the nineteenth century, the Roman Catholic church has maintained by far the largest network of parochial schools in the United States. The very earliest Catholic schools in what now is the United States were founded by missionaries in Spanish and French America under the aegis of colonial administrations. In English America, the Catholic minority established several dozen schools during the century before the Revolution.[16]

Along with their Protestant counterparts, many Catholic schools during the eighteenth and early nineteenth centuries received public funds.[17] Although the Catholic hierarchy in the United States encouraged parochial education during the first decades after the Revolution, the church initially was tolerant of parents who could not afford to send their children to parochial schools.[18]

By the 1830s, however, Roman Catholics were becoming more uneasy about the religious character of the public schools. As denominational distinctions among American Protestants eroded, public school authorities began to introduce generically Protestant religious instruction and devotions into the public schools. Horace Mann, the principal advocate of universal public education, contended that the schools could and should teach a common core of nonsectarian Christian beliefs.[19] What seemed nonsectarian to the Unitarian Mann and many Protestants, however, seemed quite sectarian to Roman Catholics. A mid-nineteenth-century Roman Catholic bishop of Cincinnati referred to that city's public schools as "Presbyterian schools."[20] Roman Catholics felt particularly vulnerable to what many perceived as Protestant evangelization in the public schools, since the Catholic church was small, weak, and disorganized in most parts of the nation. Catholics especially objected to the use of Protestant hymns and prayers in the officially nonsectarian schools and vehemently opposed the widespread practice of instruction in the King James version of the Bible.[21] Riots over Bible reading in the Philadelphia public schools left dozens of persons dead in 1844 in the most dramatic manifestation of a controversy that erupted in many places during the mid-nineteenth century.[22]

Although some Protestant educators were willing to eliminate Bible reading and other forms of religious instruction and observance in the public schools, they failed to realize that a school that ignored religion was just as offensive to many Catholics as was a school that taught non-Catholic doctrines.[23] In contrast to public school educators, who generally used religion only as a means of inculcating civic virtue, Roman Catholics viewed religion as an end in itself.[24] Catholics therefore could never be entirely satisfied with a wholly secular school.

The conflict over religious instruction in the schools emerged at the very time that a tidal wave of immigrants from Ireland and Germany was reinforcing the thin ranks of American Catholicism. Although often the immigrants were so poor that their children attended no school, the percentage of Catholic pupils in many public schools increased so significantly that the

Protestant character of those schools seemed more incongruous and unjust than ever to many Roman Catholic parents and prelates. The increase in the Catholic population likewise gave the hierarchy greater self-confidence in its efforts to resist the Protestantization of the public schools. The objections of the hierarchy received the support of the new immigrants. Tempered by centuries of oppression from the Protestant English, the Irish immigrants generally were more militant in the defense of their faith and less willing to reach accommodations with Protestants than were the Anglo-Saxon Catholics who previously had dominated the American church.[25] The German Catholic immigrants were similarly resolute in their desire to retain a distinctive cultural and religious identity.

Although the increase in Catholic immigration during the 1840s and 1850s provided an impetus for the creation of parochial schools, it helped to consolidate support for universal public education among Protestants, who began to feel economically and culturally threatened. As the vaguely anti-Catholic and antiforeign prejudices of earlier years became more pronounced, the nation experienced its first organized nativist movements.[26]

Relatively few Americans ever joined secret societies, voted for the Native American party, or seriously believed in a papal plot to control America, but many Americans experienced to some extent the nativist contempt for the immigrant. As the streets filled with strangely attired persons who spoke incomprehensible languages, the initial curiosity and wonderment of the native born often curdled into revulsion and fear toward these exotic newcomers who seemed oblivious to the mores and amenities of American life. Hostility toward the immigrant, moveover, spread far beyond working-class natives who competed with the immigrants for jobs and housing. Even the urbane New York attorney and civic leader George Templeton Strong filled his diary with frequent derogations of the shabby, rowdy, and uncouth immigrants whom he encountered on the streets of Manhattan. At the very time that the nation appeared to have secured a common identity, lasting prosperity, and the triumph of a democratic political order, immigrants seemed to threaten these achievements. Many Americans feared that most immigrants lacked any conception of democracy and willingly would submit to the authoritarian yoke that had bound them in Europe. The devotion of many of these immigrants to Roman Catholicism particularly frightened Americans, since the Roman Catholic church was an authoritarian institution that had often opposed economic liberalism and democracy in European countries.

Although some of the more racist nativists questioned whether the immigrants and their progeny ever would be able to absorb American values, the more benign critics of the immigrants were confident that they would gladly shed their primitive and obnoxious ways if only they were properly exposed to the supposedly superior American customs.[27] As Carl Kaestle has pointed out, however, many Anglo-Americans were more interested in acculturating the immigrant than in assimilating him. They "wished to Americanize the habits, not the status, of the immigrant."[28]

The school provided an efficient agent for rapid acculturation, since it enabled the state to reach children during their formative years. Recognizing that most children are eager to conform to their peers and please their teachers, the proponents of public education correctly foresaw that the schools would be powerful instruments of assimilation.[29] The use of the public school after 1840 as an agent of assimilation was a natural extension of its earlier role as a means of breaking down sectional and class differences.[30] By 1920, the sociologist John Daniels estimated that nine-tenths of immigrants who had reared a family in America regarded the public school as the most effective institutional agent of assimilation. Daniels remarked that the immigrant parent saw his children "go into the kindergarten as little Poles or Italians or Finns, babbling in the tongues of their parents, and at the end of half a dozen years or more he sees them emerge, looking, talking, thinking, and behaving generally like full-fledged 'Americans.' Vicariously, he sees himself at one with the life of America in this wonderful metamorphosis."[31]

Not all immigrant parents, however, were so sanguine about this transformation. The common school threatened to rob immigrant children of their religious and cultural heritage and to estrange them from their parents, who usually were much slower to adopt American ways. In their zeal to propagate American culture, teachers often deliberately or unwittingly denigrated Old World customs and culture.[32] Protestant prejudices and nascent nativism sometimes led to infusion of blatantly anti-Catholic and anti-immigrant propaganda in the public school curriculum.[33] As late as 1906, a Catholic newspaper in Chicago complained that textbooks "systematically misrepresented" Catholics.[34] Although immigrant leaders urged revision of curricula to present a more favorable image of Roman Catholics, Catholics recognized that curriculum reform could not purge anti-Catholic attitudes, particularly unconscious attitudes, from their children's Protestant peers and teachers in the public schools.[35] Roman Catholics could not easily counteract this prejudice from within the schools because Catholics often faced discrimination in obtaining teaching jobs and positions on school boards.[36] Faced with unremitting hostility from the dominant culture, many Catholics came to view parochial schools as what one scholar has called "a symbol of defiance against the established order that so despised their religion."[37]

After Roman Catholics failed in their attempts to remove Bible reading from the public schools, they began markedly to increase the number of their parochial schools, even though they also failed in their efforts to obtain tax assistance for the operation of Catholic schools.[38] The First and Second Plenary Councils of Baltimore, in 1852 and 1866, urged bishops to establish parochial schools throughout their dioceses.[39] During the decades after the Second Plenary Council, the trend toward founding of parochial schools was accelerated as universal schooling became more common and many states enacted compulsory school attendance laws. Parochial education also benefited from the large immigration of Germans, who hoped the parochial schools would help preserve their language.[40] In addition to using language to hold on to the secular aspects of their culture, the German Catholics believed that their language was needed to preserve their religion. "Language saves faith" became a common aphorism in German communities.[41] The creation of German-language parochial schools became possible after the Roman Catholic hierarchy permitted the establishment of German-language parishes.[42]

Although a conference of American bishops in 1874 concluded that the establishment of a school in every diocese was impracticable, proponents of parochial education in 1876 persuaded the Vatican's Congregation for the Propagation of the Faith to urge American bishops to establish parochial schools. Influenced by the ultramontanism of the period, the congregation denounced American public schools as "most dangerous and very much opposed to Catholicity."[43] Universal parochial education finally became the official goal of the Roman Catholic church in 1884, when the Third Plenary Council decreed that every parish must maintain its own school. The council also required parents to send their children to their parish school unless the children were able to receive sufficient religious training in the home or in other Catholic schools, or unless the bishop, for good cause, released them from their obligation.[44]

The council's order does not appear to have accelerated the pace of expansion of the parochial school system, but it continued to grow.[45] By 1900, more than 850,000 children attended Roman Catholic parochial schools, more than 5 percent of the American elementary and high school population.[46] This proportion was higher in the cities, where so many immigrants had settled. A survey of twenty-four major American cities by the Immigration Commission in 1908 found that some 221,000 students—more than 15 percent of the total—attended parochial schools. Nearly two-thirds of the students in those schools had foreign-born fathers.[47]

Many Catholic children, however, did not attend parochial school, since some Roman Catholics remained indifferent or hostile toward parochial education and many could not afford it. Other Catholics, notably the influential Bishop John Ireland of St. Paul, hoped that parochial schools would exist only until more satisfactory accommodations could be arranged between the Roman Catholic church and the public schools.[48] Many Roman Catholic clerics and laypersons, however, opposed the very idea of public education. These Catholics adhered to the traditional idea that education was the responsibility of parents rather than the state. The Bishop of Rochester declared that the state was incompetent to perform parental duties, and the Bishop of Trenton contended that "the idea that the state has a right to teach . . . is a pagan one."[49] The campaign for parochial education gradually had an effect, since the percentage of Roman Catholic children who attended parochial school steadily increased between the mid-nineteenth century and the 1960s, even though a majority of Catholic children always attended public schools.

The nondenominationally Protestant character of the public schools during the nineteenth century distressed not only Roman Catholics, but also some Protestant groups. During the middle of the nineteenth century, Episcopalians and Presbyterians began to develop a network of parochial schools in an effort to provide their youth with a more rigorous and orthodox religious education than the public schools could offer. The theological, cultural, and social tensions between these denominations and the public schools, however, was not sufficiently great to sustain the arduous and expensive enterprise of creating and maintaining a separate system of schools. During the late 1800s, Presbyterians and Episcopalians abandoned their efforts to establish their own schools.[50] In 1925, when the controversy over parochial education reached its climax, the Episcopal church still maintained more than one hundred schools, including many of the nation's most elite college preparatory institutions. A substantial number of the pupils at those schools, however, were non-Episcopalian,[51] and the schools were devoted more to the encouragement of moral and civic virtues than to the inculcation of Anglican religious doctrine.

Even many Protestant groups that were largely comprised of non-English-speaking persons were not willing to make the sacrifices needed for a separate school system. Though such groups as the German Baptists and Evangelicals sometimes maintained parochial schools, the similarity of their religion to the Anglo-American churches ameliorated their fears of the religious tendencies of the public schools. Many of the non-Anglo Protestant groups, however, observed religious beliefs and ceremonies that sharply differed from those of their Anglo-American neighbors. Highly distinct groups such as the Amish and the Mennonites insisted on educating their children in separate schools. Since their numbers were small and they lived in isolated communities, their parochial schools generally did not create widespread tension, even if they sometimes aroused local suspicions and hostility.

The educational problems of the Lutherans, the largest non-Anglo Protestant group in America, were more complex. Following a creed and liturgy that in many ways resembled Roman Catholicism more than the beliefs and ceremonies of other Protestant religions, Lutherans shared with Catholics a profound concern for orthodox doctrine. This emphasis on doctrine helped to isolate and even estrange Lutherans from other Protestants, most of whom tolerated doctrinal latitude and were more concerned with correct behavior than with correct belief. Many Lutherans feared that their children would convert to other faiths or bring unorthodox ideas into the Lutheran fold if they were exposed to the heterodox Protestantism of the public schools.

By the late nineteenth century, the Lutheran churches were the only major Protestant bodies in America that continued to embrace the concept and practice of parochial education. Like the Roman Catholics, the Lutherans brought to the United States a tradition of close ties between the church and the schools. In Scandinavia and much of Germany, nearly all schools were established and operated by Lutheran state churches, which had developed a system of universal public education. Settling in areas in which there usually was no public school, the earliest Lutheran immigrants built schools alongside their churches, often building the school first.[52] From the late colonial period until the mid-nineteenth century, Lutherans maintained the most extensive system of parochial schools in the new nation.[53]

Although Lutheran schools decreased in number during the early nineteenth century as Lutherans became more assimilated and public schools became more widely available, Lutheran parochial education began to grow again as German immigrants started to arrive in large numbers after 1840. The Lutherans thus expanded their parochial system at the very time that other Protestants were abandoning church schools in favor of public education.

Many of the German Lutheran immigrants were particularly eager to establish parochial schools because they had left Germany in order to preserve a distinctively Lutheran identity. A substantial number of these immigrants had fled Prussia and other German lands during the mid-nineteenth century because they opposed the recent confederation of Lutherans and Calvinists in state churches that previously had been wholly Lutheran. The generic Protestantism of the public schools reminded these Lutherans of the indistinct theology of the so-called united churches in Germany. Other Lutherans had left Germany because they opposed the erosion of orthodox Lutheran doctrine in churches that were heavily influenced by rationalism. These Lutherans likewise were distressed by the nondoctrinal Christianity that the public schools propounded.

The Lutheran Church—Missouri Synod,[54] founded by immigrants who had fled rationalism and unionism in Saxony, emphasized parochial education more than any other Lutheran denomination and established what remains the nation's most extensive system of non-Catholic parochial schools. Alone among the larger Lutheran denominations, the Missouri Synod vigorously encouraged all parents to send their children to parochial schools and required that virtually every parish support a school. Proponents of the Missouri Synod's schools during the nineteenth century blamed the influence of the public schools for the conversion of countless German Americans to non-Lutheran denominations.[55]

The heavy influx of Scandinavians between 1870 and 1890 also provided an impetus for the establishment of Lutheran schools. Like other immigrants, the Scandinavian Lutherans who established parochial schools desired to preserve a religion, language, and culture that were closely interrelated. But while many Scandinavians founded parochial schools, most were content to send their children to public schools.[56] Unlike struggling German immigrants, who often were willing to make heroic sacrifices to establish schools, the more pragmatic Scandinavians preferred to avail themselves of the state's bounty. "The doors to this country's schools are open to us," remarked Rasmus Anderson, the first professor of Scandinavian studies at the University of Wisconsin. "The American . . . invites the immigrant child to the school desk, to sit together with his own. Why not accept this generous invitation?"[57] Scandinavian immigrants also tended to favor public education because they generally were more receptive to assimilation than were the Germans and were more likely to settle in places where their numbers were so small that they could not support a school or where their concentration was so intense that they could dominate the local public school. Rather than establish many parochial schools, Scandinavians founded a multitude of colleges, which were intended in part to produce teachers who could impart Scandinavian standards and values in the public schools.[58]

Lutheran proponents of public education invoked Martin Luther's doctrine of the dualism of church and state in support of their contention that the church and the state had distinct educational tasks that were best carried out in separate institutions without interference by one with the other.[59] By 1921, only eighteen of the sixty-one Lutheran synods in the United States maintained a parochial school system, and only six of those synods—all of them German—strongly encouraged all parents to send their children to parochial school.[60]

Although religion was a principal reason why both Roman Catholic and Protestant immigrants from Germany established parochial schools, even many nonreligious German immigrants sent their children to parochial schools or established private schools in order to transmit German culture to their children.[61] In Milwaukee, for example, freethinking Germans who objected to the low standards and limited curriculum of the public schools formed private schools during the 1850s. In addition to offering German-language instruction, these schools taught a broad array of academic, artistic, and practical subjects that the public schools did not teach and pioneered progressive teaching methods that Milwaukee's public schools later emulated.[62]

In contrast to the Roman Catholic church and many Lutheran groups, few Jewish communities in the United States have supported full-time schools. The trickle of Jews who settled in the United States before the mid-nineteenth century frequently educated their children in Jewish schools or at home, since the so-called public schools were closely associated with various Christian denominations. Jews tended to send their children to the public schools that became available after 1830, even though they often joined Roman Catholics in complaining about the persistence of elements of Protestant sectarianism there. With the rise of Jewish immigration during the late 1840s and early 1850s, demand for Jewish day schools increased and some were established in major cities.[63] The secularization of the public schools in New York during the 1850s, however, soon arrested the growth of Jewish parochial education, as did financial difficulties and the founding of the Free Academy (now the City University of New York), which limited admission to graduates of public schools.[64] The proselytization of Jewish children in Protestant mission schools in New York's immigrant neighborhoods during the 1860s stimulated a brief revival of day schools, but inadequate funding quickly led to their collapse. Prosperous and assimilated Jews withheld financial support then and later in the century because they opposed the highly Orthodox character of the schools and feared that full-time Jewish schools would impede the Americanization of the newcomers.[65]

The establishment of full-time Jewish schools was further hindered by divisions within the immigrant communities themselves, in which Jews tended to cluster in small groups defined by the areas from which they had emigrated. The relative equality of opportunity between the sexes in the public schools made them a magnet for Jewish women.[66] Finally, the public schools were attractive to Jews because they offered the most expeditious means of achieving knowledge of secular subjects that would facilitate comprehensive education and economic advancement. Even though New York's public schools during the early part of the century suffered from overcrowding and inadequate facilities,[67] they may have been superior to many of the underfinanced Jewish schools.[68] Accordingly, many Jews enthusiastically and gratefully availed themselves of the resources of the public schools, where Gentile teachers admired the abilities and diligence of their Jewish students.[69] By the end of World War I, only 1,000 of the more than 200,000 school-age Jewish children in New York City attended all-day Jewish schools,[70] although a substantial number attended part-time religious schools.[71] Although day school attendance rose during the mid-twentieth century, the large majority of Jewish children have continued to attend public school.[72]

The emergence of widespread parochial education during the middle and late nineteenth century occurred while the common school was consolidating its place in the hearts of Protestants as the nursery of American values. By this time, most Protestants had rejected the old idea that education was a parental responsibility and had embraced the concept that education was a concern of the government. Although Americans always had recognized that a democracy needed an educated citizenry, Protestants increasingly came to believe that the state had a duty to provide an education for all classes. The corollary of this idea was that only public schools or educational institutions closely allied with the state could instill patriotism and democratic ideals and provide the sort of learning that was required for self-government. Public schools also were regarded as a means of inculcating virtues that would prevent democracy from degenerating into anarchy or despotism.[73] The egalitarianism of the public schools seemed to foster democratic ideals. As John Higham has pointed out, the common school by the 1890s "was becoming a potent patriotic symbol."[74]

The growing importance of public education was reflected in various forms of legislation in which the states extended their power over education. During the decades following the Civil War, legislatures centralized textbook selection, demanded loyalty oaths from teachers, prescribed patriotic exercises, adopted more stringent requirements for the education and certification of teachers, and enacted compulsory education laws. Although mandatory education laws were difficult to enforce and were largely evaded for decades in most states, such laws represented a legal recognition of the universality of elementary education and provided a goal that eventually would be largely attained.[75]

Patriotism, democracy, and assimilation of immigrants were closely intertwined with Christianity in the minds of many American Protestants, and the late nineteenth century saw a continued development of Mann's vision of a public school that would instill Christian ideals and values in the nation's youth.[76] Most public schools of the era taught only the bare fundamentals of Christian doctrine but emphasized a moral and social code that its proponents believed was based on religious principles. Many public schools continued devotional exercises that included reading from the King James version of the Bible and generically Protestant prayers. Although few public school teachers actually attempted to proselytize immigrant children, many urban Roman Catholic, Jewish, Eastern Orthodox, and Lutheran immigrants naturally viewed the religious exercises of the public schools as an adjunct to the Protestant missions that were beginning to dot the ethnic neighborhoods of the major cities and the Anglo-American churches that filled the countryside.

Although parochial education provided a means of transmitting the culture and traditions of the Old World, some parents were unable to afford the tuition and others did not subscribe to the religious tenets of the parochial schools. Parents who resisted assimilation but who were unable or unwilling to send their children to parochial schools attempted to ameliorate the homogenizing effects of the public schools by persuading them to offer instruction in foreign languages.

As early as 1840, the Ohio legislature enacted a law to require school boards to teach German whenever at least seventy-five property owners demanded it in writing. Between 1854 and 1877, at least six midwestern states passed laws to permit instruction in foreign languages in public schools when the local school board directed it or a specified number of parents requested it. Statutes in Wisconsin, Illinois, Minnesota, and Iowa permitted instruction in any foreign language, while the Kansas and Indiana statutes were limited to the German language. As a result of these laws, foreign-language instruction became common in some major cities, particularly Cincinnati and Milwaukee. In most schools, German was the most common foreign language, although schools also offered instruction in many other languages, including Polish, Spanish, Norwegian, French, Italian, and Dutch.[77]

Most public schools that taught German offered it only as a second language, although in some schools many or all of the common subjects were taught in German. In heavily German areas of the rural Midwest, public school instruction often was conducted in German even in the absence of any statutory authorization when Germans dominated the local government. The Board of Education in the Territory of Dakota lamented in its report for 1886–88 that some teachers were "not even able to speak the English language and nothing could be done about it," since "the foreign element" elected the county superintendent and controlled the schools. Missouri's superintendent of public instruction made a similar complaint in his report for 1887–88. In many urban areas, German immigrants also were strong enough to persuade local school boards to permit German-language instruction in excess of any statutory authorization.[78]

Although foreign-language instruction in the public schools often was the result of demands by ethnic parents,[79] many old-stock Americans reluctantly supported the introduction of foreign languages into the curriculum because it enabled the public schools to compete more effectively with the parochial schools, which had become so strong in some areas that they threatened the viability of the public school system.[80] Similarly, many Anglo-Americans were willing to compromise the common curriculum ideal by giving German children a small dose of their native tongue if this appeased their parents and thereby kept them out of schools that would immerse them in a foreign language and isolate them from American ideals.

Moreover, some educators believed that foreign-language instruction would foster family cohesion among immigrants and would discourage the abrupt breaks in social continuity that spawned crime and other social evils. Recognizing that Germans valued learning and had pioneered modern pedagogical methods, educators also perceived that German Americans could be valuable allies in the development of a better public school system. As Germany emerged as a strong political and economic power late in the nineteenth century, educators likewise began to believe that a knowledge of German had great commercial value. Moreover, early studies in child psychology suggested that instruction in foreign languages would enhance rather than retard a child's ability to learn English.[81]

Even though parochial schools continued to flourish during the late nineteenth century, the public schools were not unsuccessful in their attempts to lure German Americans into their classrooms by offering foreign languages. By 1870, for example, half the white public school children in St. Louis were German American, and three-quarters of those children were enrolled in language classes. Non-German children also benefited from these classes; in St. Louis during the 1870s, they comprised nearly one-quarter of the students in German-language classes.[82] Ultimately, however, the introduction of foreign languages into the public schools troubled many Americans. In addition to complaining that foreign-language instruction was unduly expensive and superficial, Americans often contended that it contravened the mission of the public schools to create a common culture and to eradicate distinctions among Americans.[83] As Heinz Kloss has observed, "these bilingual public school systems were shining achievements in the fields of language maintenance, bicultural education, and minority rights. They were very modern in their rationales—too modern to outlive the tempests and crises of developing American nationalism."[84] Moreover, the laws perpetuated foreign culture in the very areas in which ethnic children already were the most isolated from the mainstream of American society. Writing in 1913, Professor Henry Pratt Fairchild of Yale lamented that the public schools in many heavily ethnic areas were "losing their American character" because so few "children from American families" attended those schools.[85] As opposition to foreign-language instruction gained momentum during the late nineteenth century, California, Kansas, and the Dakota Territory enacted statutes that required the exclusive use of English in the public schools.[86] During the late 1880s, the teaching of German also was discontinued in the public schools of many major cities, including Louisville, St. Louis and St. Paul.[87]

Meanwhile, the growth of the network of Roman Catholic and Lutheran parochial schools continued to alarm many Protestants. As Paul Kleppner has pointed out, the establishment of a separate parochial school system "struck at the very heart of the pietist's attempt to create the moral society."[88] The use of foreign languages in the parochial schools was particularly vexing, for language above all else set the immigrant apart from the mainstream of American society. Americans often feared that immigrants never would adopt the mores of the dominant American culture if they did not learn to speak English. Indeed, the use of foreign languages itself irritated many Americans, who resented their inability to understand what the immigrants were saying and feared that the immigrants used their strange tongues to transmit unwholesome and dangerous ideas. Anglo-Americans also worried that the public school system would collapse if parochial school enrollment continued to rise, since parents of parochial school children might become sufficiently numerous to demand public support for parochial schools or exemption from taxes to support the public schools. The substantial enrollment of non-Catholic children in Catholic schools also caused some alarm, since many non-Catholics were afraid that Catholics used their schools to win converts. Like Catholic fears that Protestants used the public schools to proselytize Catholic youth, these concerns were not entirely groundless.[89]

The simmering controversy over parochial schools flared up during the late 1860s and early 1870s, when Roman Catholic leaders again began to call for public funding of their schools. President Ulysses S. Grant and the Republican party vigorously opposed public support of parochial education. In his annual address to Congress in 1875, Grant proposed a constitutional amendment to forbid any legislature to appropriate funds to any religious institution for any purpose. The amendment, which also would have required each state to establish and maintain free elementary schools, was clearly aimed at preventing the diversion of public funds to parochial schools and it appears also to have been intended to discourage parochial education. Grant explained in his address that the survival of democratic government required educated voters. Ignorant citizens would inevitably succumb, he warned, to the tyranny of "the demagogue or . . . priestcraft."[90] In the following year, the Republican platform called for a constitutional amendment to forbid the use of public funds for sectarian schools.[91] Although public apathy doomed the proposed amendment, Roman Catholics discontinued their calls for public funding in the face of Republican opposition.[92]

Public hostility toward parochial schools flared up with a new intensity during the late 1880s and early 1890s, as nativism was stoked by resurgent waves of immigration, growing radicalism among immigrant laborers, and ethnic domination of big-city politics. At its 1891 convention, the National Education Association expressed concern that parochial schools perpetuated foreign traditions and governmental principles that threatened "distinctive Americanism." The antidote, according to the NEA, was the "assimilating power of a public free-school system," which "should be protected from every corrupting influence and every political or religious entanglement."[93] Although public school advocates always had viewed common education as integral to republican virtue, many prominent educators now embraced a statist view of education that rejected the idea that parents had the right to decide what education was best for their children. The public schools also began to abandon religious instruction, although they continued to emphasize moral virtue. Espousing a secular and statist view of education that abandoned the traditional religious role of the schools and was at odds with American notions of individualism and limited government, advocates of public education more than ever viewed the parochial schools as a threat to the public school ideal.[94]

In several major states during the late 1880s, nativists began to wage campaigns against the parochial schools. Attempting to exercise greater control over parochial education, nativists advocated legislation to establish state inspections of parochial schools and to require them to use the English language for instruction in the basic academic subjects. Massachusetts was the first battleground. A bill for state inspection of parochial schools died in the state legislature in 1888 in the face of opposition among a curious coalition of Roman Catholics and Brahmins. In the following year, nativists supported another bill for the inspection of schools that also provided for the imposition of fines against any person who encouraged a parent to withdraw a child from public school or attempted to influence a parent to send a child to parochial school by threatening social, moral, political, or ecclesiastical disabilities. This provision, of course, would have exposed all Roman Catholic clergy to prosecution. After bitter and protracted hearings, Catholics and tolerant Protestants joined forces to defeat the measure.[95]

Meanwhile, opponents of parochial education in Wisconsin supported a state senate bill that provided for public control of private schools. After intense public opposition, the measure died in committee. Later in the year, however, both Wisconsin and Illinois enacted statutes to require the use of English in parochial schools. The Wisconsin statute, known as the Bennett Law, required elementary schools to teach reading, writing, arithmetic, and United States history in the English language.[96] The Illinois statute, known as the Edwards Law, required every child between the ages of seven and fourteen to attend a public school for at least sixteen weeks per year, unless the child had received equivalent instruction in a school approved by local authorities. The statute also required parochial as well as public schools to teach the common subjects in English.[97]

The statutes created a storm of protest among Lutherans and Roman Catholics, especially in heavily German Wisconsin.[98] The controversy over the statute became intertwined with partisan politics, with the more nativistic and moralistic Republicans championing the measure and the more libertarian Democratic party opposing it. Swift and vigorous opposition to the Bennett Law led to its repeal in 1891 after the Republicans suffered a crushing defeat in legislative elections. The statute's repeal enraged proponents of English-language education, who inveighed against the influence of alien ecclesiastics and vowed to reenact the law. The political muscle of Wisconsin's large German and Scandinavian population, however, prevented any reenactment, and a measure to improve the quality of parochial schools was defeated in 1912.[99]

In Illinois the provisions of the Edwards Law for use of the English language may have created less outrage among German Americans since most German schools there already taught the common subjects in English. Roman Catholics and Lutherans nevertheless vigorously opposed the law on the principle that parents should have the right to control the education of their children and that interference with education violated freedom of conscience. In a controversy that presaged the language conflicts of the post–World War I period, many ethnics feared that the Edwards Law augured broader assaults on their churches and schools, while Anglo-Americans defended the need for the law because it encouraged assimilation. As one Congregational minister explained, "Men cannot . . . think American thoughts in other than the American language . . . the language of liberty." After German defections led to an overwhelming defeat for Republicans in the 1892 elections, the Edwards Law was repealed. A new statute guaranteed the rights and privileges of the private schools while providing for limited state regulation.[100]

Bills similar to the Wisconsin and Illinois measures were introduced in other state legislatures in response to agitation from various nativist groups, particularly the American Protective Association, a rabidly anti-Catholic secret society. Opposition by Lutherans led to the defeat of bills in South Dakota, Minnesota, and New York in 1891. An 1894 bill in New York to prohibit instruction in any language other than English was amended until the final measure enacted by the legislature required only the teaching of English grammar. Roman Catholics and Lutherans also succeeded in defeating or modifying bills in Michigan and North Dakota during the first decade of the twentieth century.[101] Measures to require the use of English in instruction in all basic subjects were successful in several other states. California had enacted such a provision in 1872, and similar laws were enacted between 1897 and 1915 in Arizona, Colorado, Indiana, Iowa, Kansas, Massachusetts, Montana, New Mexico, Ohio, Rhode Island, Texas, Utah, and Washington.[102] Meanwhile, the National League for the Protection of American Institutions, a genteel version of the American Protective Association, revived earlier proposals for a constitutional amendment to prohibit allocation of public funds for parochial schools.[103]

The success of parochial schools in fending off nativist assaults during the 1890s was particularly remarkable because the acute economic depression of the mid-1890s exacerbated nativistic sentiments. As in previous times of economic hardship, native-born Protestants found that their ethnic neighbors provided convenient scapegoats for the nation's ills. But though the populist fury that swept rural America during the 1890s contained a notable streak of xenophobia and anti-Catholicism, the numerical strength of ethnic voters in the East and Middle West inhibited most successful politicians outside the South from indulging in overt nativism.[104] Indeed, ethnic voters, especially in the central plains states, were important components of the populist movement.

With the return of prosperity after 1896, nativism waned for nearly two decades, and political agitation against parochial schools largely disappeared. During this period, however, social and economic forces quietly laid the foundation for a recrudescence of nativism and a renewed hostility against parochial education. Beginning in about 1890, immigration from northern and western Europe had begun to decline, and immigration from eastern and southern Europe had markedly increased. Since the nation's thriving economy needed the cheap labor that these immigrants provided, Americans at first were loath to complain about their arrival. Gradually, however, many Americans became fearful that the new immigrants would more radically change the national character than had earlier immigrants from northwestern Europe. Accordingly, the mission of the public school became more important than ever before. The American public school, Fairchild observed in 1913, was the "one great assimilative agency" but was not "a panacea for all ills." Although "a wise and tactful teacher" could instill principles of Americanism during school hours, the public school could never "take the place of both birth and home training," and the isolation of ethnic communities further tended to perpetuate alien traditions.[105] These obstacles against assimilation magnified the importance of public education, since the public schools were the only means by which native Americans could reach many immigrants and their progeny.

The impact of continuing large-scale immigration and the persistence of tight-knit ethnic communities particularly bothered many supporters of the progressive movement who valiantly strove to reform the nation's political and social character during the decade before the American entry into the First World War. Although ethnic voters, especially German Americans, were significant constituents of the progressive movement, middle- and upper-class Anglo-American Protestants dominated the movement. These progressives were imbued with the same moral zeal and nationalistic vision that had animated their ancestors during the pre–Civil War years. Like the antebellum reformers, the progressives viewed public education as a crucial means of transmitting peculiarly American political and cultural values that seemed threatened by rapid social change. Believing that the urbanization and industrialization of the nation after the Civil War imperiled individualism and democracy, the progressives hoped that schools could help to restore the republican virtues of a bygone era. In addition to working for improvement of the public schools and establishing adult education programs, the progressives advocated broader compulsory education laws and crusaded for prohibitions on child labor to transfer impoverished children from the factories to the schools.

Although most prewar progressives were too genteel and optimistic to recite the hateful and ugly litanies of traditional nativism, their profound suspicions of their ethnic neighbors found expression in their attempts to "Americanize" the immigrants and their children by inculcating in them the values and attitudes that progressives cherished. Like the antebellum reformers who supported the common school movement, the progressives often embraced the "melting pot" theory of assimilation. Although some progressives, particularly settlement workers such as Jane Addams, had genuine respect for ethnic cultures, many knew little and cared less about the alien traditions of the immigrants. Few progressives were willing to look beyond the poverty, crime, filth, and chaos that often afflicted ethnic life to see that the immigrant communities were struggling to plant and preserve in American soil the rich and ancient heritages of their European homelands. Even those progressives who took the time to examine ethnic traditions often failed to respect them out of a lack of understanding or a fear that they would supersede American traditions.

The tensions between progressives and ethnic Americans often were exacerbated by the ethnic communities' efforts to thwart the reform measures for which the progressives worked. Progressives particularly resented the political machines that had corrupted politics in many large cities and often had displaced Anglo-Americans from their traditional municipal leadership roles. Progressive efforts to make city governments more honest, rational, and scientific—and to restore power to the Anglo-American elites—often ran afoul of the network of highly personal relationships that supported political machines.

Progressives also found to their dismay that many ethnics opposed reform measures, such as legislation to regulate factory safety and child labor, wages, and hours, that were intended to ameliorate the plight of the poor. Although ethnics often were the principal beneficiaries of these reforms, many preferred to reap the extra income that they believed they could derive from child labor, long hours, and unregulated factory conditions. Progressives therefore found that the ethnics often were willing accomplices of the large-scale industrialists whom the progressives blamed for many of the ills of modern society. In addition to challenging the social position of the professionals, small businessmen, and persons of "old wealth" who comprised the heart of the progressive movement, modern industrialism seemed to the progressives to have corrupted American society by glorifying materialism and promoting special interests that were at odds with broader communal values. Although the efforts of progressives to achieve constructive reform may at first have contributed to a decline of nativism early in the century, an upsurge of nativism during the mid-1910s reflected economic unrest and the failure of progressivism to fulfill the expectations that it had aroused.[106] The attitude of many Protestants toward parochial schools was summarized in a

1913 book, published by a Methodist press, suggesting that the allegedly low standards of the parochial schools threatened democracy. Although the author conceded "the wisdom of a purpose that makes religion an integral part of a child's education for life," he contended that "no patriotic American can view with equanimity the parochial school as ordinarily conducted in this country among the foreign communities." Citing a survey of Polish schools in Buffalo which found that the schools were overcrowded and many teachers were deficient in English, the author explained, "The fact that few Polish families speak English at home makes the need of early and proper instruction of the children all the more important."[107] The persistence of Anglo-American biases against ethnic Americans and the lingering hostility toward foreign-language instruction and parochial education would erupt with virulence when the First World War provided a catalyst for a major revival of nativist sentiments.

2   The War against German America

The lingering controversy over parochial schools and instruction in foreign languages intensified after the start of the war in Europe in 1914 as the Anglo-American world became increasingly hostile toward the German people and their culture. This antipathy for German society and all its manifestations inevitably made German-American parochial schools the target of suspicion and suppression and changed forever the character of instruction in those schools. The animosity of many Americans for German-American schools and other institutions that preserved ethnic identities is impossible to comprehend unless one understands why Britons and Americans turned so ferociously into implacable foes of the German culture that they had so recently admired and emulated. It is therefore useful to explore the British reaction to the Germans, since British propaganda greatly influenced Americans during the thirty-two months before the United States entered the war and served as the foundation for anti-German activities by Americans after their country joined the conflict.

In a gradual and complex process, a war that was motivated by political and economic rivalries and triggered by diplomatic accidents was transformed into a moral crusade. British and later American propaganda relentlessly portrayed the war as an Armageddon in which the forces of freedom were arrayed in a fight to the death against autocracy. In this Manichean conflict, the Allies sought to liberate the human spirit while the Central Powers worked to enslave it. The war, as Woodrow Wilson ultimately explained, was a war to keep the world safe for democracy and a war to end all wars. Allied propaganda tried to identify the Germans with cruelty, ignorance, irreligion, sexual perversion, mendacity, and every other imaginable vice.

Ironically, the high regard for Germany that had prevailed in England and America before the war may have contributed to the virulence of hostility toward Germany after the war began. The prewar admiration of Anglo-Americans for German achievements in scholarship, music, art, literature, and the sciences was tempered by more than a little envy and a gnawing fear that Germanic culture was superior to their own. Thoughtful Anglo-Americans sometimes admitted that the German intellect and temperament seemed more sublime than did their own ostensibly mundane mind and spirit. In his 1910 novel *Howards End,* E. M. Forster explored the differences between the English and the Germans in his portrayals of the prosaic and stolid Wilcox family and their neighbors, the intellectual and artistic Schlegels, who were half-German. Willa Cather drew a similar contrast in her 1922 novel *One of Ours,* in which the Nebraska farm boy Claude Wheeler during his prewar college days was enchanted with the Erlichs, a vibrantly cultured German-American family in Lincoln.

Although Britons and Americans generally agreed that they were better governed than the Germans and that their more solid character shielded them from the excesses for which the Germans had an unfortunate proclivity, they often conceded that Germany and Austria-Hungary led the world in many cultural endeavors. Fears of Germanic cultural hegemony did not, however, prevent Anglo-Americans from maintaining a keen fascination with their prodigious Saxon kin. Throughout the nineteenth century, German universities had pioneered modern methods of scholarship, and study at a German university was almost obligatory for any serious American scholar. The superiority of Germanic music was axiomatic, and Germanic achievements in art generally exceeded those of the Anglo world even if France and the Latin countries may have outdistanced the Germans. In science and technology, Germany enjoyed increasing primacy at a time when these areas were transforming the world as never before or since and faith in the correlation between scientific discovery and human progress was reaching its zenith. German accomplishments in literature also were impressive.

Germanic intellectual achievements, moreover, were leading the world into a modernism that challenged traditional values. Best symbolized by the work of Sigmund Freud in Vienna, these new ideas and forms particularly threatened the complacency of many Anglo-Americans. German cultural superiority was especially troubling to minds that were nursed on the nationalistic ideas and racist theories that pervaded late nineteenth- and early twentieth-century thought.

As Germany advanced to the economic level of Britain and America, fears of cultural inferiority were aggravated by commercial competition. In America, Anglo-Saxon resentment of German economic success was directed against both Germany and the German Americans, whose prosperity was increasingly notable. And although their political institutions remained a special point of pride for Anglo-Americans, even this source of satisfaction was eroded by German advances toward democratic government and the rise of political unrest in Britain and America.

Although the fin de siècle today is remembered as a halcyon time, contemporaries were far less sanguine in their assessment of their age. The optimism and vigor that had characterized the Western world during the past century had begun to give way to malaise and self-doubt. Britain was particularly afflicted with new woes. At the very time when the country stood at the height of its power, British society seemed threatened by disintegration. Intense unrest among the working classes and the growing radicalism of the trade unions threatened the nation's existing political and economic order. The intractable dispute over Irish home rule and the divisive struggle over female suffrage further tattered Britain's social and political fabric. Britain's leaders were keenly aware that the advent of a major war during a period of such unrest could serve as a catalyst for revolution. The danger of revolution was especially great because the trade union movement embraced a vigorous internationalism and its members had vowed not to bear arms against their working-class brothers and sisters in other lands.

The British government also recognized, however, that war might help to reunify a divided country. Sensing the superficiality of the trade union movement's internationalism and recalling that the British working classes had passionately embraced jingoism during recent colonial conflicts, the British government successfully transformed danger into opportunity by appealing to the patriotism of British workers. Rallying behind the Union Jack, the workers of Britain deferred their social and economic demands until the end of the war. Meanwhile, the British government needed to generate support for the war among the middle classes, which admired German culture and had been influenced by the peace movement of recent decades.

From the start of the war, the British government therefore tried to persuade the British public of the essential wickedness of the Germans. The need for mass enlistment in the military—unique in British history—made broad public support imperative. The German invasion of neutral Belgium provided the British with a potent propaganda weapon at the outset of the conflict, and German reprisals against Belgian civilians for resisting the German advance provided further support for British attempts to portray the Germans as atavistic Huns. German attacks on Belgian civilians and their property shocked the civilized world, because armies in modern Europe had generally avoided terrorism. The burning of the great library of the University of Louvain shortly after the start of the war particularly seemed to show that Germany was barbarous. As Albert Marrin has observed, "it would be difficult to overestimate the impact of this seemingly gratuitous display of Teutonic fury on educated opinion the world over."[1] The initiation of German aerial raids over England in December 1914 intensified Britain's moral outrage against its foe. These indiscriminate raids, the first aerial attacks in history, caused substantial civilian casualties and therefore seemed to confirm the growing belief that the Germans were a beastly race. With an imprudent lack of regard for their world image, the Germans continued throughout the war to commit acts that cost more in terms of public relations than they won in terms of military advantage. During 1915 alone, the initiation of gas warfare, the execution of the English nurse Edith Cavell, and the sinking of the *Lusitania* provided the Allied Powers with decisive examples of the brutality from which they were trying to save the world.

As the conflict lapsed into the stalemate of bloody and protracted trench warfare, the staggering human and economic costs encouraged the British government to intensify its propaganda campaign against Germany. Both the government and the people needed to believe that their sacrifices were sanctified by moral imperatives that transcended petty economic and political considerations. Thus more and more British were therefore willing to believe that German society itself was evil. The actions of the German troops increasingly came to be seen as a paradigm of the German character. Not content to cite merely the many authentic examples of German outrages, the insatiable British propaganda machine began to invent them. Exaggerating the incidence of both official and unauthorized German crimes against civilians, the British charged that pillage and rape were endemic to the German military. Cartoons of wild-eyed German soldiers, crowned with spiked helmets and sporting large, kaiser-like mustaches, portrayed the Germans as savages who routinely ravished fair Flemish and French maidens and slew babies in their cradles.

Like the false alarms of Aesop's shepherd boy, the hyperbolic atrocity reports later had tragic consequences, for they encouraged Allied skepticism about reports of massive German atrocities during World War II. Memories of the discredited anti-German propaganda of the First World War may have retarded efforts to stop the attempted genocide of the Jews and other acts so ghastly that they strained credulity until the liberation of the death camps at the end of the war shattered incredulity. It is a tragic irony that reports of German barbarism during World War I were often wildly exaggerated, whereas even the most lurid rumors of German atrocities during World War II failed to convey the full horror of the Holocaust and other crimes.

By the time the United States entered the war in April 1917, most Americans had long been exposed to accounts of German barbarism, both real and imagined. American admiration for the German people already had been seriously eroded by nearly three years of reports and propaganda from anti-German sources. Even many newspapers that favored neutrality had a natural bias in favor of the mother country, and apologists for Britain were far more skillful in manipulating American public opinion than were the heavy-handed Germans and their American sympathizers. The efforts of the German-American press to present a balanced or pro-German view of the conflict inevitably failed to reach the mass of Americans who were not within the German-American community.[2] Unremitting anti-German propaganda eroded respect for German Americans, who until now had been widely admired for their work ethic and the high cultural standards they had brought from the Fatherland.[3] Moreover, repeated warnings by President Wilson and the pro-British against the subversive character of so-called hyphenated Americanism had already aroused antagonism toward German Americans and laid the foundations for the intolerance and persecutions of the war years.[4]

The widespread American outrage against German atrocities and the declining American admiration for German culture did not necessarily translate into broad public support for the war. Although the First World War today is remembered as a popular war that aroused mass enthusiasm among Americans, the rows of flags, streams of bunting, and throngs of rallied patriots that one sees in the old newsreels concealed large-scale opposition to the war. Though many Americans before 1917 had clamored for intervention on behalf of the Allied Powers, a significant number had supported intervention on behalf of the Central Powers. Many German Americans favored intervention on behalf of Germany, as did many Irish Americans, who hoped that the defeat of Britain would secure independence for Ireland. Wilson's policy of neutrality was so popular that it enabled the Democratic president to secure reelection in 1916 against a reunited Republican party. Having shifted abruptly from the neutrality that had allowed the nation to remain aloof from the slaughter in Europe for nearly three years, the government had good reason to be apprehensive about public reaction to the war.

Although the German provocations of late 1916 and early 1917 ensured that Wilson's request for a declaration of war received overwhelming support in Congress, the opposition of six members of the Senate and fifty members of the House provided a sharp reminder of lingering antiwar sentiment. The Wilson administration and prowar members of Congress recognized that this sentiment would not easily disappear and might actually grow as Americans began to suffer the burdens of the conflict. In particular, the government feared that Americans' traditional antipathy toward foreign entanglements would undermine support for the war, which represented a sharp break with the nation's historic policy of nonintervention in European conflicts. Recalling the bitter opposition that military conscription had aroused during the Civil War, officials also worried that a selective service law enacted during the spring of 1917 might provide a catalyst for organized opposition to the war. Although support for the war was widespread and probably grew broader and deeper as the conflict continued, dissent never was entirely silenced. Most German and Irish Americans quickly rallied around the flag, but pacifists and anarchists generally remained opposed to the war. Many socialists also refused to support the war, and the Socialist party officially condemned the war and urged resistance to conscription. Sharp increases in the socialist vote in local elections during 1917 indicated that many Americans harbored hostility toward the war.[5]

In an effort to stifle dissent, Congress enacted laws to punish interference with the war effort. The Espionage Act, which was passed two months after the war began, prescribed penalties for causing insubordination in the armed forces, attempting to obstruct enlistment and recruitment efforts, or conveying false statements with the intent of interfering with military operations.[6] The act also gave the postmaster general the discretion to ban from the mails materials that he deemed treasonous or seditious.[7] One year later, Congress enacted the Sedition Act, which included a section that made it a felony to say or publish anything denigrating the American form of government, the Constitution, or the military forces.[8] Violation of these acts carried penalties of fines up to ten thousand dollars and imprisonment for a maximum of twenty years. More than one thousand convictions were obtained in the more than two thousand cases arising under the two statutes,[9] and countless other persons were convicted in state courts under a multitude of state and local laws. Only a few federal judges, notably Charles A. Amidon of North Dakota and Learned Hand of New York, refused to impose penalties for mere criticism of the war effort. Hand's brave declaration that the state must tolerate any speech that does not directly incite unlawful action was reversed by the court of appeals.[10]

The government recognized, however, that mere suppression of antiwar activity would not be enough to ensure the success of the war effort. It was also necessary to rally widespread positive support for the conflict. In an effort to generate such support, the federal and state governments strove to foster a chauvinistic patriotism that deliberately emphasized America's superiority to Germany. In fanning enthusiasm for the war, the government exploited the energies of the progressive movement, which had flagged in its drive for domestic reform but retained its crusading spirit. Not content merely to assail Germany's army and leaders, the U.S. government and many voluntary organizations followed the example of British propagandists by denouncing all aspects of German culture and transforming the war into a moral crusade. Efforts to disparage German culture reflected widely held fears that the war effort would fail to receive sufficient popular support or would be sabotaged by its numerous opponents.

The government's massive propaganda effort had no precedent in American history. Early in the war, the government formed the Committee on Public Information (CPI), which generated mountains of propaganda to keep patriotism at a heated pitch.[11] Private citizens reinforced the government's activities by forming a multitude of patriotic associations and undertaking various activities to facilitate the war effort. The two largest voluntary societies were the National Security League and its offshoot, the American Defense Society. Both organizations called for unquestioning support for the war and denounced German-American institutions as agents of a pan-German conspiracy. Not surprisingly, the two organizations were hostile toward use of the German language.[12] As the president of the National Security League stated in July 1918, the "animosity, clannishness and the propaganda of undemocratic ideas are sources of injury to the community and the substitution of other languages for our own clearly fosters them."[13]

Having been exposed for so long to anti-German propaganda emanating from Britain, American citizens were well prepared for the anti-German campaigns of the federal government and the patriotic societies. Anti-German hysteria spread rapidly. The animosity soon was directed not merely against Germans and German-American opponents of the war, but against all German Americans who retained a visible ethnicity. As John Higham has pointed out, the "war seemed so encompassing, so arduous, that the slightest division of purpose or lack of enthusiasm appeared an intolerable handicap to it."[14] The hostility against German Americans, which waned in some places as the prospects for Allied victory improved after May 1918, also may have reflected uncertainty about the outcome of the war.[15]

The German-American community particularly frightened many Americans because it was so large, prosperous, and self-confident. Of the 92 million Americans counted in the 1910 census, two and a half million were born in Germany and many millions more were the children or grandchildren of German immigrants. The immense size of the German community and its concentration in a swath of territory stretching from the Middle Atlantic states through the Great Plains enabled German Americans to maintain a distinctive ethnic identity. Even as German Americans adapted themselves to their new home and adopted American ways, they cleaved to their German customs and established a multitude of churches, businesses, social clubs, and other voluntary associations that had a distinctively Germanic character. As one study of ethnic America has observed, German Americans were "one of the few immigrant groups which had sought to 'colonize' the United States, believing their 'culture' was superior to the one they found in the New World."[16]

As the parochial school controversies of the nineteenth century had demonstrated, German attempts to maintain a separate identity always had aroused some suspicions among Americans. As early as the mid-eighteenth century, when large numbers of Germans settled in central Pennsylvania, Benjamin Franklin railed against "the Palatine boors" and expressed fear that the German settlers would become "so numerous as to Germanize us, instead of our Anglifying them."[17] By the late nineteenth and early twentieth centuries, German opposition to prohibition and Sabbatarianism was a special source of tensions between German Americans and many Americans of British ancestry. Despite these tensions, however, the German Americans were widely admired for their work ethic and the high cultural standards that they had carried from the Fatherland.

The advent of the war precipitated a paroxysm of hostility toward German ethnicity. Although part of this frenzy reflected the revival of old nativist impulses, much of it arose out of fears that Germans did not loyally support the war effort. These fears were not entirely unfounded. Many Germans naturally opposed a war against their Teutonic kin, and more than a few had the temerity to continue to disparage the war publicly even after the United States entered it. Other Germans, however, were hostile to the German government since they or their ancestors had come to America to escape political or religious repression. A small but prominent group of German Americans, for example, proudly traced their ancestry to the so-called Forty-Eighters, who had fled Germany after the Revolution of 1848. Since, as Frederick C. Luebke has pointed out, German Americans were "anything but uniform in their response to the war," generalizations about German-American loyalty to the war effort were difficult to make, although it seems fair to say that the large majority of German Americans remained loyal to the United States.[18] Many Americans simply assumed, however, that German Americans naturally would be sympathetic toward Germany.

Hostility toward German Americans during the war provided a new focus for the nativism that had festered in American life during the past several decades. German Americans replaced Roman Catholics and aliens as the nativist bogy for the duration of the war. The animus against German Americans distracted attention from the traditional objects of nativist fury, and wartime unity and commonality of purpose helped to break down traditional social barriers between Anglo-Americans and ethnic Americans other than Germans. As Higham has observed, any xenophobia that was not related to the war was an unaffordable luxury.[19]

In addition to attracting the antagonism of unabashed nativists, German Americans became the focus of attention among progressives and other Anglo-Americans who often had worried about the baneful effects of ethnic culture on traditional American values. The crusading zeal of the progressives that had been directed against corruption by ethnic political bosses was easily transferred to the effort to destroy "kaiserism" both abroad and at home. Similarly, fears of the tyranny of kaiserism supplanted fears about the traditionalistic authoritarianism of Rome and the socialistic authoritarianism of labor movements in which immigrants were prominent. German Americans also symbolized ethnic opposition to the forces of social reform and regeneration. In the words of one scholar, the First World War enabled American Protestant churches "to link their domestic campaigns against immigrant influence with wartime patriotism."[20] Accordingly, both pietistic and Social Gospel clergy were among the most vociferous supporters of the war.[21] As in Britain, German atrocities, both real and imagined, facilitated ecclesiastical efforts to present the war as a moral crusade and to provide a religious justification for it. Americanization of immigrants, the temperance movement, and the fight to extend democracy thus were "woven into one great moral endeavor."[22] Although most clergy refrained from the more extreme manifestations of militancy, most denominations offered unstinting support for the war, organizing chaplaincy programs and assisting with such war efforts as food conservation and the purchase of war bonds.[23]

The widespread use of the German language was the most visible aspect of German ethnicity and became the primary target of anti-German hysteria. Although the use of German among German Americans already was waning before the First World War,[24] it remained the language of a multitude of social clubs, newspapers, churches, and parochial schools. In many rural communities and in large parts of such cities as New York, Philadelphia, Baltimore, Cincinnati, St. Louis, and Milwaukee, German was the principal language. The nation also was dotted with local chapters of the Turnverein, the German-American Alliance, and other organizations through which German-speaking Americans sought to perpetuate the German language and culture in America and to carry on their campaigns in opposition to a pietistic social agenda. The German language, moreover, was widely preserved through a powerful press. As of 1917, there were 522 German-language periodicals in the United States.[25] German also continued to be used extensively in the churches. In 1916, approximately two hundred Roman Catholic parishes in the United States used the German language exclusively and another two thousand partially used it. The use of German was even more widespread among the Lutherans, since they, unlike the Roman Catholics, were able to form ethnically homogeneous denominations. On the eve of the First World War, approximately half the nation's two million German-American Lutherans worshiped in the German language,[26] although there was a strong trend toward the use of English.[27] German also was widely used among the small German Reformed and Mennonite bodies.[28]

The use of the German language by the Lutheran churches and schools particularly aroused the suspicion of nativists because Lutheranism was a principal target of nativist hostility during the First World War. Since Martin Luther was German and nearly two-thirds of the population of Germany was at least nominally Lutheran, "German" and "Lutheran" were virtually inseparable terms to many persons, even though only half the world's Lutherans were Germans and substantially fewer than half the German Americans were Lutheran. Lutherans were a minority among German Americans because many Lutheran immigrants were unchurched or had joined other Protestant denominations. Moreover, Jews, Protestant sectarians, and freethinkers may have been disproportionately represented among German immigrants, since many members of those groups had left Germany in pursuit of greater religious and political freedom. Although there probably were more Roman Catholics than Lutherans among America's Germans, non-German Americans did not identify the Roman Catholic church with Germany since Catholicism in the United States and the rest of the world was primarily non-German. Unlike Roman Catholicism, however, American Lutheranism was heavily German.

Although some Lutherans were descended from early immigrants and were highly Americanized, a substantial number lived in the largely unassimilated German communities that the Americanizers so distrusted. Many other Lutherans lived in Scandinavian ethnic communities that likewise aroused nativist suspicions, since the physical characteristics, customs, mores, and religion of the Scandinavians seemed closely to resemble those of the Germans. Lutheran aloofness toward other Protestant churches also raised nativist fears, as did their parochial schools and the bitter opposition of some synods to the fraternal lodges that were so popular and prominent in small-town America during the early twentieth century.[29] The movement of Lutheranism into the mainstream of American society was further retarded by the tendency of assimilated Lutherans to convert to other Protestant denominations.

After the war began, suspicions about lack of patriotism among Lutherans were reinforced by the refusal of many Lutheran clergy to cooperate with activities such as the sale of war bonds. Failing to appreciate Lutheran sensitivity toward any sign of "unionism," Anglo-American Protestants were insulted that Lutheran clergy often refused to sit on the same platforms with clergy of other denominations at patriotic rallies, even though many Roman Catholic priests and Jewish rabbis in this pre-ecumenical age were willing to appear alongside Protestant clergy at these events. Anglo-American Protestants also failed to comprehend that appeals for the sale of war bonds during church services would have violated Lutheran liturgical propriety.[30] Anglo-American Protestants likewise did not understand that American Lutherans shunned political involvement, partly because Luther taught a form of quietism and also because many Lutherans, particularly German Lutherans, had come to the United States in order to escape entanglements between church and state. Despite their initial reluctance to cooperate with the war effort, however, Lutherans recognized the importance of dispelling fears about their lack of patriotism. As one Missouri Synod pastor observed, "if our church gets into disrepute during the war, it will kill our future missionary success among Americans—the greatest mission field we have."[31] Ultimately, Lutheran churches became enthusiastically engaged in wartime activities.[32]

Meanwhile, Lutherans of German extraction vigorously sought to eliminate the erroneous but widely held belief that their synods maintained official ties to the state churches of Germany and that the kaiser was a Lutheran. In a pamphlet published in 1918, Theodore Graebner, a professor at the Missouri Synod's seminary in St. Louis and editor of the *Lutheran Witness,* explained that the Missouri Synod opposed the unionistic religious policies of the German government and was estranged from many Lutherans in Germany. Graebner emphasized that the kaiser was a Calvinist and pointed out that some American Presbyterians before the war therefore had proudly counted him within their fold.[33] Although Graebner's editorials in the *Lutheran Witness* pointed out the need for Lutherans to avoid criticism of the war, the *Witness* did not encourage patriotic activism and Graebner privately admitted five months after the nation went to war that he had been unable to determine "which nation has a righteous cause."[34]

Despite the efforts of Graebner and other enlightened Lutheran leaders, rational arguments failed to dispel the growing hysteria against all manifestations of German culture or to halt the harassment of German Americans.[35] Hostility was particularly pronounced in the states of the Great Plains and the upper Middle West, where the German-American population of the United States was concentrated. But while the mere size of the German community in those states helps to explain why Germans were the targets of much abuse, many other elements contributed to the patterns of hostility against German Americans.

Hostility toward Germans tended to be especially intense in areas where Germans were the most distinctive and alien ethnic group. Thus, although the percentage of first- and second-generation German Americans in New

York was nearly as high as it was in Nebraska, South Dakota, and Iowa,[36] which witnessed significant acts of animosity toward German communities, there never was any great upsurge of hostility against Germans in New York. The presence of high numbers of other and less assimilated ethnic groups in New York may have made the German community there less visible than it was in middle western states, in which Germans and their Scandinavian cousins tended to be the largest ethnic groups. German-American communities in the East often were more fragmented than were the German communities of the Middle West. In the major eastern cities, German communities included immigrants from a wide range of German-speaking locations and embraced Jews, Catholics, Calvinists, Lutherans, and freethinkers. In the Middle West, Germans tended to cluster in settlements that were ethnically and religiously more homogeneous. In a few states, particularly Wisconsin and Minnesota, German Americans may have been protected from the more extreme manifestations of discrimination because they were so numerous that they constituted a formidable political force. In states such as Nebraska and Iowa, however, the German community was large enough to attract the attention and fears of nativists but not large enough to protect itself easily from nativistic assaults.

Antagonism toward German Americans was aggravated in the Great Plains states because many German Americans there were emigrants from Russia, descendants of the industrious Germans whom Catherine the Great had lured to her underdeveloped realm during the eighteenth century with promises of free land and perpetual exemption from military service. These immigrants aroused particular suspicion among their neighbors because they "held on more tenaciously to their German language and their curiously blended heritage of German and Russian customs" than did other German immigrant groups.[37] The war against Germany intensified distrust of these immigrants, and the Bolshevist scare that followed the war further exacerbated this hostility.[38]

The concentration of German Americans in the Middle West enabled Germans there to hold fast to their ethnic traditions and to resist assimilation more effectively than did their counterparts elsewhere. Anglo-Americans in the Middle West during the war often expressed outrage because second-, third-, and fourth-generation German Americans continued to cleave to their ethnic ways. In a 1918 letter to the editor of the *New York Times,* the chairman of the Iowa Council of National Defense explained that "the language question in States like New York and in Western States like Iowa is entirely different," because "you are struggling to make Americans out of foreigners, and we are struggling to prevent Americans from being converted into foreigners."[39]

Antagonism toward German Americans also may have been especially intense in the Middle West because the elites in those states were less secure than were their counterparts in the East and the South. Like many frontier societies, the Great Plains states were characterized by a paradoxical combination of toleration and conformism. The lack of well-established social institutions, the absence of any ancient ruling class, and the constant influx of newcomers created an environment that eroded tradition and was receptive to social and economic mobility and cultural diversity. But although a frontier society could not afford social rigidity, neither could it sustain cultural deviations that threatened a fragile social fabric. Recognizing the need for common values that would help to forge identity and foster social cohesion, the Anglo-American elites promoted fundamental practices such as the use of the English language and apotheosized simple symbols of patriotism such as the flag. In newly settled areas in which Yankees were scarcely more entrenched than were their immigrant neighbors, Anglo-Americans felt threatened by ethnics who refused to honor the verities of Americanism. A Boston Brahmin who disdained the increasingly numerous Irish was buttressed by inherited wealth and could retreat to his clubs, charities, hobbies, and network of influential friends in America and abroad. An Anglo-American Nebraska merchant whose county was heavily populated by Germans might fear that he faced social and economic extinction.

Hostility toward the use of the German language was particularly pronounced in Iowa, where large numbers of German Americans lived in closely knit communities that became targets of suspicion and resentment among their Anglo-American neighbors. A businessmen's club in a small Iowa town, for example, complained to the State Council of Defense in February 1918, "You do not know what we out in these rural districts have to put up with." Expressing frustration over the apparent failure of diplomatic efforts to inspire greater enthusiasm for the war effort among local Germans, club members declared that the time had come to use the "hickory club" and that only a "hanging bee" would wake up "some of these old moss-backed Germans . . . to the fact that they are living in America." In reply, the State Council urged the local leaders to continue to use diplomatic means to try to persuade Germans to discontinue the use of the German language.[40] Late in 1917, H. J. Metcalf, the secretary of the Iowa Council of National Defense, had advised "extreme caution" in dealing with German clergy since "we have no power to say to these men that they may not preach German in their churches and it would not be right to do this."[41] By early 1918, however, the council was warning individual Lutheran ministers and teachers to refrain from teaching and preaching in German. "In all cases this has proven effective," Metcalf observed late in April.[42]

This tactic was not effective enough, however, for Iowa governor William L. Harding. On May 23, 1918, Harding issued a proclamation that prescribed English as the sole medium of instruction in public, private, and denominational schools and as the sole means of communication in public addresses and conversations in public places, on trains, and over the telephone. Persons who could not understand or speak the English language were instructed to conduct religious worship services in their homes. The proclamation discussed and attempted to dismiss the obvious constitutional objections that the decree created. Although Harding acknowledged that the federal and state constitutions protected freedom of speech and freedom of religion, he contended that no person had the right to speak or worship in a foreign language during a time when the use of foreign languages might "excite suspicion or produce strife among the people."[43]

Despite his peremptory language, Harding and the Iowa Council of National Defense interpreted the proclamation with some flexibility. Two weeks after issuing his proclamation, Harding permitted a Lutheran pastor in Davenport to preach his sermon in German after the regular service for the benefit of elderly parishioners who spoke little English. Attendance at the German sermon, however, was limited to persons who had attended the English-language service. The same congregation eliminated unnecessary ceremony from its monthly Communion services and offered the essential elements of its eucharistic liturgy in both English and German. Harding agreed to these concessions because the congregation already had demonstrated its desire for anglicization by conducting most of its services in English and eliminating German from its parochial school.[44] Harding later extended a similar dispensation to other congregations.[45] Although a few ministers defied the order,[46] most congregations attempted to comply with it. A Missouri Synod leader reported in October that "conditions are different in the various sections of the state. Some sections are quiet, others unruly, still others under actual mob rule."[47] The fluidity of the situation was demonstrated by the changing practices of one Lutheran pastor in Sioux County. This pastor originally complied with the decree by using only English. Then, for a while, he offered German translations of his sermons. By October, the county council of defense asked only that he conduct an English-language service on the same day on which he led a German service.[48]

Despite the growing relaxation of the order, however, some congregations were forced to disband. Meanwhile, Harding continued his crusade against the use of foreign languages, declaring in June 1918 that "there is no use in anyone wasting his time praying in other languages than English. God is listening only to the English tongue."[49] Recognizing that Harding's extremism embarrassed their state, many Iowans ridiculed the language proclamation. Calling for its revocation, the *Des Moines Register* denounced its "enormous injustice"[50] and explained that "America is not primarily a piece of land, nor a language, nor a church, nor a race," but rather "a high level of human attainment."[51]

Although Iowa was the only state that banned the German language altogether, other Great Plains states imposed significant restrictions on its use. In Kansas, the State Council of Defense in January 1918 called for the exclusive use of English in public meetings and urged the elimination of the German language from church services.[52] The council did not, however, insist on the elimination of the German language in churches or in any other public places other than elementary schools.[53]

In South Dakota, the State Council of Defense during the spring of 1918 prohibited the use of the German language in both public and private schools and in all public meetings, including church services. The council stated, however, that it would grant permits for the use of German in meetings and worship services on a showing that "the use of the German language upon such occasions is necessary and is not detrimental to the best interests of the state and nation."[54] Two months later, the council extended its order to prohibit the use of German over the telephone and in assemblies of three or more persons in any public place, except in instances of emergency. Violation of the order carried a maximum penalty of one year in jail and a fine of one thousand dollars.[55] Although the governor was reported to have believed that these measures were too extreme, he acquiesced to political pressure and refused to make concessions to the German-American community.[56]

In neighboring Montana, hostility toward the German language likewise was intense. In March 1918, a mob in Lewistown stormed the local high school, harassed the principal for continuing to allow German instruction, and seized German textbooks, which were burned as the mob sang patriotic songs.[57] In the following month, the Council of Defense issued an order prohibiting the use of German in church services.[58] In Missouri, the Council of Defense in July 1918 expressed its opposition to the use of German in schools, churches, and public meetings but did not expressly prohibit it.[59]

Much depended on the attitudes of state and local officials. In North Dakota, Governor Lynn J. Frazier prevented official interferences with the use of the German language, and there was relatively little local agitation against the teaching of German.[60] Likewise, in Utah, a state with a much smaller German American population, hostility against German-Americans may have been ameliorated by the influence of the governor, a highly respected native of Germany who actively supported the war effort.[61] Animosity toward Germans and their language may have been tempered in Minnesota by the presence of a governor, superintendent of public instruction, and public safety commissioner who as Swedish Americans were sensitive to the needs of their German-American cousins.[62] Similarly, hostility toward German Americans in Kansas may have been ameliorated after Martin Graebner, Theodore Graebner's brother, was named to the State Council of Defense at the behest of the German community during the summer of 1918.[63] In Illinois, Governor Frank O. Lowden provided a restraining influence.[64] Unfortunately, President Wilson probably fanned the flames of intolerance. On several occasions during the war, Wilson publicly exaggerated the extent of German-American disloyalty, and his denunciation of mob violence mid-1918 was too little and too late.[65]

Restrictions on the use of German created hardships for elderly persons who were unable to speak English. After the Franklin County Council of Defense in Iowa requested the discontinuation of German-language church services, a German Baptist minister complained to the Iowa Council of National Defense in April 1918 that "the aged people should not be deprived of the benefit of worship." Assuring the council that members of the congregation supported the war effort and had purchased large amounts of war bonds, he predicted that they would be thankful "and do even more if the use of the German language is allowed to them in public worship."[66] A Lutheran minister in Oklahoma who favored the use of English as the primary language in church services and supported the abolition of German in parochial schools nevertheless complained that the elimination of German in church services would constitute "religious persecution" since it "would be tantamount to hindering me from preaching the Gospel to quite a few" of the elderly parishioners, who knew little or no English.[67] As Graebner ob-

served to another correspondent, however, "the plea of constitutional violation is valid, but it will not avail in time of war."[68]

As the anti-German hysteria spread, acts of violence against German
Americans and their property increased. In perhaps the most egregious incident, a mob in Collinsville, Illinois, lynched a young German immigrant in
April 1918, even though the victim protested his loyalty to America and does
not appear to have given anyone any reason to doubt his patriotism.[69]
Countless other Germans, including some clergymen, were beaten or were
tarred and feathered.[70] Shortly before the end of the war, a German Lutheran church in rural Kansas was burned to the ground by a mob, and a Lutheran church in Indiana that had refused to stop teaching German was destroyed by dynamite.[71] A Lutheran school in Lincoln, Missouri, that had
continued to offer instruction in the German language was destroyed by ar-
sonists. The local pastor had advised his parishioners to eliminate the use of
German in the school, but they had refused to listen to him.[72]

It was the use of German in the parochial schools that most aroused the
ire of self-styled patriots. The more realistic proponents of Americanization
recognized that there was little that they could do to eradicate the use of
German among adults, but they hoped that the schools would break the
German language cycle. The Americanizers particularly feared that children
could not properly absorb American values and become good citizens unless they received instruction in the English language. A bank president who
asked the Minnesota Commission of Public Safety to close the local Lutheran school contended, for example, "We must be one united people and
we will never be as long as these people are permitted to carry on their
school and their church in their Mother tongue."[73] Moreover, many persons
alleged that German-language schools tried to instill in their students a loyalty toward Germany and an admiration for autocracy. As one county attorney complained to the Minnesota Public Safety Commission, the German-
language schools taught "principles destructive of democracy" to children
"at the most impressionable age."[74] Similarly, a Congregationalist minister
in a small town warned the commission that a local parochial school was
"teaching our American boys and girls to be good Germans."[75] And a public
school teacher insisted that "those children are getting lessons in disloyalty
that will stick by them *all their lives,* and . . . the rabid pro-Germanism of
some these young men born in America comes from such schools."[76] The inability of many military conscripts to read or write in English especially con-

tributed to fears that vast segments of the population were politically unreliable.

Critics of German-language education also contended that the German-language schools undermined the quality of public education. The alleged opposition of German Americans toward tax increases and bond issues for the support of public education particularly inspired resentment. In areas where German Americans comprised a large segment of the population, supporters of public education complained bitterly about German Americans who erected fine new parochial school buildings after helping to vote down revenue measures for the improvement of the public schools.[77] By keeping students away from the public schools, the private schools also reduced the number of public schools that the states could maintain. This especially was a problem in rural areas, where a reduction in the number of public schools might force public school children to travel a long distance to school. In middle western states, for example, many citizens complained to state officials that the German schools were interfering with public education and had forced the closing of public schools.[78] A Minnesota school superintendent alleged that the Germans were trying "to kill the public schools."[79]

Hostility toward the parochial schools also arose out of the widespread belief that the quality of the schools was low. One public school teacher in rural Minnesota reported that German schools often had only one teacher for as many as 120 students and that the students learned "*next to nothing* in those schools except German reading, writing and their catechism."[80] Critics of the parochial schools also believed that graduates of parochial elementary schools often were poor students in the public high schools, if they attended high school at all. In Garfield County, Oklahoma, where the Council of Defense attempted to close Lutheran schools, the county school superintendent was able to demonstrate that there was a county high school in every district in which there was no parochial school but that no district that had a parochial elementary school had a high school.[81] Lutheran leaders privately admitted that criticism of the quality of the parochial schools was not unwarranted. Martin Graebner believed that the fault lay not with the schools but with German-American parents who were indifferent toward education.[82]

The network of German parochial schools was extensive. In 1910, the Missouri Synod operated more than two thousand elementary schools enrolling more than one hundred thousand students. One thousand schools were operated by other Lutheran synods, and the German Evangelical Synod of North America maintained another three hundred.[83] The Roman Catholic church also maintained many parochial schools in predominantly German parishes. The extent to which German was used in parochial schools differed widely among congregations and denominations. Although the German language was taught in virtually all these schools, many of them taught all basic subjects in the English language. Responding to the pressures and exigencies of assimilation, many schools during the early twentieth century had therefore begun to do voluntarily what they had so bitterly resented being forced to do in the late nineteenth century. English-language instruction was the norm in the Missouri Synod schools. Although some other denominations provided instruction only in German, many of the students who attended those schools also attended English-language public schools during at least part of the year.[84]

Some Lutheran leaders believed that it was natural that the use of German in parochial schools created public hostility. Theodore Graebner commented that "two thousand German schools in France or Italy or England at this time would be unthinkable."[85] Like other assimilationist Lutheran leaders, Graebner perceived that the war presented a welcome opportunity to hasten the process of Americanization of his church and its schools.[86] To Graebner, the use of German in the schools was "an anachronism"[87] that had caused the church to suffer "staggering losses" of members. He believed that even religious instruction in German was unwise since children were more conversant with English.[88] Another Lutheran minister observed that the continued use of German in the churches was "suicidal to the future of the Lutheran Church in this country."[89] And a Lutheran attorney in the U.S. Department of Justice remarked in 1918 that opponents of a transition to the English language in the church "seem to be more concerned about their grand-fathers than their grand-sons."[90]

Graebner complained that many other synod leaders failed to understand the urgency of the need to make a transition to the use of English,[91] and he expressed fear that stubborn insistence on the continued use of German would encourage authorities to close parochial schools.[92] Although Graebner admitted that he felt "a sharp pang of regret" when his young son brought home a stack of German books after the St. Louis parochial schools eliminated German instruction, he observed, "In the vast world-movements now taking place we must [be] prepared to give up dear possessions, if only the free preaching of the gospel is not hindered."[93] In an effort to persuade federal authorities to protect this liberty, he provided the Department of War with information about interference with German-American religious activities.[94]

Other Lutheran leaders privately acknowledged that public antipathy toward the church was not wholly unjustified since many clergy were hostile toward the American cause. One Lutheran pastor in South Dakota confided to Graebner shortly before the armistice that "we are to blame to a great extent for the hatred that fills the hearts of the English element in our country." Recalling "vicious remarks . . . concerning our government" that he had heard at conferences of clergy, the pastor remarked, "If the government had clever detectives out on the lawn, a half dozen of our ministers would now be at Leavenworth." He added that disloyal "preachers can lie like thunder if confronted with the Defense Council."[95] Graebner admitted privately that "Germany did actually try to establish a Germany" in America.[96]

Anglo-American reactions toward parochial education during the war varied widely within states. In Idaho, for example, local authorities closed Lutheran parochial schools in at least two small towns, and the school in another village was closed after the Lutheran church received anonymous threats to destroy church property. In several other communities, however, schools and churches were not molested even though at least some of them continued to use German. Other parishes may have avoided trouble by switching to the exclusive use of English. A Lutheran minister predicted in June 1918 that "it seems as if we shall have no further difficulty so long as the German language is discontinued."[97]

In Minnesota, the state superintendent of education, Carl Gustav Schultz, advised the Commission of Public Safety in October 1917 that private and parochial schools should be required to offer instruction only in English.[98] In response to Schultz's recommendation and various citizens who had complained about the use of German in parochial schools, the commission in November 1917 officially urged all schools to use English exclusively, except in foreign-language and religion classes.[99] In May 1918, however, Schultz reported that fewer than one-third of the 307 private and parochial schools used English as the exclusive language of instruction. Nearly two-thirds of the schools used both German and English, and a smattering of schools conducted classes in English and Polish, French, Dutch, Bohemian, Norwegian, or Danish.[100] With the blessing of the commission, Schultz in August 1918 requested all private, parochial, and public schools to use only English as a medium of instruction during the coming school year.[101] The commission decreed that religious instruction in foreign languages had to be limited to forty-five minutes.[102]

In states that restricted the use of any language other than English, members of non-German ethnic groups complained about unfair discrimination. In Minnesota, for example, a Roman Catholic priest in a heavily Polish parish warned in May 1918 that the proposal to make English the exclusive medium of instruction would create resentments that would dampen Polish-American enthusiasm for the war.[103] A Franco-American resident of Minneapolis complained that the elimination of French in his children's parish school would emulate "Prussian methods." Contending that "we are in this war for liberty . . . [n]ot to make the world English," he told the Public Safety Commission that the state should strive to "produce world citizens."[104]

Parochial schools generally acquiesced in the elimination of German from the schools. As Graebner pointed out to a Kansas pastor in April 1918, "it is useless to argue with state officials or Councils of Defense when the public mind is set against the use of German."[105] A South Dakota pastor who had tried to persuade the Council of Defense to condone German-language services for the aged observed that "anyone who appreciates what a task it has been to get even such a small concession can easily conclude that it would be the height of folly to try to get the larger concession of being permitted to teach German in the schools."[106]

Parochial schools also usually yielded to informal pressures. After a Lutheran pastor in Mt. Leonard, Missouri, received an anonymous note threatening that he could expect a "committee" visit if the church and its school did not refrain from the use of German, the pastor dryly told Graebner, "We found it to be [a] wise move to preach and teach in the English language only." Graebner commended his prudence. "Anything else," Graebner assured him, "would have meant the end of your congregation, so you had no choice."[107] Graebner explained, "No state governor or president of the United States can protect you against popular sentiment. They might place a regiment of soldiers around your church to protect you but you would have no people in church." On Armistice Day, Graebner complained to a South Dakota pastor that many Lutherans had called the *Witness* cowardly because "the editors, sitting safely ensconced in a big city with ample police protection, did not tell their brethren elsewhere to dare the mob and call upon the 'authorities' for protection on 'constitutional grounds.'"[108]

Parochial school teachers who asked for protection often found that it was not available. After a mob in Steeleville, Illinois, warned a teacher to close a Lutheran school that already had discontinued the teaching of German, the teacher sought help from local authorities, who replied that they could offer no protection. "This was a very fine thing to hear from your government," the teacher complained to Graebner. After the authorities refused to intervene, the mob returned to the teacher's house one evening and ordered him to leave the town within twenty-four hours. He left early the next morning, accompanied by two armed men.[109]

Opposition to the use of German in nonpublic schools was less pronounced in the eastern states. A Massachusetts pastor reported to Graebner in October 1918 that there had been virtually no hostility against the teaching of German in parochial schools in New England and that there was no discernible animosity toward the Missouri Synod.[110] In New York, the Board of Regents decreed in 1918 that all instruction in private, parochial, and public elementary schools should be in the English language. The superintendent of schools later advised a Lutheran minister that nonpublic schools had a legal right to give instruction in foreign languages after the regular school hours.[111]

Opponents of the use of the German language also attempted to eliminate German from the public schools. At the outset of the war, German instruction was not widespread in public elementary schools. Only 19 cities out of 163 that reported to the Bureau of Education in 1917 taught foreign languages below the seventh grade, and only twelve offered instruction in German.[112] The use of German was much more common in the high schools. Nearly 95 percent of the more than one thousand secondary schools accredited by the North Central Association in 1917 offered German courses.[113]

After America entered the war, German-language instruction in the public schools became highly controversial. "Judging from the conduct of the German government in this war German ought to be the prevailing language in hell, but our schools are not supposed to be preparing students for a future abode in that locality," observed a 1918 editorial in a midwestern farm journal.[114] Some opponents of the continuation of German-language instruction contended that there was a close correlation between language and thought patterns and that students who learned to speak German therefore would tend to think like Germans.[115] Opponents also expressed fear that instruction in German would subconsciously encourage admiration of German culture and society.[116] They claimed, moreover, that instruction in German provided a means for German propagandists to infiltrate the educational system.[117]

Some prominent organizations also opposed German-language instruction. The American Defense Society in February 1918 called for the prohibition of compulsory study of German in the public schools.[118] The National Security League conducted a similar crusade and boasted of its successes in persuading school authorities to discontinue instruction in German and to disband German musical and literary clubs.[119] The Union League Club of New York and the Sons of the American Revolution passed resolutions calling for the expulsion of German from the public schools,[120] and an Americanization conference attended by eighteen governors urged Congress to enact legislation to prohibit instruction in the elementary subjects in German.

Although the agitation for abandonment of German-language instruction in the schools received some support from professional educators, most leading educators defended German-language instruction.[121] Early in 1918, the U.S. Commissioner of Public Education, Philander P. Claxton, declared that elimination of German-language instruction in the high schools and colleges was irrational and impractical. He contended that the war had not diminished the cultural and scientific value of German writings and that it would be "very foolish" to "rob ourselves of the ability to profit by them." Claxton also predicted that postwar Germany would become a major economic power and that Americans thus would "need a knowledge of the German language more than we have needed it in the past."[122] Other federal authorities likewise firmly opposed prohibitions on German in the public schools.[123]

Similarly, John Preston Hoskins told the Modern Foreign Language Conference of the National Education Association in July 1918 that Americans would enter the postwar period with "one hand tied behind our back" if the nation neglected the study of the German language, since Germany was certain to reemerge as a formidable economic competitor.[124] Likewise, a teacher at Washburn College in Topeka, Kansas, declared that "the people that produced Luther and Melanchthon, Goethe and Schiller, Beethoven and Wagner will always be worth hearing about."[125] Urging moderation on the part of the Minnesota State School Board, a local school board contended that the elimination of German from the high school curriculum would not hurt the Germans but would "be to our own impoverishment."[126] Advocates of German instruction also argued that the study of German provided mental discipline and enriched students' understanding of the English language.[127]

Advocates of German instruction contended that patriotic teachers could instill admiration for the German language and civilization without promoting the evils of kaiserism.[128] Hoskins, for example, explained that the German government's "autocratic methods, its violation of treaties and the brutality of its methods of waging war have no necessary and organic connection with the language and the literature." The study of German, he insisted, would no more inculcate those qualities in American children than had the study of Latin inspired gladiatorial combats or the study of Spanish encouraged bullfights and an inquisition.[129] A Miami University professor maintained that teachers could avoid the German contagion by shunning any discussion of modern Germany and teaching only about the glories of the German past.[130]

Advocates of the continuation of German-language instruction also pointed out that Britain and France had not diminished instruction in German and that Germany had not discouraged instruction in English and French.[131] Indeed, English-language study in Germany was reported to have increased since the start of the war. The French inspector-general of schools declared that a knowledge of German was essential to understanding Germany and guarding against the blandishments of German propaganda.[132] Similarly, a British government committee urged more extensive study of the German language,[133] and many American educators noted that a knowledge of the German language would facilitate the defeat of Germany.[134] As Professor Allen Wilson Porterfield of Columbia commented, "to understand the Germans it is necessary to know their language."[135]

A survey of a thousand public school superintendents by the *Literary Digest* during early 1918 revealed strong sentiment for preserving German-language instruction at levels beyond the elementary schools.[136] In a statement issued late in 1917, the Bureau of Education of the Department of the Interior declared that "a knowledge of the German language is more important now than it was before the war." The bureau explained, however, that educators generally questioned the use of teaching any foreign languages in the lower grades.[137]

The bureau helped persuade the governor of Kentucky to veto a bill prohibiting the teaching of the German language in the public schools.[138] President Wilson privately dismissed the agitation to ban German-language instruction as "ridiculous and childish,"[139] but he refrained from making any public comment on the controversy.[140]

Although it was easy for advocates of German instruction to ridicule the attitude that "the German word, like German beer, once taken into the mouth, steals away the brains,"[141] rational discourse failed to withstand the onslaught of impassioned patriotism. Despite broad support among educators for German-language instruction, enrollment in German-language courses plummeted throughout the war, and many schools abandoned German instruction. In March 1918, the *Literary Digest*'s survey on the teaching of German revealed that German had been dropped from the curriculum in at least 149 school districts throughout the nation. Although German continued to be taught in 868 districts that responded to the *Digest*'s survey, many superintendents in these districts reported that there were plans to remove German from the curriculum during the coming school year, and reports of declining enrollment were legion.[142] Four months later, a *New York Times* survey estimated that enrollment in German had fallen by at least 50 percent since the start of the war and that it would virtually disappear in the elementary schools during the coming year. The *Times* found that action to reduce or eliminate German had been taken in three-quarters of the states.[143]

Since educational policies were controlled by different units of government in different states, the means of curtailing German instruction varied widely. In most states, authority to eliminate German was vested entirely in the local school boards.[144] Policies concerning German instruction therefore often differed widely within states or even within counties. In California and Iowa, the study of German was discontinued by resolutions of the state boards of education during the spring of 1918.[145] In the same period in South Dakota and Montana, the state councils of defense ordered the suspension of all instruction in German. Florida terminated German instruction by simply eliminating all German books from the list of state-adopted texts.[146] In Missouri, after the governor and the State Council of Defense had called for the elimination of German in schools and all other public places, the state superintendent of schools announced that no units of German instruction would count toward requirements for high school graduation.[147] In banning or discouraging the use of German, state authorities reiterated widespread arguments concerning the evils of the German language. The California State Board of Education, for example, declared that German was "a language that disseminates the ideals of autocracy, brutality and hatred."[148] On a more constructive level, state and federal authorities introduced patriotic exercises in the public schools and used them to help coordinate wartime activities.[149]

Even many educators who deplored the unreasoning hatred of the German language were willing to acknowledge that elimination of German from the public school curriculum might produce some benefits. Although the *School Review* declared in October 1917 that "to withdraw our attention from the tongue of Luther, Gutenberg, Goethe, Kant, Schiller, and Beethoven, is the height of pettiness," its editors questioned whether school districts should continue to spend large sums to teach German to children when they lacked adequate funds to teach English to foreign-born citizens.[150] In the following year, the *Review* acknowledged that some of the more far-reaching efforts to prohibit the use of German seemed hysterical but that the exigencies of the war might justify restrictions on German instruction.[151] Many Americans agreed with this conclusion, and support for extreme measures continued even after the end of the war.

3   The Postwar Hysteria

By the time of the armistice in November 1918, numerous campaigns against the German language in America had substantially reduced its use. Although German Americans naturally hoped that the hysteria against the German tongue would subside with the end of the war, the hostility actually intensified during the first two years of peace, reflecting an upsurge of nativism. The widespread social, political, and economic dislocations that followed the war created an ideal climate for the fears and frustrations on which nativism traditionally feeds.

The year 1919 was one of the darkest in the history of the modern world. Famine threatened much of Germany and eastern Europe, civil war tore apart Russia, and an influenza pandemic claimed tens of millions of lives in every part of the globe. Among Americans, the enthusiasm and idealism of the war period gave way to disillusionment as politicians met in Versailles to carve up the map of the world. The sense of unity and national purpose that had exhilarated many Americans faded as domestic conflicts broke out over subjects as various as the rights of labor and the League of Nations. Despite America's victory in the war, foreign menaces continued to haunt the United States: the Bolsheviks were winning the civil war in Russia, and Communists were making significant inroads in Germany and Hungary. The danger of domestic subversion seemed even greater than it had during the war, as the Communists threatened to export their revolution to America and a multitude of revolutionary organizations actively worked to overthrow the government. Meanwhile, the nation continued to suffer from the high inflation that had started during the war, and unemployment and recession began to wrack the land as the economic demands of the war disappeared. With President Wilson lying prostrate in the White House for months following two strokes during the autumn of 1919, the nation lacked effective leadership. During this period of drift, one of the most visible public officials was Attorney General A. Mitchell Palmer, whose raids on radicals and deportations of radical aliens did much to inflame the so-called Red Scare and to heighten the public sense of crisis.

The nativism that manifested itself in the immediate postwar period in many ways was uglier and more intense than the version that had arisen during the war. As John Higham has pointed out, "a coercive zeal to maintain absolute loyalty" survived the war, but the disappearance of an overriding need for national unity freed nativists from the restraints that had ameliorated wartime nativism. The persistence of nativism during peacetime also may have represented an extension of the aggressive impulses that had been channeled into more constructive endeavors during the war.[1]

Opponents of the use of the German language in the schools vowed that they would continue to work for its removal. Even though the use of German had sharply declined during the war, the armistice encouraged many German Americans to test the limits of public tolerance, and superpatriots discerned a growing ethnic confidence among their Teutonic neighbors. The wife of a Minnesota rancher who had been sued for harassing German Americans on Armistice Day informed Senator Knute Nelson five weeks after the armistice that some German Americans "who never knew how to speak German are learning it now and others are talking it who didn't talk it much before." Complaining that local German children attended a Lutheran school rather than the public school, she declared, "It is disgusting the way they act[. Y]ou would think this was Germany."[2] Similarly, the owner of a hardware store in a small Minnesota town complained to the Commission of Public Safety early in 1919 that a local German school that had closed during 1918 had reopened. Contending that the school ought to be able to teach religion in "the American language," he asked the commission if there was any way to close the school.[3]

A Lutheran pastor in a small Missouri town told Graebner in February 1919 that the long-suffering older members of his congregation were "getting somewhat restive" over the suspension of German-language services, but that the local council of defense continued to discourage the use of German and that the church would "run the risk of being mobbed" if it resumed German services. "Our people have shown themselves to be exceptionally loyal," he observed. "Still the use of the German language is denied us."[4] In

Montana, the order of the council of defense restricting the use of German remained in effect for many months after the armistice. In March 1919, a German American reported to Theodore Graebner that the Montana council had persistently refused to rescind or modify the order.[5]

The prohibitions on the teaching of German had destroyed one of the principal purposes for the existence of the parochial schools and had forced many of them to close. On Armistice Day, Graebner observed, "If a tornado had destroyed all our school buildings in three Western states, the loss would not be what it is now. Our work has been dealt a staggering blow."[6] Graebner correctly had foreseen that hostility against the German language would only grow after the war, and he had warned in October 1918 that "it is absolutely necessary that we prepare for the shock" by accelerating the transition toward the use of English in schools and churches.[7]

Even many Americans who were not specifically nativistic were vexed or frightened by the persistence of lumps in the melting pot. The war had provided a vivid reminder that unassimilated ethnics might present a menace during a time of national crisis. After the war, Americans of many political persuasions resumed the work of Americanizing all immigrants, a mission that had been suspended among many non-German ethnics during the war. As the *Journal* of the National Education Association observed with dismay in 1924, "there are communities in this country containing more Italians than Rome, and more Russians than Moscow. These men and women— potentially good citizens—have had little contact with American life and often have failed to appreciate the purposes and ideals of our American democratic institutions."[8]

Many proponents of Americanization believed that restrictions on foreign-language instruction would hasten the assimilation of the children of immigrants and help to inculcate democratic ideals. Contending that "the English language is essentially democratic," the Masonic journal *New Age* warned in 1924 that "the danger and gravity" of large pools of non-English-speaking Americans "cannot be overestimated." The editors expressed the belief that no language other than English should be permitted in the schools until a child had obtained a working knowledge of English.[9]

Many Americans also favored restrictions on the use of German because they blamed parochial schools and the persistent use of foreign languages for the widespread illiteracy that had been revealed among military conscripts. Of ten million registrants for the draft during the war, some

700,000 could not sign their own name,[10] and many others were literate only in a foreign language, usually German.

Andrew F. West, dean of Princeton's graduate school, stated in 1919, "One language for all our people is a strong bond of national union. To loosen it is to weaken our national life." Although West favored toleration of immigrants who still spoke their native tongue, he declared that it was intolerable "that they should be unwilling to learn and use English" and that "they should fail to have their children promptly learn what is now their language as well as ours."[11]

A survey of fifty heads of college English departments during 1919 revealed widespread support for laws to make English the sole language of instruction in all schools—public, private, or parochial—and a virtually unanimous belief that foreign languages should not be offered at all in the grade schools. A survey of school officials in 130 small western cities likewise showed extensive opposition to instruction in foreign languages in the grade schools. The superintendent of schools of Ogden, Utah, who conducted the surveys, told the 1919 meeting of the National Education Association that a grade school child "should not be allowed to do anything that might weaken his Americanism" and that "the child needs to pay more attention to his own tongue, if he is to speak it well."[12] Similarly, Earl C. Arnold, a University of Florida law professor, in 1919 urged that states prohibit the use of any foreign language, except for foreign-language instruction in the advanced grades. Although Arnold acknowledged that older immigrants could not be expected to learn English, he advocated "every discouragement" of the use of other languages "in the home, newspaper or church."[13]

A newly formed organization of veterans, the American Legion, also was vocal in its calls for Americanization of the foreign born. After its formation in 1919, the American Legion quickly became a potent force, with millions of members and thousands of posts in every corner of the nation. The Legion, according to the preamble of its constitution, was established in part "to foster and perpetuate one hundred percent Americanism." Not willing to forget animosities toward the German culture, the Legion's official publication in October 1919 demanded a continuation of bans on performances of German operas and vowed to "fight this nuisance to the limit." The "sound of German gutterals" in opera reminded the editors of the "shrieks of the *Lusitania*'s dying" and conjured up a "picture not of human emotions but a firing squad marching at the goose step upon defenseless women and children."[14]

Generally, however, the American Legion's national organization was restrained in its efforts to promote Americanization. As the *American Legion Weekly* declared early in 1920, "the country must discriminate between ignorance and inherent viciousness. It must apply intensive education as an antidote against alien agitators and imported red propagandists."[15] At its first convention in 1919, the Legion endorsed some fairly moderate Americanization measures, including laws to require aliens to acquire knowledge of the "American language" and to make citizenship a course in every public school.[16] Since the American Legion strove to be an inclusive organization, it remained mindful that more than 20 percent of the Great War veterans were Roman Catholic and 6 percent were Lutheran. The Legion's national organization made no attacks on parochial education or the teaching of foreign languages. State and local branches, however, were not always so circumspect, and the Legion in some areas became one of the primary vehicles for harassment of German Americans and the movement to continue restrictions on the teaching of German.

During 1919, nineteen states enacted laws that imposed restrictions on the teaching of foreign languages. This legislation, together with more than a dozen statutes that were enacted before the start of the war and the four that were enacted during the war, brought to thirty-seven the number of states that restricted the teaching of foreign languages by the end of 1919.[17] The content and scope of the laws differed from state to state. The most extreme legislation was enacted by Louisiana, which in 1918 prohibited the teaching of the German language in any institution, including private schools and universities.[18] Aside from Indiana and Ohio, which prohibited the teaching of German in all elementary schools, other states that passed language laws did not specifically refer to the German language. Like the statutes enacted before the war, most of those enacted during and immediately after the war merely required that all the basic subjects be taught in the English language. With the exception of New Hampshire's new statute, all these laws applied to private and parochial schools as well as to public schools. In addition to the ban on German in Indiana and Ohio, only Alabama, Colorado, Delaware, Iowa, Nebraska, North Dakota, Oklahoma, and South Dakota explicitly prohibited the teaching of foreign languages in the elementary schools. Several of these states, as we have seen, had substantial German-American populations and had witnessed some of the most virulent anti-German sentiment during the war. In 1917, Wisconsin, which had the nation's largest concentration of German Americans, enacted a law that permitted the teaching of foreign languages for a maximum of one hour per day in public schools, and heavily German Minnesota instituted a similar law in 1919 that applied to all schools. Agitation for language restrictions subsided as quickly as it had began, and no more language laws were enacted after 1919, except for a 1921 statute in Delaware and a 1923 law in Connecticut.

Catholics and Lutherans actively opposed the enactment of language laws, and their lobbying campaigns helped to defeat or ameliorate measures to restrict the teaching of foreign languages. In Iowa, for example, the Missouri Synod was able to persuade legislators to refrain from adopting any measure that interfered with religious education. In preventing the enactment of more extreme measures, Lutherans faced an uphill struggle, since anti-German sentiment in Iowa was intense. Early in 1919, Governor William Harding proposed legislation that would have prevented the teaching of any foreign language in elementary schools.[19] House and senate bills introduced in the legislature would have prohibited instruction in any foreign language in any school.[20]

The Missouri Synod's Schools Committee failed in its early efforts to persuade Iowa legislators to permit religious instruction in German. "But [then] our men got busy," an Iowa Lutheran reported to Graebner. "Not a little time was spent by our men and in particular a prominent layman and attorney in informing the solons. Most of them were open to conviction."[21] In a letter to the Iowa legislature, Missouri Synod officials argued that proposed bills to restrict the teaching of German would violate the state constitution by interfering with the ability of the parochial schools to impart religious instruction in the German tongue in order that children could worship and receive religious edification from their German-speaking parents. They also argued that such laws would violate the federal Constitution, although, as we shall see, the free exercise clause of the First Amendment had not yet been applied to the states. "It is of the utmost importance," the synod explained, "that the whole family, parents and children, should worship at the same altar." Although the synod advocated English-language instruction in the common subjects, it argued that a prohibition on the teaching of German would destroy parochial schools, since "there is no gain in maintaining a private school that teaches identically what is taught in the public school."[22]

Following the Lutheran lobbying campaign, the Iowa house voted 63 to

40 to amend its bill to limit to secular instruction the prohibition on the teaching of foreign languages. After the bill as amended passed the house by a unanimous vote, the senate approved it without amendment by a vote of 36 to 12. Although the senate narrowly rejected an amendment that would have expressly provided that the law was not intended to interfere with religious instruction in parochial schools, the limitation of the statute to secular subjects seemed to offer a measure of protection to German-language instruction in the parochial schools.[23]

Lutheran efforts also bore fruit in Missouri, where Missouri Synod pastors met with the chairman of the state senate's committee on education during February 1919 to oppose a bill to prohibit the use of languages other than English in parochial schools.[24] Graebner later told the chairman of the committee that parents had the right to provide religious instruction to their children in any language that they chose, since "it is the undoubted right of all parents to supervise the education of their children. This is a basic principle of Anglo-Saxon law."[25] In April, the house defeated the bill by a vote of 59 to 46. One newspaper contended that early support for the measure had melted in the face of intense opposition among German Americans, who were particularly successful in persuading Republican legislators to vote against the measure.[26]

In Kansas, Martin Graebner took the initiative to draft a successful bill that prescribed English as the only lawful medium of instruction in all schools but that did not specifically prohibit the teaching of foreign languages as languages and did not subject parochial schools to additional state regulation. Although superpatriots had warned Graebner that Lutheran schools were doomed, Graebner arranged for his local legislator to introduce this bill and then obtained the critical support of the council of defense. With the council's backing, Graebner was able to persuade state school officials to withdraw their support for more radical measures.[27]

Lutheran opposition likewise helped to defeat language legislation in Montana, where the governor and state council of defense had recommended laws to restrict the teaching of foreign languages. One such measure passed the house on the first two readings but was defeated on the final reading after Lutherans testified before the committee on education and spoke privately with some of the legislators. In explaining their votes, lawmakers stated that the bill would violate the Constitution and was an insult to the nation's non-English-speaking allies, particularly the French. Another measure that would have banned the teaching of foreign languages in the public elementary schools passed the senate but was killed in the house. One prominent legislator contended that the bill would have countenanced ignorance.[28]

Martin Graebner reminded his brother Theodore that "the proper way to get something is *not* to wait until some of the worst enemies have the game about won, and then protest, for that is a negative method." Graebner explained, "We must write our own school legislation . . . and we should have men of influence in every State, who can get the necessary backing to put it over." He averred that it was easy "to get something if you work constructively. . . . Most people are lazy, and these legislators are mostly willing to let you do the work of writing the bills. That is what most of them are used to on the part of teachers, manufacturers, labor, corporations, farmers, etc." Graebner emphasized that Lutherans should learn a lesson from the Roman Catholics, "who go about their task quietly," and that parochial school supporters likewise should "avoid useless protests."[29]

Few legislators were inherently hostile toward parochial schools, and public officials in states that had sizable Lutheran and Roman Catholic populations obviously had no desire to offend large blocs of voters. For example, U.S. Senator Warren G. Harding of Ohio in January 1920 told a Lutheran minister from Toledo that he was surprised "that any one was seriously combatting the idea of the parochial school"; Harding affirmed his belief "in the fullest religious liberty" and "the complete separation of church and state."[30] Legislators who opposed restrictions on foreign languages may have believed that hostility toward parochial schools was likely to cost more votes among ethnic voters than it would win votes among chauvinistic Anglo-Americans. Nevertheless, the enactment of so many laws to restrict the teaching of foreign languages demonstrates that nativistic opinion was highly potent and that significant numbers of lawmakers either shared this animus against their ethnic neighbors or were willing to be swept along by the prevailing sentiment.

The reluctance of some legislators to support extreme antilanguage laws was supported by prominent educators, who continued to point out the follies of removing German from the schools. Although Professor Percy E. Davidson of Stanford agreed that the United States should have a common language, he argued in 1920 that legislation to prohibit the teaching of second languages could be justified only "by reason of a very grave danger to the total community." Davidson contended that no such menace existed, since exposure to the German language was not likely to shake the innate

Americanism of the nation's youth. He averred that attempts to remove German from the schools represented "a radical break with a liberal educational tradition" that had permitted local communities to exert a high level of control over the curriculum of their public schools.[31] Despite these warnings, the agitation against German-language instruction took a heavy toll. Although most statutes that restricted German instruction applied only to elementary schools, the proportion of high school students studying German fell from 25 percent in 1915 to 1 percent in 1922.[32]

Although proponents of Americanization believed that removal of foreign languages from the classroom would facilitate good citizenship, many contended that widespread illiteracy demonstrated the need for more fundamental reforms in the educational system. Even before the war ended, educators, politicians, and social reformers had begun to propose remedies. In the summer of 1918, for example, a former member of the Chicago Board of Education advocated the enactment of a criminal statute to compel schooling for every American between the ages of sixteen and forty-five who was unable to read and write English. Although he acknowledged that this measure would raise constitutional questions, he insisted that "lesser remedies do not afford a satisfactory substitute."[33]

Many proponents of educational reform believed that federal intervention was necessary to mitigate the deficiencies of state school systems. Since the war had vastly expanded the powers of the federal government, it was natural to look there for a solution. If the federal government could conscript millions of men for military duty, operate the nation's railroads, and ban the use of alcohol as part of its effort to win the war, why should it not take extraordinary efforts to combat the domestic enemy of illiteracy? Even before the war, the federal government had begun to expand its intervention in educational affairs: in 1914, Congress had enacted the Smith-Lever Act, which provided financial support for agricultural studies. Three years later, the Smith-Hughes Act provided for federal intervention in vocational training programs. In March 1918, Thomas H. Briggs of Columbia's Teachers College urged that the federal government establish national educational goals, which would be carried out through an expansion of the Department of the Interior's Bureau of Education.[34] During the same month, Interior Secretary Franklin K. Lane called for increased federal attention to the problems of education, since "an uninformed democracy is not a democracy."[35] Meanwhile, the National Education Association appointed a commission that proposed legislation to provide federal aid to education in an effort to promote good citizenship, assimilate ethnic Americans, and ameliorate the problem of illiteracy.[36] The recommendations of the NEA were embodied in a bill that Senator Hoke Smith of Georgia, the chairman of the Senate committee on education, introduced on October 10, 1918. Smith's bill, the first of many similar measures that were introduced in Congress during the next decade, called for the creation of a cabinet-level department of education and the appropriation of matching grants to the states. The grants were to assist programs to diminish illiteracy, Americanize immigrants, equalize educational opportunities, encourage physical education, and improve teacher standards.[37] Advocates of the measures also contended that they would ameliorate the problem of child labor by encouraging the enactment and enforcement of compulsory school attendance laws.[38]

The federal education bills received enthusiastic support from a remarkably broad array of persons and organizations. The scattered remnants of the old progressive movement tended to unite behind this reform, which was quintessentially progressive insofar as it ostensibly was designed to use the power of government to strengthen democracy by enlightening and uplifting every segment of society. In addition to the NEA, supporters of the bills or similar legislation included the American Federation of Labor and its affiliate, the American Federation of Teachers; the National Association for the Advancement of Colored People; the National League of Women Voters; the National Council of Jewish Women; the YWCA; and the Women's Christian Temperance Union.[39] The Masonic lodges were particularly assiduous in their advocacy of the bills,[40] as were nativists who opposed parochial education. Urging Senator William E. Borah of Idaho to support a federal education bill, a Klansman who was a former DePauw University dean warned that the Catholic hierarchy was "gradually enclosing upon the Public Schools like an octopus."[41]

Like the proponents of restrictions on foreign-language instruction, advocates of the federal education legislation contended that it was necessary for the preservation of democracy. As the NEA's *Educational Record* observed in 1921, a "nation can be properly governed only when it is intelligently governed." Expressing dismay that five million out of the fifteen million foreign-born Americans were illiterate in English, it declared that illiteracy was "an active source of danger to the Republic," since communities in which English was not widely understood "constitute a rich soil in which are sown the seeds of unrest and revolt."[42]

This seemingly benign legislation, however, encountered intense opposition. Many educators feared that it would lead to federal control of education and create a dictatorial bureaucracy that would stifle local initiative. The presidents of a multitude of leading universities opposed the bills,[43] as did the Special Committee on Education of the Chamber of Commerce and a majority of members of the chamber who were polled in 1923. Among rank-and-file teachers, of whom only 20 percent were NEA members, there was considerable opposition to the bills.[44] Some lawyers questioned the constitutionality of the legislation, arguing that education was within the exclusive power of the states and that federal intervention would invade the powers reserved to the states under the Tenth Amendment.[45]

The most vociferous opponents of the measures, however, were Roman Catholic and Lutheran officials, who believed that the legislation would lead to the suppression of the parochial schools.[46] As the executive secretary of the Missouri Synod's School Board told a congressional committee in 1928, the legislation "may easily become a tool of private and church school enemies, and of religious propaganda."[47] James H. Ryan, the executive secretary of the National Catholic Welfare Conference, expressed fear that centralized control of education would permit "a well-organized minority" to "obtain control of the whole American system of education," and he warned that such a minority "would be next to impossible to dislodge."[48] Parochial school advocates also may have resented having to pay additional taxes for public education and secretly may have feared that the legislation would detract from the competitiveness of parochial schools by markedly improving the quality of the public schools. In public pronouncements, however, clerical opponents tended to minimize their religious objections to the legislation and emphasize their pedagogical, economic and constitutional objections. In testimony before the Senate's education committee in 1924, for example, Ryan barely mentioned the church's fear that the bills would lead to suppression of the parochial schools.[49] The Catholic attorney and parochial school advocate William D. Guthrie argued that the legislation would invade the rights reserved to the states, and he warned against entrusting educational policy to "obscure and irresponsible politicians."[50]

Although proponents of the measures vigorously denied that they would lead to federal control or standardization of education,[51] opposition to the education bills ensured that they were unsuccessful. As one Capitol Hill correspondent observed in 1923, "the reluctance of Congress to take sides in what has come to be essentially a religious controversy is quite understandable."[52] Support for a cabinet-level department of education and greater federal aid to education remained strong, however, and ultimately resulted in greater federal intervention in education and the creation of a Department of Health, Education, and Welfare in 1953 and a Department of Education in 1979.

In addition to calling for restrictions on the teaching of foreign languages and greater federal support for public education, many of the so-called Americanizers advocated compulsory public education. In contrast to the language laws, which were motivated by anti-German prejudice and directed against Lutherans, the movement for compulsory public education reflected the xenophobia and anti-Catholicism that animated nativism during the early 1920s. As the anti-German hostility of the First World War receded, Roman Catholics replaced Lutherans as the principal target of nativist antagonism, resuming their traditional role as a nativist bogy. In 1922, a nativist newspaper in Missouri praised the "splendid achievements" of the Lutheran schools but maintained that the only way to cure "the papal cancer" was to "abolish all parochial schools" and that Lutherans should sacrifice their schools for the common good.[53] Nativists feared Catholics more than they feared Lutherans because so many Catholics were unassimilated members of ethnic groups from southern and eastern Europe whose customs and values seemed far more alien to Anglo-Americans than did those of German Americans. Moreover, the sheer size of the burgeoning Roman Catholic church intimidated nativists. Catholics already constituted a majority in many large cities, and nativists feared that continued immigration and high birth rates would enable Catholicism to overwhelm Protestantism.

Proponents of compulsory public education were categorical in their insistence on the evils of parochial education. One anti-Catholic publication alleged in 1923, for example, that textbooks used in Catholic schools taught that the pope could nullify laws enacted by Congress and the state legislatures. Universal public education, the journal urged, would "quickly Americanize the alien Roman Catholic hordes." Meanwhile, a Methodist bishop in Detroit declared that "the parochial school is the most un-American institution in America, and must be closed."[54]

Anti-Catholicism was aggravated during the 1920s by the growing visibility of Roman Catholics in all corners of America and also by the dispute over prohibition of alcohol, which intensified with the enactment of the Eighteenth Amendment in 1919. The cultural clash between an increasingly assertive urban Catholicism and a defensive rural and small-town Protestantism was best exemplified by the rancorous Democratic national convention in 1924 and the presidential contest between Herbert Hoover, the western Protestant, and Al Smith, the New York City Catholic, in 1928. The most enduring legacy of the resurgence of nativism during the postwar years was the enactment in 1924 of highly restrictive immigration legislation, discriminating against southern and eastern Europeans, which remained in force until 1965.

Gaining momentum at a time when hostility toward German Americans was waning, the campaign against parochial schools represented a virulent new phase of nativism. The campaign had significant antecedents, however, since it renewed and magnified the antagonisms toward parochial schools that were manifest in the language controversies of the 1880s and 1890s and the years immediately following the First World War. As Arthur F. Mullen had feared, the initial success of the movement to prohibit the teaching of foreign languages encouraged nativists to promote a far more extreme measure, the abolition of parochial education. The movement for compulsory public education attracted support from a broad spectrum of persons and organizations, ranging from the Ku Klux Klan to the Order of Free Masons.

It is natural that the Klan should have supported compulsory public education, since the Klan that flourished throughout much of the United States during the 1920s was virulently anti-Catholic. Although the original Klan of the Reconstruction era was primarily southern in membership and anti-black in its activities, the Klan that was reborn in 1915 and thrived during the early postwar years attracted members throughout the nation and subscribed to a traditionally nativistic ideology. The new Klan thrived on the insecurities and dislocations produced by the war and its success reflected fears inspired by Russian Bolsheviks, home-grown radicals, and immigrants whose cheap labor and alien customs seemed to threaten the jobs and folkways of native-born Protestants. By its zenith in the mid-1920s, the Klan had a membership in excess of one million and enjoyed a high degree of political influence in a substantial number of states throughout the nation.[55]

Like nativists of earlier generations, the Klan recognized that schools were crucial agents of socialization and feared that the hyphenated Americans whom Klansmen so distrusted never would adopt American standards if permitted to retain their parochial schools. Believing that the Roman Catholic church was conspiring to destroy democracy, many Klansmen worried that Rome would strike first at the public schools, the foundation of democracy. The widespread faith among Klansmen in the redemptive aspects of public education reflected their ambivalence toward persons of other races and religions. Like some nativists of the nineteenth century, some were motivated by a genuine desire to assimilate the alien population and were willing to accept persons who conformed to traditional American codes of behavior. At the same time, however, many Klansmen were hostile to these persons merely because their ethnic and religious backgrounds differed from their own. They also were motivated in part by envy, since many newcomers to the country were visibly more prosperous than were the members of the Klan, who primarily were drawn from the lower middle and working classes. Like nativists in other periods of rapid social change, Klansmen also may have envied the ceremonies and rich cultural traditions that offered a security and solace to immigrant peoples.

Even many Americans who did not join the Klan experienced hostile feelings toward foreigners for the same reasons that animated the hostility of the Klan. The fear of foreigners that gripped Protestant America during the early postwar years helps to explain why many Masonic lodges supported the movement for compulsory public education. In May 1920, the Supreme Council of the Scottish Rite Masons, representing thirty-three southern and western states, adopted a resolution that proclaimed its active support for "free and compulsory education" of all children in public primary schools. It averred that universal public education in the English language "without regard to race or creed" was "the only sure foundation for the perpetuation and preservation of our free institutions."[56] In the following summer, the Imperial Council of Shriners adopted the same platform, and various local Masonic organizations likewise endorsed it.[57]

Masonic publications during the early 1920s tirelessly crusaded for compulsory public education. Virtually every issue of the *New Age,* for example, contained at least one article or editorial that advocated mandatory public schooling. Masons warned that Roman Catholic education endangered democracy. "Once concede that an alien church can interfere with the education of the citizen," a prominent Montana Mason declared, "and you must concede that an alien political committee or dictator can do the same."[58] Brushing aside the Roman Catholic argument that parochial schools relieved the public of a tax burden, a Mason who taught in a Florida public school argued that any saving on expenditures for public schools was more than counterbalanced by increased public spending for the "children's homes, reformatory schools, charity hospitals, insane asylums, courts of justice and prisons" that were needed to accommodate parochial school alumni and their progeny.[59] In addition to claiming that a parochial education had a deleterious impact on Catholics, some Masons further warned that the Roman Catholic church might be seeking to undermine and even destroy public education. As one Mason explained, the "militant clerical machine" was a "real menace" to the continued existence of the public school.[60]

The Masonic appeal for compulsory education, however, was not entirely negative. Universal public education, the Masons emphasized, would have a salutary effect on the Republic. As the *New Age* explained in August 1920, "the public school is the place of all others where children who are to be future citizens can mingle together, acquiring true democracy and banishing the prejudices of race, creed, religion, and whatever else tends to bring about antagonism among humankind."[61] Similarly, one Mason maintained that public schools would create greater social harmony, because "much of the misunderstanding and unrest of the present time is the result of the failure on the part of people in different walks of life to really understand each other" and public schools were the one universal place where citizens could "meet each other on a common level and on terms of equality."[62] The *New Age* contended that the public school was "the best and greatest of all our institutions and the most effective safeguard of our liberties," and that the parochial school "separates children into religious groups, fosters dislike and enmity and destroys the very taproots of democracy."[63]

The Masonic campaign for compulsory public education was part of a larger educational campaign that included advocacy of the creation of a national university[64] and support for the various bills to increase federal support to education.[65] Masons recognized that federal education legislation would be a boon to the universal public education movement. As the Grand Commander of the Supreme Council of the Scottish Rite, Southern Jurisdiction, explained, "the creation of a federal department of education will do more than any one thing toward establishing the prestige and extending the influence of the public schools."[66]

Masonic support for compulsory public education demonstrates that hostility toward parochial schools was not confined to hatemongers, the unlettered, or the lower classes, since many Masons were prosperous, well educated, and enlightened in their political and social views. The movement for compulsory public education was inspired by many of the ideals that had animated the progressive movement. It sought to use the power of the state for the intellectual improvement and moral regeneration of the citizenry. By inculcating democratic virtues, it would help to unify an increasingly fragmented society and would rescue the body politic from the grip of plutocratic industrialists and urban clubhouse bosses. Consistent with the progressive flavor of the Masonic educational program, the Masons and other proponents of compulsory public education also continued to crusade for restrictions on child labor.[67] They called for more extensive efforts to Americanize the immigrant[68] and supported restrictions on immigration from southern and eastern Europe.[69]

The widespread Masonic support for compulsory education also reflected in part a longstanding antagonism between the Masons and the Roman Catholic church. Established in its modern form during the Enlightenment of the eighteenth century, the Masonic movement traditionally has advocated individual freedom and democracy. Masonic championship of intellectual and religious freedom created conflict with Roman Catholic hierarchies, particularly in Europe. The Roman Catholic church has remained suspicious of the heterodox religious practices of the Masonic lodges and has forbidden its members to become Masons. Many Lutheran churches also have objected to the Masons, because their religious practices do not conform to Lutheran tradition. In the United States, the Lutheran Church—Missouri Synod during the early twentieth century was especially vocal in its opposition to the Masons. Since the Missouri Synod maintained more parochial schools than any organization except the Catholic church, Masonic hostility toward parochial schools may in part have reflected the tensions between the synod and the Masons.

Although both the Klan and the Masons supported compulsory public education, the two organizations generally did not cooperate in their campaigns against private schools. The Masonic lodges abhorred the violence and bigotry of the Klan and often were outspoken in their denunciations of it. Many individual Masons championed the rights of private schools, perceiving that freedom of choice in education was consistent with the cherished Masonic ideal of individual liberty. By 1922, the grand masters of the grand lodges in thirty-five states had denounced compulsory education measures.[70]

Although the editors of the Jesuit weekly *America* stated in 1924 that "the sole motive of this campaign against the private school is hatred of the Catholic Church,"[71] the motivations of advocates of compulsory public education were more complex. The movement throughout the nation reflected the organized efforts of the Klan and some Masons, clergymen, and educators, but it never would have gone so far if it had not tapped a well of nativism that extended deeply into the population. As the Jesuit publication

America observed in 1922, the success of the Oregon initiative for compulsory public education painfully demonstrated to Catholics that "their friends are few and far between."[72]

To Lutherans and Roman Catholics, the compulsory education movement, language legislation, and the proposals for extending federal control over education were all part of a unified assault on parochial education that threatened the foundations of their religious and cultural life. As one Catholic noted in 1924, "the Catholic school in America is in danger, not merely locally but nationally. . . . The war has begun."[73] Roman Catholics recognized, however, that not all critics of parochial schools were blind bigots. As one writer in *America* observed in 1924, the foes of the parochial schools were embraced in two classes. "The smaller is actuated by bigotry, hatred and malice," he contended, but a "much more numerous" group, a "splendid body of fair-minded Protestants," had been misled about the parochial schools and were "open-minded and anxious to protect the citizen in the exercise of his rights."[74] It was this second body of Protestants who ultimately ensured the defeat of parochial school legislation. Unlike hardcore anti-Catholics, many Protestants were inclined to favor compulsory public education for genuinely idealistic reasons.

Hoping to appeal to the intelligence and tolerance of their neighbors, Roman Catholics tried to remain alert to new forms of bigotry while attempting to convince fellow citizens that parochial schools promoted American ideals and that religious instruction helped to inculcate moral virtues. In 1922, for example, Ryan denied "that the only safe way to Americanize foreigners is to dump them pell-mell into the public school hopper." He explained that "the private school has been doing, without recompense, a great deal of effective Americanization during the last one hundred years."[75] And the editors of *America* pointed out that "in these days of social unrest, it is bad public policy for any community to disturb the schools which make religion their cornerstone."[76] But though ethnic Americans tried to discourage the enactment of hostile legislation, their ultimate refuge lay in the courts. Since *Meyer v. Nebraska* was the principal decision that emasculated the movements against parochial education, we next examine the background of chauvinism and nativism that led to the enactment of the law that the Supreme Court struck down in *Meyer*.

4 The "Americanization" of Nebraska

It is not altogether accidental that Nebraska was the scene of the principal judicial challenges to prohibitions on the teaching of foreign languages. As in neighboring Great Plains states, hostility toward German Americans during the war was more virulent than in most other parts of the nation, and the measures to suppress manifestations of German ethnicity were more extreme. Nebraska, like other states in which German Americans faced great abuse, had a German population that was large and powerful enough to attract suspicion and resentment but was too weak to ward off assaults engendered by wartime frenzy. Moreover, Nebraska Germans were particularly vulnerable to nativist enmity because many lived in tightly knit enclaves. Although even the most isolated German Americans were making significant strides toward assimilation before the war, this process was too subtle for many Anglo-Americans to appreciate. To the eyes of Nebraska's native stock, the German Americans stubbornly resisted Americanization and sought to preserve all aspects of their ethnicity forever.[1]

At the behest of the federal government, the state of Nebraska early in the war established a twelve-member State Council of Defense, which undertook a multitude of projects to facilitate the war effort. Among other activities, the council promoted the sale of war bonds, encouraged the increased production and conservation of food, and assisted the work of various federal agencies, draft registration boards, and the Red Cross. The council's Woman's Committee conducted canning schools, investigated moral and health conditions at army camps, recruited army nurses, conducted a campaign to reduce infant mortality, found war jobs for women, and undertook many other public service activities. County councils of defense, which were established in every Nebraska county, facilitated the war effort at the local level.

In addition to their economic and humanitarian work, the state and local councils promoted patriotism and loyalty. Many of these efforts were benign. The state council, for example, organized Liberty Choruses to encourage public singing of patriotic music, and the Woman's Committee established night schools for aliens and helped foreign-born women secure naturalization papers.[2] As in other states, however, the state and county councils of defense became the principal vehicle for harassment of opponents of the war and German Americans who insisted on preserving a distinct ethnic identity. Ever vigilant to detect and investigate signs of disloyalty, the councils often confused dissent with subversion and convinced themselves that German ethnicity endangered the war effort. Armed with the statutory authority to subpoena witnesses, compel the production of documents, and punish for contempt, the state council had formidable powers to ensure public cooperation with the war effort.

The council's attempts to promote conformity received enthusiastic support from many influential persons and institutions, including private businesses, the clergy, and the press. Declaring that criticism of the war "indicates that there is need of rigid repression," the *Lincoln Daily Star* in June 1917 urged the council to "silence and restrain copperheads and traitors."[3] Constitutional guarantees of speech, the *Star* contended, would not protect enemies of the Constitution.[4]

Shortly after its formation, the council conducted an investigation in an effort to measure the extent of public support for the war. The results of the investigation deeply troubled members of the council. On July 10, 1917, it reported that its survey of "discreet and responsible men" had revealed "a very general misunderstanding of the purposes and the necessity of this war" among both native and foreign-born citizens. Although the council acknowledged that most German Americans supported the war effort, it suggested that a substantial number sympathized with Germany. Its report also alleged that opponents of the war had obstructed the war bond campaign by failing to purchase bonds and by using intimidation to keep patriotic citizens from buying bonds. The council's report complained that "several professors" of the University of Nebraska and "conspicuous representatives" of the Lutheran church were helping to turn public opinion against the war. Charging that these Lutheran clergy had "shown marked partiality for the cause of America's enemy," the council appealed to Lutheran laymen to demonstrate their church's devotion to the American cause. The council acknowledged that it was extraordinary for a public body to "single out by name a great church organization" and appeal to its members over the heads of its leaders, but explained that hundreds of "reliable reports" from every section of Nebraska had questioned the loyalty of prominent Lutheran clergy. Although the council emphasized its preference for voluntary compliance with war aims, it promised to "employ its power and authority to the limit" to suppress opposition to the war.[5]

There can be no doubt that some Lutheran clergy in Nebraska openly opposed the war. While many of these pastors served small flocks in remote regions, the pastor of Omaha's Kountze Memorial Lutheran Church, the largest English-speaking Lutheran congregation in the world, had declared shortly after the declaration of war that "this is Mr. Wilson's war." Despite calls for resignation from some members of the congregation, the church council did not ask the pastor to resign.[6] Most clergy, however, appear to have at least acquiesced to the war.

The council's allegations of widespread disloyalty caused much comment. The director of the local branch of the Federal Bureau of Investigation declared that the council's "statement[s] regarding treasonable activities in Nebraska are mild compared with the truth."[7] Meanwhile, the *Star* alleged that the German Lutheran clergy were the "mediums through which pro-German literature is being peddled" and that "the minds of their congregations are being poisoned by the tenor of their sermons."[8]

Although the council had carefully refrained from attacking the Lutheran church itself, Lutherans were alarmed by the condemnation of unnamed clergy and vigorously attempted to demonstrate their patriotism. Shortly after the council promulgated its statement, twenty-seven clergymen representing nine Lutheran church groups adopted a resolution declaring that Lutherans were loyal to the government. They pointed out that the charter of the Lutheran faith, the Augsburg Confession of 1530, commanded civil loyalty and that Luther's Small Catechism likewise instructed Christians to submit to temporal uthority.[9]

In the following week, eight Lutheran clergymen received an audience with the Council of Defense to respond to its allegations. Several members of the delegation explained that the Lutheran church required strict obedience to civil authority but maintained a clear dichotomy between the realms of religion and politics, a division that prevented clergymen from using their pulpits to promote the war. Although the clergymen protested their loyalty to the American government, they admitted that "a lack of enthusiasm for the present war has been noticeable among citizens of German birth or descent," since "it is a hard thing for human beings . . . to take up arms and wage war against their kindred." The clergymen admonished the council, however, that "it would be unfair to stamp such sentiment as a proof of their disloyalty," and they promised to try to eradicate any form of disloyalty from their churches.[10]

The council later explained that its allegations were directed only toward some disloyal Lutherans and not toward the church itself. The council acknowledged the loyalty of the representatives with whom it had met and predicted that "the example of these faithful citizens will have the effect so earnestly urged in the original statement of the Council."[11]

In addition to investigating the loyalty of the churches, the council attempted to restrict the German-language press. Denouncing its "insidious methods," the council in August 1917 called for federal legislation to censor or suppress the press.[12] *The Star* also waged a campaign to suppress German-language newspapers. It declared that the German-language press had "spread poison through the minds of its readers" and had "kept American Germans under the spell of the kaiser."[13] In the following month, the German-language press was vehemently criticized at a statewide conference of county councils of defense.[14]

The council likewise waged a successful campaign to eliminate the state's thirty-six German-language lending libraries, which contained about twelve hundred volumes and circulated in fifty towns in heavily German areas.[15] The secretary of the state library commission insisted that the books contained nothing objectionable and that they were read mostly by older persons. "There is no more harm in these German libraries than in a band playing German music," she declared,[16] apparently unaware that even German music was beginning to fall into disfavor.[17] The *Star,* however, urged that that "every miserable German book should be thrown out," since the books encouraged tens of thousands of the state's German Americans to remain as "German in their language, habits and sympathies, as if they had never left their fatherland."[18] Presaging later attacks on the use of the German language, the *Star* declared in August 1917 that "one may well and always question the citizenship of a foreigner who insists upon maintaining his native language."[19] After several months of controversy and a formal request by the council for suspension of the libraries, the state library commission in November 1917 announced that circulation of the German-language books would cease for the duration of the war.[20]

Meanwhile, the council continued to scrutinize carefully the activities of the Lutheran church. As the war progressed, the council became increasingly concerned that parochial schools operated by the churches were not instilling patriotism in their students. During the early autumn of 1917, Sarka Hrbkova, the chairwoman of the council's Woman's Committee, quietly conducted an investigation of parochial schools in several counties and was distressed to find that "little or no English was being taught" in many schools.[21] Meanwhile, the council had become increasingly concerned about the effects of foreign-language instruction in the parochial schools, since many young second- and third-generation German Americans who were summoned before the council to explain allegedly disloyal deeds or remarks could not speak English. The council found that nearly all these men had been educated in Lutheran parochial schools.[22] On November 13, Hrbkova reported to the council that she had surveyed sixty counties and found 137 German Lutheran schools, some of which used little or no English. The council directed Hrbkova to prepare a report on the subject of grade school education. Richard L. Metcalfe, a council member, advised her to avoid any suggestion that she was attacking parochial education itself.[23]

In December, Hrbkova reported to the council that 379 teachers in 262 schools taught foreign languages to more than ten thousand students. Although a handful of these schools offered instruction in Swedish, Danish, and Polish, the overwhelming majority taught German. Her report contained much information that disturbed the council. Schools in at least seven counties offered instruction entirely in German, and approximately two hundred schools devoted three hours each day to instruction in the German language. School superintendents in three counties reported that the German national anthem was sung in some schools, and students in about one hundred schools did not sing American patriotic songs. More than one hundred schools were reported to lack an American flag. Moreover, instruction in these schools was reputed to be inferior. County school superintendents generally reported that eight years of instruction in these schools was equivalent to only a sixth-grade education in public schools. Less than 4 percent of the teachers were certified by the state.[24]

The schools operated by the Missouri Synod, which enrolled more than half the students who were taught foreign languages, offered a more rigorous and Americanized caliber of instruction than did the schools operated by some of the smaller Lutheran synods. Early in December, representatives of the Missouri Synod met with the council[25] and submitted a report stating that all the 151 Missouri Synod schools in Nebraska taught all secular courses in English, except for courses in the German language.[26] English-language instruction occupied at least four hours per day in the schools, and the teaching of German and the teaching of religion in German occupied no more than two hours per day. All the schools flew the American flag, and students at all schools sang American patriotic songs. None sang the German anthem. The Missouri Synod representatives also assured the council that the schools' German-language textbooks were published in St. Louis and "contain nothing that could be used in any way to make propaganda for the cause of the enemy." They explained that the schools were maintained not for the teaching and perpetuation of the German language, but rather "to give our children a thorough religious instruction and training, such as the Sunday School cannot give and the public school very properly does not attempt to give."[27]

Other Lutheran clergy and teachers likewise tried to reassure the council that they were willing to cooperate with its desire to make certain that parochial schools instilled patriotism in their students. In late November, a delegation of Lutheran pastors and educators met with the council to discuss the teaching of German in the parochial schools. One pastor predicted that English would be the exclusive language of the parochial schools within ten years and that they would abandon German at once if the council objected to its continued use in the schools. A German-American Lutheran who served as the Gage County school superintendent declared that the exclusive use of German in parochial schools should be abandoned, for their students otherwise could not become truly American.[28]

At the same time that the council was investigating the use of German in the parochial schools, public hostility toward continued German instruction in the public schools reached the boiling point. The teaching of German in the public schools had become particularly widespread after 1913, when the legislature enacted a statute that required schools to offer foreign-language instruction for a maximum of five hours per week starting in the fifth grade if the parents of at least fifty students requested it.[29] The statute, the so-called Mockett Law, was the product of lobbying by the German-American Alliance, and no one was surprised that German became the language most commonly requested by parents. The use of public funds to help perpetuate the teaching of a foreign language was highly controversial, especially after the start of the war in Europe in 1914. Opponents of the law challenged its constitutionality, but the state supreme court in 1916 upheld its validity. The court explained that students of all backgrounds would profit by the study of a foreign language.[30]

In the face of mounting hostility against German-language instruction in the public schools, the house in 1917 voted to repeal the Mockett Law. The senate failed to act on the proposal, perhaps because German-American legislators agreed to support a limited women's suffrage bill in return for votes to save the Mockett Law.[31] In 1918, the legislature finally repealed the law after Governor Keith Neville denounced it as "vicious, undemocratic and un-American."[32]

By the time of the law's repeal, opponents of German-language instruction in the public schools already had succeeded in eradicating German from the curriculum of most public schools. Even before America entered the war, the Omaha Board of Education had unanimously expressed opposition to the teaching of German; barely one month after war was declared, the board abolished the position of supervisor of German studies.[33] By November, German had been dropped from the curricula of many high schools and most grade schools. The annual meeting of the German-language section of the state teachers' association in November was a forlorn affair, attended by only one hundred teachers rather than the four to five hundred who had attended in past years. Although Professor L. E. Fossler in an address to the gathering protested against "the craze . . . to throw German out of the schools" and argued that there was no connection between knowledge of German and sedition,[34] his plea was futile. Even as he spoke, self-styled Americanizers were successfully assaulting German courses in Lincoln, the only major Nebraska city that still offered German instruction in its public schools.

As in other efforts to eliminate all traces of Germanic culture in Nebraska, the *Star* led the pack, editorializing relentlessly in opposition to German courses.[35] According to the *Star*, German teaching was "a traitorous device" that had been "promoted for the secret and insidious Germanization of this country, as part of the great propaganda for the Germanization of the world."[36] The generous funding of German courses in the public schools was particularly vexing. According to the *Star*, Lincoln pupils were "getting more German in the public schools than they could ever acquire by attending a parochial school."[37] Meanwhile, parents who had been virtually unaware that their children were receiving German instruction began to demand the elimination of German from the schools, and enrollment in German courses slumped.[38] Enrollment in German courses also plummeted at the University of Nebraska. No German course was offered during the summer of 1918 because of lack of demand.[39]

A committee that studied the parochial schools proposed that they be more extensively regulated but acknowledged that they had a right to teach foreign languages and religion.[40] The council, however, chose to advocate a more sweeping measure. On December 11, 1917, it issued a statement requesting all public, private, and parochial schools to discontinue all foreign-language teaching from the courses of study below high school. The council explained that compliance with the order would "represent the correct attitude of patriotism which should endeavor to Americanize the youth of our land to the fullest extent possible."[41] One week later, the council adopted an additional resolution requesting that "no foreign language shall be taught in any of the private or denominational schools of Nebraska and that all instruction, whether secular or religious, shall be given in the English language." The resolution reiterated its admonition to the public schools to discontinue foreign-language instruction.[42] The council's opposition to the continued teaching of German reflected the opinions of many Nebraskans. The *Evening State Journal and News* contended that the elimination of German would not interfere with religious instruction and would injure only those schools that sought to instill in their students the ideals of the German government.[43]

Many Nebraskans were overtly hostile to the very existence of the parochial schools. In November 1917, the pastor of a Methodist church in Lincoln received applause at a public meeting when he called for the closing of German parochial schools.[44] A woman in rural Nebraska told Hrbkova that German parochial schools should be abolished since instruction in the catechism was merely a ruse for indoctrination in kaiserism.[45] A public school teacher in a heavily German community wrote to Hrbkova that "the public school and no other institution on earth can prepare our children to exemplify American, democratic ideals."[46] And the Thurston County attorney warned Metcalfe that some residents of the county had threatened to close the schools if the state failed to do so.[47]

The council recognized that it had no legal right to ban German in the schools and would need to rely on the voluntary cooperation of school authorities. Although the special session of the legislature that convened in 1918 unanimously adopted a resolution approving the council's request that German not be taught in the elementary schools,[48] the council never enjoyed any specific legal authority to prohibit German instruction. During the months following its resolutions, the council was heartened by the widespread compliance from both Roman Catholic and Lutheran schools.[49] Immediately after the council promulgated its first resolution, a member of the Missouri Synod's parochial school governing board publicly announced that there was "no doubt" that the synod's schools would abide by the council's request.[50] Three weeks later, a conference of Missouri Synod teachers and pastors unanimously recommended the abandonment of the use of German during the war in the synod's 151 parochial schools in Nebraska.[51]

During the following months, many parish clergy wrote to the council to express their willingness to comply with the resolution and to report that they were abandoning the use of foreign languages. A Lutheran minister in rural Nebraska, for example, explained, "We, of course, would like to be permitted to further use the german language in our Church and School—but we are willing . . . to give it up, if it would cause trouble and disturbance of the peace."[52] The same pastor served on the Iowa Synod's Committee on Information, which admonished the synod's clergy to refrain from asking whether instruction in English violated their rights and to accept English-language teaching as a wartime measure that would discourage violence against German Americans.[53] The *Star* praised the clergy for their "proper spirit" and admitted that "it is very doubtful if these schools could have been lawfully compelled to do their teaching in the language of the country had the church leaders been at all stubborn about it."[54] As in other states, many Nebraska clergy may have welcomed the opportunity to impose the English language on congregations that had stubbornly clung to German even though young people were defecting to English-language churches.

The acquiescence of many clergy, however, masked considerable anguish. Writing to Theodore Graebner in April 1918, a pastor in Waco, Nebraska, lamented the "fiendish cyclone" that had placed Lutherans in "a precarious situation" and forced them to "suffer for conscience' sake." The pastor told Graebner that his congregation had decided to postpone building a much-needed school building until after the war.[55]

Since much of the hostility against the use of German in Nebraska reflected fears that German Americans were insufficiently patriotic, churches and parochial schools that visibly supported the war effort by cooperating with Liberty Loan drives or other patriotic activities often found that public animosity quickly evaporated. A Lutheran parish in Scottsbluff that included many Russo-Germans who spoke little or no English even found that it could retain the use of German after it presented a lively and well-publicized patriotic skit.[56]

At the same time that the parochial schools were eliminating German-language instruction, German was disappearing from the few remaining public schools in which it was taught. Enrollment in German courses had fallen precipitously. The *Star* reported that elimination of German from the public schools of Lincoln inspired few protests even in predominantly German areas of the city.[57] When the school board of the heavily German town of Seward indicated that it would wait until the end of the school year to drop German, advocates of immediate suspension stole one hundred German textbooks from the local high school.[58]

In order to prevent interference with preparations for German-language confirmations that were scheduled for Easter or Pentecost, the council expressed its willingness to tolerate the use of German during the present school year. The council also explained that the resolution was not intended to call for the discontinuation of foreign-language instruction on Saturdays and Sundays to children who were enrolled full time in the public schools.[59] Although the council did not oppose the teaching of foreign languages in high schools, Hrbkova expressed the opinion that high school students should commence the study of a foreign language only after they had "attained a thorough foundation in English."[60] By mid-March, Hrbkova privately stated that the council knew of no parochial elementary school in the state that continued to teach German.[61]

Despite its gratification over the results of its appeal, the council took nothing for granted. It vigilantly investigated reports concerning the continued use of German. In response to an inquiry from the council, a Roman Catholic priest in rural Nebraska reported in May 1918 that the school in his parish had abandoned the use of German, except for the instruction of a few small children from German-speaking homes who were taught in German until they could learn a little English. This explanation failed to satisfy the council, which demanded more information about the children who received German instruction. The council was placated only after the priest provided a more detailed account of conditions in his parish and assured the council that children from German-speaking homes would receive instruction in English from their "very first school day."[62]

Having succeeded in removing foreign languages from the schools, the council commenced a broader attack on the use of foreign languages in the churches and other public places. As Robert N. Manley has pointed out, the council moved more slowly against church services since there were many churches that used Swedish, Danish, and various other non-German languages. The council also may have been reluctant to interfere with religious worship. Moreover, it may have been more tolerant of German-language services because they principally were for the benefit of the old rather than the instruction of the young.[63]

As in other states, German-American churches in Nebraska at the start of the war were engaged in a slow but steady transition toward the use of English in church services. In 1906, the Nebraska District of the Missouri Synod had acknowledged that it would not be possible to maintain German as the language of the church and that the use of German was not essential to the church's mission. The district emphasized the importance of incrementalism, since many of the church's literary treasures had not yet been translated into English and too abrupt a change might permit unorthodox ideas to creep into the church.[64] The war, however, encouraged German-American churches of all denominations and sects to accelerate the pace of change. Many churches voluntarily abandoned German-language services shortly after the outbreak of the war. By December 1917, for example, Trinity Lutheran Church in Lincoln, the largest German-American church in the city, had substantially increased its use of English, and a group of dissident parishioners who wished to use English exclusively had withdrawn from the congregation and begun plans to start a new parish.[65]

The gradual transition to English-language services, which had been well under way in Nebraska's ethnic churches before the outbreak of the war, was insufficiently rapid to satisfy the most vehement advocates of Americanization. The continued use of foreign languages in the churches particularly troubled advocates of assimilation since the churches were the most visible and powerful agents of ethnic culture. By removing foreign languages from the schools, the Americanizers hoped to ensure that upcoming generations would be Americanized. By removing foreign languages from the churches, they could immediately take a major step toward the Americanization of entire ethnic communities. Reluctant to interfere with religious liberty without legal authority, the council believed that the licensing of alien clergymen would provide an opportunity to control the use of German in religious services. At the council's behest, the legislature at its special session in 1918 enacted a statute that required alien teachers and preachers to obtain a license from the nearest district court. The statute, which was part of a new Sedition Act, permitted local councils of defense to investigate each applicant. Some clergymen received licenses only after agreeing to permit a representative of the local council of defense to attend each foreign-language service.[66] In denying permits to preach to two Roman Catholic priests, a Dodge County judge in May stated that the burden was on applicants to prove their loyalty rather than on the county council to prove disloyalty.[67] At the end of April 1918, the council began to request that applicants for preaching licenses abandon German preaching for the remainder of the war.[68] The council was not patient with clergy who persisted in preaching in German. In early June, for example, it dispatched a curt note to a small-town pastor, demanding to know whether there was any truth to a report that he continued to preach in German.[69] Likewise, a minister who had outraged many persons in his community by delivering a short German sermon at an English-language service for a deceased soldier was called to account by the council, which commended the minister after he humbly promised never to repeat his mistake.[70]

Restrictions on foreign-language services created a genuine hardship for parishioners who knew little or no English. It is ironic that the council's policy may have affected non-Germans more harshly than Germans, since many of the former were more recent immigrants. The restrictions were particularly irksome to persons who spoke languages other than German. A Bohemian American complained to Hrbkova in July that "Bohemians have shown their patriotism in every way and . . . I don't see any reason why their mother tongue should be taken away from them in churches."[71]

Similarly, a Danish American who was fluent in English and preferred to attend English-language church services told the council in May 1918 that his elderly mother was "now entirely cut off" from sermons at her Lutheran parish since they were given in English. He complained that "denying her the right to hear God's Word in the only tongue she understands is certainly sad for her and many others." His mother, who had invested seven hundred dollars in war bonds at the behest of the county council of defense, had tearfully told her son that she also was unable to understand the proceedings of a ladies' aid meeting that had been conducted in English. He pointed out the irony that the Germans had prohibited the speaking of Danish in the Danish territories they had seized in 1864. "That was the iron hand we are fighting now," he reminded the council. "Let us not do as they did for if we give just a little time all people will be glad to talk American," he pleaded.[72]

The council's efforts to discourage the use of foreign languages in church services also created a hardship for clergymen who were not fluent in English. The council had little patience with these men. When a forty-nine-year-old Swedish Lutheran minister explained that he was not sufficiently fluent in English to abandon his use of Swedish, the council urged him to resign from the pastorate at the parish at which he had served for twenty-three years. The need for rapid Americanization was so great, the council explained, that no compromise was possible and the emergency demanded that he sacrifice his livelihood for the greater good of the nation. In response to the council's request, the startled pastor humbly asked permission to continue to conduct his Sunday morning services in Swedish for a while longer while he practiced his English in the evening services. When the council then reiterated its request that he convert at once to the exclusive use of English or resign and urged him to display more affection for his adopted nation, the pastor expressed indignation that the council had impugned his patriotism and curtly reminded it that it lacked any legal authority to require him to abandon the use of Swedish. The council's explanation that growing public opposition "to everything foreign" justified its demand also angered the pastor, who chided the council for succumbing to the demands of a mob. In reply, the council tacitly apologized for the tone of its second letter but told the pastor that he voluntarily ought to join the "one large American family" without the force of either mob spirit or law.[73]

In order to accommodate the needs of persons who spoke little or no English, the council suggested that special services be conducted only for them.[74] It urged persons who attended such services also to attend English-language services "in order to familiarize themselves with the language of the country." The council believed that the allowance of a separate service for non-English-speaking persons would "guarantee the constitutional right of religious worship" while giving "due response to the popular demand of our citizens for the exclusive use of the [English] language."[75] The council generally was pleased with the results of its efforts to discourage the use of German in church services.[76] In mid-June, the council's secretary stated that "the numerous preachers in all foreign languages are adjusting themselves to the Council's attitude readily and cheerfully."[77]

Meanwhile, on June 8, 1918, the state council had issued a proclamation that called for the exclusive use of English in all public places in Nebraska. In addition to reiterating its request for the sole use of English in schools, the council stated that nothing but English should be spoken in sermons and public speeches, on railroad trains and streetcars, and over the telephone.[78]

Although the council cautioned that citizens should exercise "great patience and care" in complying with this plan and that "every good citizen" should discourage "resort to harsh measures," the proclamation helped to exacerbate public hostility against German Americans. In July, an Albion man whose brother had been killed in action in France struck to the ground two men whom he found conversing in German on a public street. The local newspaper warned that persons who had been speaking German in public should learn a lesson from this incident and "remember they are in America where that language has no place, and avoid personal danger."[79]

The widespread hysteria against use of the German language was fanned even by clergymen. In a sermon late in June, for example, the pastor of the Congregational Church at Leigh called for the complete suppression of the German language throughout the nation. "The Germans have seen fit to load down and disgrace their language with such an awful weight of infamy," he declared, "that the only appropriate place for it would seem to be in hell itself." The pastor argued that elimination of German was justified not only as war measure, but also on general principles, since "we should talk the language of the people and country where we live." He further complained that the German language helped to propagate German Lutheranism, which he excoriated as un-Christian and immoral.[80]

By July, the crusade against the use of foreign languages had gone so far that even Hrbkova was moved to protest to the council about the needless harassment of loyal Americans who spoke a foreign tongue. As an example of such "distinctively unfair and unjust treatment," Hrbkova told the council that one woman was threatened with arrest after a fellow Bohemian American greeted her in public in the Bohemian language. Hrbkova reminded the council that "language is not the only thing that makes true citizenship." Although Hrbkova acknowledged that "English should be the language of this country," she declared that "it is absolutely wrong to persecute individuals of nationalities which have been friendly throughout the course of the war, just because they happen to speak the language of one of our allies on the street or some other public place." She warned that "we cannot afford to cause resentment among those who have so bravely and outspokenly stood for America's cause," and she admonished the council to refrain from the use of "Prussian methods."[81]

Although German Americans generally acquiesced to the council's foreign-language proclamation, its request for the suspension of the use of German over the telephone was highly controversial because telephone communications were conducted in private. Some German-speaking persons discontinued their phone service,[82] but many others resisted the council's request. The council conceded that "one unable to use our language cannot be denied the right to converse in his native tongue" over the telephone. It warned, however, that "those who [also] speak English must not be given this privilege."[83] Late in August, the state railway commission advised the telephone company to refuse to comply with any request by a county council of defense for the removal of any telephone that had been used for communication in German. The commission explained that the company had a common law duty as a common carrier to provide services to the public, except where those services would be used in furtherance of a crime. Since no law prohibited the use of German over the telephone, the company had no right to remove phones into which German had been spoken, unless the communication had been seditious.[84]

Although the council lacked any specific legal authority to suppress the use of the German language and ostensibly relied on voluntary cooperation to accomplish its ends, its campaign against foreign languages became increasingly coercive and acquired a quasi-legal character. While recognizing that its directives enjoyed broad public support, the council remained acutely aware that it lacked any specific power to prevent the use of foreign languages. In an opinion in August 1918, Attorney General Willis E. Reed stated that a town would lack the power to enact a valid ordinance forbidding the speaking of any foreign language. Reed predicted, however, that "prudence and public policy" would "prompt those of foreign birth to desist as far as possible in the use of their native language."[85] Reed understood, moreover, that the exigencies of the war dictated compliance with the council's so-called requests. In a letter to a German-American minister in June 1918, Reed acknowledged that no statute prohibited German preaching, but he stated that "it is essential that the public should do many things or omit to do others which are not commanded or prohibited by law." He observed that failure to obey public norms usually resulted in the "subsequent enactment of laws to meet the general will of the public."[86] Both during and after the war, the council lobbied for legislation that would provide a legal foundation for its opposition to the use of foreign languages. Meanwhile, it tried to avoid any confrontation that would provoke a lawsuit challenging its authority. As the vice-chairman of the council explained in confidence to a county council chairman shortly after the end of the war, "we have not desired to test our legal standing because of a fear that we might fall down."[87]

The council's combination of confidence and circumspection was reflected in its admonitions to the county councils to discourage all public use of foreign languages. Although it admitted that there was no legal ban on the use of German, the Council declared that lack of legal authority need not have any effect on the efforts of the state and county councils to discourage "the use of foreign languages on the street, in the home or over the telephone." The council urged the county councils, however, "to avoid the use of force" or "unnecessarily harsh" methods and to explain to persons who used foreign languages that the use of English would enable them to avoid public reprobation.[88]

The county councils often were even more aggressive than the state council in attempting to prohibit the use of foreign languages. County councils often forgot, if they ever knew, that no law prohibited speaking German. Accordingly, they often issued peremptory directives that made no pretense about taking the form of a mere request. At the end of May 1918, for example, the Cedar County Council of Defense commanded a Roman Catholic priest to discontinue immediately the use of any foreign language in public worship and instruction, except for the use of Latin in the Mass. The priest at once agreed to abide by the terms of the council's order.[89] In its report in December 1918, the legislature's Americanization Committee stated that some county councils had prohibited the use of foreign languages in church services and that members of the home guards had stopped Swedish-language funeral services.[90]

During the summer of 1918, the Americanization Committee convened to consider the feasibility of legislation to restrict the use of foreign languages. At its first hearing in September, more than two hundred persons appeared to express opposition to any legislation that would prohibit the use of foreign languages. Roman Catholic priests from German, Polish, and Italian parishes testified that such legislation would create hardship for older persons who could not speak English. After a German Catholic priest argued that a legislative ban on the use of foreign languages by churches would be unconstitutional, the chairman of the committee announced that it would refuse to hear any more references to constitutional rights because the state clearly had the right under the police power to prohibit any language other than English. Several witnesses pointed out to the committee that there was a clear trend toward the use of English in the churches and parochial schools and that it would be better to allow the use of foreign languages to disappear naturally. Other witnesses complained that loyal ethnic Americans resented measures that seemed to impugn their patriotism. An Italian-American priest warned, "You are estranging these people from the stars and stripes if you do this."[91]

As the 1918 gubernatorial election approached, the foreign-language question became a campaign issue. The state's suppression of the German language threatened the reelection bid of Governor Neville, a Democrat who had been elected in 1916 when many normally Republican German voters supported the Democratic ticket because they believed that Wilson had kept the nation out of the war. In an apparent effort to return German voters to the Republican fold, Republicans criticized some of the more extreme forms of hostility toward German Americans. In particular, Republicans castigated the council of defense for impugning the loyalty of German Americans and the Lutheran churches.[92] In late September, Neville admitted that German Americans had been the victims of "some unreasonable things," such as the suppression of the use of German in church and over the telephone. He warned that "we must have patience" with loyal Nebraskans who were "too old to rapidly change the habits of a life time." Neville contended, however, that the exclusive use of the "American language" in all elementary schools would ensure that the next generation of Nebraskans would all speak one language,[93] and he praised the council for removing foreign languages from elementary schools.[94] Although German-American Democrats professed to have been insulted by Republican allegations that the council had impugned the loyalty of German Americans,[95] the German vote swung decisively toward the Republicans in the election and may have been responsible for Neville's defeat.[96]

As in other states, the demonstrated patriotism of German Americans and the cessation of hostilities in November 1918 did not immediately end the campaign to suppress the German language. A woman in one small Nebraska town complained to the council early in December that local Germans were "resuming their former german customs" and that they were "determined that their little germany's [*sic*] must survive." Alleging that nine-tenths of the Germans in her community were disloyal, she predicted that "there will be trouble in this community" if "the Americans must contend with their disloyal enemy language."[97] Similarly, the chairman of the Otoe County Council of Defense warned the state council late in November that Germans would resume using their language if the council did not make clear that it was "still hunting the Hun."[98]

Despite agitation for stringent measures to suppress the German lan-

1. Arthur F. Mullen (1873–1938), an Omaha attorney, served as counsel for the opponents of the laws that prohibited the teaching of German. Mullen, a devout Roman Catholic, recognized that the language laws were part of a broader assault on parochial education. Active in Democratic politics, Mullen served as a Democratic national committeeman from 1916 to 1920 and 1924 to 1934 and acted as Franklin D. Roosevelt's floor manager at the 1932 Democratic presidential convention. Nebraska State Historical Society.

2. Above: William D. Guthrie (1859–1935), a New York attorney, served as counsel for the opponents of Oregon's compulsory public education law. A devout Roman Catholic and staunch proponent of individual freedom, Guthrie was an ardent advocate of the merits of parochial education. He also was a champion of conservative political causes and served as president of the New York Bar Association and the Association of the Bar of the City of New York. Library of Congress.

3. Right: Theodore C. Graebner (1876–1950), a Lutheran clergyman, educator, and journalist, helped to coordinate opposition laws that impeded and imperiled parochial education. He served as coeditor of the Missouri Synod's *Lutheran Witness* from 1914 to 1949 and was professor at Concordia Seminary from 1913 to 1950. Concordia Historical Institute.

4. Left: Robert T. Meyer (1878–1972) defied Nebraska law in 1920 by teaching German to elementary school students so that they could participate in German-language worship services. Convicted and fined twenty-five dollars, Meyer fought his case to the U.S. Supreme Court, which overturned his conviction in a landmark case that charted new boundaries of personal liberties. Concordia Historical Institute.

5. Above: James C. McReynolds (1861–1947) was the author of decisions in 1923, 1925, and 1927 in which the Supreme Court invalidated restrictions on parochial education. In the first of these decisions, *Meyer v. Nebraska*, McReynolds enunciated a remarkably broad vision of personal liberty under the First Amendment. McReynolds, who served on the Court from 1914 to 1941, is better known for his vehement opposition to social and economic legislation. Library of Congress.

6. Left: The Zion Lutheran Church near Hampton, Nebraska, was the congregation that supported the parochial school in which Robert Meyer defied Nebraska law by teaching German in 1920. The church remains the nucleus of a vibrant German-American community. Concordia Historical Institute.

7. Above: Zion Lutheran Church's South School was the scene of Robert Meyer's fateful encounter with the county attorney who arrested Meyer for teaching German. This building has been razed, but Zion still operates a school. Nebraska State Historical Society.

8. A tract published by a Ku Klux Klan member in Oregon shortly after the enactment of Oregon's compulsory public education law in 1922 depicted the fancied destruction of the venerable Old Cedar School by clergy of several denominations. In this cartoon, a torch-wielding Roman Catholic prelate triumphantly departs from the school while Amos Parker, an elderly teacher, rings the public school bell as he lies dying in the vestibule. Like the author of this tract, some nativists who advocated compulsory public education unfairly accused proponents of parochial education of seeking to destroy the public schools. Oregon Historical Society.

guage, the Americanization Committee urged a policy of relative leniency in a report that it issued in December after completing its investigations. The committee's report tacitly criticized the council's heavy-handed policies and warned that "harsh and oppressive methods" would not facilitate the Americanization process. Only "an intelligent regard for human sensibilities" would instill genuine patriotism, the committee argued. Although it recommended that instruction in all schools be given in English, the committee concluded that parochial schools should be permitted to teach foreign languages to the extent necessary to enable students to receive religious instruction from their parents. It predicted that foreign-language instruction would disappear as more parents became fluent in English.

The committee also opposed any restrictions on the use of foreign languages in religious services. It explained that any attempt to require a church to conduct services in a language that some parishioners did not understand would constitute "a flat denial of freedom in religious worship." The committee contended that the council's policy of allowing separate services for non-English-speaking persons was impracticable because it was impossible to identify those parishioners who needed to attend the special services. Urging persons who knew English to speak it in public places, the committee nonetheless advocated "a spirit of kindness and toleration" toward foreign-language conversations in public involving one or more parties who did not understand English.[99]

The committee deliberately withheld the release of its report until after the election, since it feared that the council would allege that the report was designed to help the Democratic administration. Believing that a Republican victory was inevitable, the committee feared that antagonists of the German-American community would contend that the Democratic defeat was a repudiation of the moderate position of the committee. The president of the Lutheran teachers' college in Seward held that this "would have been the death-blow to our schools, not to mention the use of any foreign language, perhaps even in church."[100]

Even though it could not interpret the election as a mandate for suppression of the German language, the council continued to call for restrictions on its use. Three weeks before the committee issued its report, George Coupland, the council's vice-chairman, privately stated that "the State Council has not changed its attitude on the language question in the least."[101] In a final report issued shortly before it disbanded in January 1919, the council tacitly expressed disagreement with the lenient program advocated by the committee, defended its own repressive policies, and warned that the menace of subversion by foreign elements would continue as long as the use of foreign languages was tolerated.[102]

In a letter to the state legislature, the council recommended legislation to prohibit the use of foreign languages in parochial schools,[103] and many Nebraskans supported laws to suppress the use of foreign languages. Late in December, Coupland hinted that mob violence would occur if the incoming legislature did not enact laws to restrict the use of foreign languages, and the *Star* continued to call for renewed efforts to ensure that all children would learn the English language.[104] Meanwhile, ethnic communities lacked official guidance regarding their use of foreign languages. In response to an inquiry from a pastor in January 1919 as to whether he could offer more services in German, Attorney General Reed could only advise him to do what was "best for the peace of the community" and the welfare of his congregation.[105]

Nebraska, like the rest of the nation, faced the ravages of influenza, inflation, and economic recession during the early postwar period.[106] The state had also begun to experience racial tensions, a relatively new phenomenon in Nebraska. In Omaha, where significant numbers of blacks had come from the South during the war to help relieve a labor shortage, a riot erupted during the autumn of 1919.[107] Racial and ethnic animosities were exploited by the Ku Klux Klan, which established numerous klaverns and attracted hundreds and perhaps thousands of members in Nebraska beginning in 1921.[108] As in other states, the fears of political radicalism that followed in the wake of the Bolshevik Revolution in Russia and the renewed radicalism of socialist groups in America after the end of the war helped to keep alive the spirit of intolerance toward political dissent that the war had engendered.

In their addresses to the session of the legislature that convened in January 1919, both Neville and Samuel McKelvie, the incoming governor, emphasized that schools were the key to Americanization. Neville recommended legislation prohibiting the use of any foreign language in the teaching of all secular subjects in the lower elementary grades of all public, private, and parochial schools. Similarly, McKelvie stated that all instruction in all schools should be conducted in English but that schools should be allowed to teach foreign languages as separate subjects. McKelvie added that "churches should also be used as a medium through which the use of the English language should be aided and encouraged," but he warned against the abridgment of religious freedom. Though McKelvie maintained that the state should seek the "universal use of the English language," he pointed out that any attempt to accomplish this goal at once would "work undue hardship" and risk the "defeat of the desired end." McKelvie therefore endorsed "the tolerant methods" that the Americanization Committee had advocated.[109]

German-American leaders were relieved by the relatively moderate tone of the gubernatorial speeches. McKelvie's views may have been influenced by a private conference with Missouri Synod leaders.[110] Widespread press support for the report of the Americanization Committee also seemed to augur well for the German Americans. But though the president of the Missouri Synod teachers' college in Seward stated early in the legislative session that the trend of public opinion opposed nativistic measures, he acknowledged that nativistic furor was far from exhausted.[111]

Responding to popular agitation for Americanization, legislators introduced a spate of bills to facilitate the assimilation of ethnic communities. Some of the bills had a distinctively nativistic flavor. One, for example, would have prohibited "involuntary service" and "forcible detention in convents, monasteries," and other sectarian institutions and would have permitted public inspections of those institutions.[112] Many of the bills were aimed at the education of the young. The most radical measures threatened the very existence of parochial schools. At least three measures would have required that all children attend public schools.[113]

One of these bills was passed by a vote of 75 to 11 in the house.[114] Alarmed at the imminent threat to their schools, a coalition of Roman Catholics and Lutherans vigorously fought the measure while it was under consideration by the senate. Arthur F. Mullen worked with C. Petrus Petersen, a Lutheran Republican state senator, to devise amendments that would regulate rather than prohibit parochial education. Although many Roman Catholics were willing to acquiesce to such regulations, one Catholic pamphlet alleged that the amendment's provisions for public inspection of the schools and public control over textbooks and curriculum would "take away from the Catholic authorities every vestige of management and leave them only the privilege of selecting the teachers and paying the bills."[115]

After the senate defeated the original bill by a margin of one vote, the house rejected the amendments proposed by the senate and the bill went to a conference committee, where it remained for several weeks. According to Mullen, Petersen finally won agreement to the amended bill by persuading advocates of the original bill that "its passage meant the starting of a religious war in Nebraska."[116] The final measure required parochial school teachers to obtain state certification and required parochial schools to comply with state standards for attendance, equipment, and supplies and to offer courses in American history and government. It also permitted local school superintendents to inspect parochial schools and to report any violations of the statute or subversive activities.[117] Expressing dismay that "a few bigots" had come so close to destroying Nebraska's parochial school system, a Roman Catholic newspaper noted that the fight over the school bill demonstrated that "Catholics must be more alert in protecting their own interests."[118]

Various bills were introduced to restrict the use of foreign languages in the schools. Most were aimed only at elementary schools, since German instruction in the high schools was not generally perceived as helping to perpetuate the linguistic isolation of the German-American community. School authorities in Lincoln opposed measures to restrict foreign-language instruction in the high schools.[119] German Lutheran clergymen actively opposed bills that would have prohibited German-language religious instruction and the teaching of the German language.[120] The bills also were opposed by a Swedish Lutheran synod, which adopted a resolution declaring that the measures would abridge religious freedom in violation of the federal Constitution.[121]

The statute eventually enacted, the Siman Act, prohibited instruction in any foreign language in any public, private, or parochial school, except that foreign languages could be taught as languages to students who had passed the eighth grade. The penalty for each offense was a fine of between twenty-five and one hundred dollars or confinement in jail for not more than one hundred days.[122] The Siman Act passed the senate by a margin of 29 to 2 and the house by a margin of 76 to 15, with 9 members absent or excused.[123] A minority report of the conference committee that considered the bill proposed that the statute specifically state that it should not be construed to forbid the use of a foreign language in any Sunday school, or in any private or parochial school on Saturdays or after the usual school hours for the religious instruction of pupils who were able to speak and understand such language.[124] At least some members of the house opposed the act because it failed to include this reservation. One representative denounced the measure as "vicious and uncalled for religious persecution," and another legislator explained that the restriction on religious instruction in foreign languages offended his "sense of fairness." One lawmaker who voted against the measure warned that European foes of America were attempting to divide the nation along the lines of "lingo and religion." Another house member noted that the valiant military records of German Americans proved that "language has nothing to do with good citizenship."[125]

In addition to the statutes regulating parochial schools and prohibiting grade school instruction in foreign languages, the Nebraska legislature enacted statutes to require the exclusive use of English in all public meetings and legal notices and to prohibit aliens from holding public office or teaching in any public, private, or parochial school. In response to Protestant complaints about Roman Catholic nuns who wore habits in public schools in which they taught, the legislature prohibited public school teachers from wearing the garb of any religious order.[126]

Attempting to reduce the political influence of German Americans, legislators enacted laws in 1919 and 1921 that emasculated the direct primary system and enhanced the power of party officials. German Americans particularly had outraged orthodox Republicans by crossing party lines to provide crucial support for Senator George W. Norris, a maverick Republican and war critic, in a closely contested primary in 1918.[127] Hostility toward the political behavior of German Americans was exacerbated by widespread support for the radical Nonpartisan League among German Americans, who briefly flocked to its radical banner more out of frustration over their harsh treatment by the mainstream parties than out of any commitment to socialism.[128]

Although the wave of anti-German and antiethnic legislation enacted during the years immediately following the war demonstrated that many Nebraskans were bitter about the past and fearful of the future, the success of ethnic Americans in averting even more extreme measures showed the effectiveness of organized action carried out in concert with moderate Anglo-Americans. This lesson would prove useful as ethnic Nebraskans mounted legal challenges to restore their right to teach their children in the language of their forebears.

5   The Fight against the
Language Laws

Although Nebraska's parochial schools survived the nativistic assaults of the
1919 legislature, the Siman Act significantly interfered with the mission of
those schools. Both nativists and ethnics were keenly aware that foreign-language instruction in the parochial schools had perpetuated Old World cultures and had ensured the survival of distinct ethnic communities. Despite
their compliance with the Council of Defense's requests to refrain from the
teaching of foreign languages, Nebraska's ethnic communities had hoped
that the wartime restrictions would not continue beyond the duration of the
conflict. This hope was dashed by the peacetime codification of the restrictions. The ethnic communities now recognized that proponents of Americanization sought not merely to protect national security and initiate ethnic
children into American ways, but to eradicate the foundations of ethnic culture. By removing foreign language instruction from the schools, the Siman
Act struck at one of the principal roots of the ethnic communities. The act
also threatened the vitality of the Old World religions that sustained these
communities. Although the state after the war no longer actively discouraged foreign-language services, the Siman Act's prohibition of foreign-language instruction virtually forced churches to continue to offer English-language services for the sake of children. A child who learned only English
obviously would receive inadequate spiritual nourishment in a church that
conducted its services in a foreign tongue. Many church leaders recognized
that such children might later forsake any religion or follow many of their
kin into the fold of other Protestant denominations. Even the most vociferous advocates of Americanization resented the language laws. As Martin
Graebner wrote to his brother Theodore, "while theoretically we can get

along without the German in the schools, we nevertheless should resist all usurpation of power and should not give up a single one of our liberties without a fight. Whether we wish to use our rights, that is our business."[1]

Early in May, the attorney general of Nebraska issued an opinion that the Siman Act did not prohibit the teaching of German in Saturday or Sunday religious classes.[2] This opinion, however, did little to allay the fears and resentments of many of Nebraska's German Americans. Pointing out that the legislature had explicitly rejected an amendment that embodied the attorney general's interpretation of the statute, Pastor C. F. Brommer informed Graebner that this "liberal interpretation of the law seems to have only the one purpose of dividing the opponents of the law [and] in this he has succeeded to some extent."[3]

Although the Siman Act was bad enough, ethnic communities feared that nativists would press for even more extreme measures. The narrowness of the defeat of the bill to require all children to attend public schools presaged future assaults against the very existence of the parochial schools. Brommer believed that the new statute to require all teachers to have state certificates might be used as a weapon in such assaults. He feared that some teachers would need to work hard to acquire certification in so short a period of time and that some would fail to do so. Although Brommer noted that the state superintendent was inclined to help the parochial schools as much as he could, opponents of parochial education were keeping a careful eye on him and some were attempting to compel him to resign from office on account of illness. Brommer told Graebner in May 1919 that "all means are resorted to, to kill our schools. Its [*sic*] a battle of life or death."[4]

Many other Nebraskans likewise regarded the Siman Act as merely the first step toward destruction of the parochial schools. According to Mullen, the real question was whether the state should control all education. Mullen helped to persuade the Roman Catholic hierarchy of the need to challenge the law. Well organized, generously financed, and politically sophisticated, the Roman Catholic church was amply prepared for protracted litigation. In order to fight an effective battle, however, the Catholic church needed allies, and its most obvious choice was its ancient nemesis, the Lutheran church. Many Lutheran leaders in addition to Martin Graebner were eager to challenge the Siman Act. Brommer told Theodore Graebner one month after the enactment of the statute that Missouri Synod leaders in Nebraska intended "to use all legal means" to defeat it insofar as it applied to religious instruction. But although Roman Catholics and Lutherans from the first seemed willing to cooperate with each other, any coordination of legal efforts was badly hampered by Lutheran decentralization and factionalization. Even the Missouri Synod, the largest and most powerful German-American Lutheran denomination, was largely congregational in its polity.

Opponents of the language laws in the Missouri Synod recognized that major litigation would require the creation of a more intensive bureaucratic infrastructure in the synod, a development that many of them already had been advocating. Graebner observed that the church could not "expect some small congregation to carry their suit to the Supreme Court," and he proposed that the synod hire a full-time legal adviser who would coordinate the litigation of test cases in all states in which a language statute jeopardized personal liberty.[5] The Graebner brothers and other advocates of modernization of the Missouri Synod also worked for the establishment of a central bureau for parochial schools. Complaining that "the apathy of our people is terrifying," Graebner stated in 1920 that the synod had lost five hundred schools since 1917 because it had failed to coordinate efforts to protect them.[6]

Despite Lutheran organizational problems, Mullen began to work almost immediately after the passage of the Siman Act for a joint Roman Catholic and Lutheran challenge to the statute. Proponents of parochial education believed that time was precious, for wartime restrictions on foreign-language instruction had demonstrated that many parents would withdraw their children from parochial schools that no longer offered instruction in German. Once parents began to send their children to public school, they were unlikely ever to resume the costs of parochial education. As Martin Graebner asserted, "we must *keep* our schools open. Once they close, they will be very difficult to reopen."[7] The ban on foreign languages also tended to demoralize the parochial schools, which had been under assault ever since the war began. Martin Graebner observed in April 1919 that a strong stand by the Missouri Synod on behalf of parochial schools that wished to defy the language laws would lift the spirits of struggling schools.[8]

Only five weeks after Governor McKelvie signed the Siman Act, several synods, schools, parishes, and laymen of the Lutheran and Roman Catholic churches commenced a lawsuit to enjoin its enforcement. Theodore Graebner confided to Pastor Brommer that "the lack of a definite policy in our Synod regarding the issues involved does not argue [*sic*] well for a coordination of efforts."[9] Brommer agreed that the outcome was uncertain.[10] He explained to Graebner that the lawyers for the schools did "not intend to make a serious effort" to obtain the injunction and would present their arguments only for "stage effect." He predicted that "the main fight will be in Supreme Court."[11]

Although the trial court of Douglas County in June 1919 entered a temporary injunction against enforcement of the law, the court dissolved the injunction after further consideration of the case,[12] and the plaintiffs appealed to the state supreme court. The plaintiffs represented a cross-section of ethnic culture, including the German, Polish, Bohemian, and Danish communities.[13]

In their brief on appeal to the state supreme court, the opponents of the Siman Act argued that the statute violated both the federal and Nebraska constitutions because it deprived them of their liberty and property without due process of law. The appellants therefore contended that the statute violated the Fourteenth Amendment to the United States Constitution, which prohibits any state from depriving any person of life, liberty, or property without due process of law, and that the law violated an analogous provision in the Nebraska constitution. In arguing that the statute deprived them of due process, the appellants did not allege that the statute violated procedural due process; they tacitly acknowledged that the law had been properly enacted and that they were accorded an opportunity to challenge its enforcement. Rather, they claimed that the statute violated substantive rights inasmuch as it unduly interfered with the schools' use of their property and the teachers' pursuit of their vocation. In making this substantive due process argument, the opponents of the Siman Act recognized that the well-established constitutional doctrine of the so-called police power permitted the state to interfere with liberty or property if it had a compelling need to protect the public health, safety, welfare, or morals. The statute's opponents contended, however, that the state had failed to demonstrate the existence of any interest that would justify the deprivation of liberty or property. Instruction in foreign languages, they maintained, was not harmful per se and did not imperil the safety of the nation.[14]

The appellants had good reason to suppose that an argument based on deprivation of property was more likely to succeed than one based on personal liberty. Although the due process clause of the Fourteenth Amendment appears originally to have been intended to protect the procedural rights of newly freed southern African Americans, the U.S. Supreme Court began during the late nineteenth century to construe the amendment to confer substantive rights on business and commercial interests. Invoking this doctrine of "substantive due process," the Court in numerous decisions protected business interests from regulation and control by states that enacted legislation to ameliorate some of the abuses of the Industrial Revolution. At the same time, states had likewise begun to invoke state due process clauses as a means of invalidating regulatory legislation, and the U.S. Supreme Court had used the due process clause of the Fifth Amendment as a shield for businesses against federal regulation. Although the federal and state courts had upheld much more legislation as a valid exercise of the police power than they had struck down as a violation of substantive due process, courts in both systems had struck down many significant pieces of social and economic legislation as constituting a violation of substantive due process. Accordingly, the appellants in the Nebraska case wisely emphasized that the statute interfered with their property interests. They recited the dollar value of their school buildings and alleged that the statute prevented them from exercising full dominion over this property and interfered with the right of teachers to engage in the practice of their vocation.[15]

The opponents of the Siman Act also contended that the statute violated the U.S. and Nebraska constitutions by interfering with their religious liberties. The appellants argued that the statute hindered non-English-speaking parents from giving religious instruction to their children and prevented families from worshiping together in a common tongue at home and at church.[16] In making this argument, the appellants wisely relied primarily on the protection of religious freedom guaranteed by the Nebraska Bill of Rights rather than the First or Fourteenth amendments to the federal Constitution. As of 1919, the U.S. Supreme Court never had applied the Fourteenth Amendment to protect personal liberties outside the context of race, and the Court specifically had refused to apply the freedom of religion clause of the First Amendment to action by states. By its own terms, the First Amendment acts as a prohibition on Congress rather than the states, and the Supreme Court as early as 1833 had held that the Bill of Rights did not act as a check against actions by states.[17] Twelve years later, the Court had stated that the "Constitution makes no provision for protecting the citizens of the respective states in their religious liberties. This is left to the state constitutions and laws."[18] After the enactment of the Fourteenth Amendment, the Supreme Court had refused to construe it to protect against state infringement of the liberties guaranteed by the Bill of Rights.[19] It therefore is somewhat surprising that the opponents of the laws bothered to invoke the federal Constitution in support of their argument that the Siman Act violated their religious rights. But they did, and, as we shall see, this argument proved to be prophetic in view of the ultimate outcome of the case.

In opposition to the appellants' argument, the state contended that the Siman Act did not deprive the appellants of property because it did not confiscate any tangible property or impair any goodwill. According to the state, parents would prefer to send their children to a parochial school in which religious instruction was offered in English rather than to a public school that provided no instruction in the tenets of their faith. The state argued that the statute did not impair religious freedom since religious instruction could be given in English.[20] The state emphasized that the law was needed to provide "equality of opportunity" among the state's children by ensuring that they were not handicapped by a deficiency in English. During oral argument, the state's counsel also contended that the statute was needed to encourage loyalty to America, since "foreign sympathies are kept alive through the foreign tongues and to that extent Americanization is retarded."[21]

In a decision handed down in the last week of 1919, the Supreme Court of Nebraska affirmed the lower court's denial of an injunction.[22] The court, however, gave the statute a very narrow reading. While holding that the statute was a valid exercise of the government's police power, the court maintained that the legislature could not have intended to prohibit foreign-language instruction at times that did not interfere with instruction under the state's mandatory education law. The court explained that such a sweeping prohibition of any foreign-language instruction would be unconstitutional since it would be an unreasonable exercise of the police power and an interference with personal liberty.

The court's narrow interpretation contravened the plain language of the statute and also its legislative history. Since the Siman Act arose out of the Council of Defense's wartime attempts to banish all foreign-language instruction, the legislature presumably intended to codify the same extensive restrictions that prevailed during wartime. Even more conclusive was the legislative conference committee's rejection of a minority report to amend the statute to permit foreign-language instruction for religious purposes on Saturdays or after the regular school hours.[23] The court's specious interpretation of the statute constituted a form of judicial legislation. As Robert Meyer's attorneys later explained, the court in construing the Siman Act "had to tone it down, write into it a meaning the legislature did not give it, and by judicial construction hold that it did not mean what it said, in order to save its constitutionality."[24] The court's failure to abide by the statute's language and purpose suggests that the justices, who served four-year elective terms, feared that nativists would defeat them for reelection if they invalidated the statute.

Accordingly, the court upheld the statute in a manner that gave the proponents of parochial education virtually everything they wanted while acknowledging that the state had a compelling need to enact measures promoting Americanization. Taking judicial notice of the fact that many military recruits during the war could not speak English and that communities in which English was not spoken were centers of alien sympathies, the court emphasized that the state had a legitimate and compelling need to enact statutes that would ensure the loyalty and patriotism of its citizens. If the state could enact banking regulations and workers' compensation laws, the court explained, the state surely could insist that its citizens understand the nation's language, history, and government and prohibit anything that interfered with such education.[25]

Although Nebraska Lutherans rejoiced over the state supreme court's decision, the official publication of the Nebraska District of the Missouri Synod urged that "we must now, more than ever, equip our children to do their duty toward their fellowmen by making them familiar with the English religious language."[26] Lutheran schools meanwhile continued to try to raise their educational standards. Brommer confided to Theodore Graebner in June 1919 that harassment by the legislature could turn out to be a blessing in disguise to the extent that it shook the synod out of its lethargy. During the spring of 1919, more than one hundred of the synod's teachers and ministers enrolled in a ten-week course at a teachers' college in Fremont in order to obtain teachers' certificates. Brommer observed that the "gray-haired men" enjoyed their instruction, although they suffered from homesickness, the added expenses, inadequate food, and bedbugs. Brommer and other clergy made periodic visits to cheer the spirits of the students. In response to the crisis, the Nebraska District of the Missouri Synod also decided to educate women teachers at its seminary in Seward. Brommer reported in June that the morale of the schools was improving and that congregations, clergy, and teachers were "showing loyalty" to the schools and making sacrifices to keep them open.[27]

Supporters of parochial schools also derived courage from the gradual diminution of anti-German sentiment in Nebraska. The conciliatory tone of the court's opinion, from which one justice dissented, demonstrates the persistence of opposition to the more extreme forms of nativism that swept the state during and immediately after the war. The judges' contrived effort to avoid invalidation of the statute, however, indicated that the nativists still constituted a powerful force in Nebraska politics.

The strengths and weaknesses of nativist forces were revealed during a constitutional convention that was held between December 1919 and March 1920. Both opponents of the Siman Act and proponents of more extreme measures attempted to obtain seats on the convention's education committee. In an apparent effort to prevent the language and parochial school controversies from disrupting the convention, the selection committee excluded from the education committee all persons who had been actively identified with either side of those controversies.[28] Although this tactic may have kept the language and parochial school questions from emerging as leading controversies at the convention, it could not suppress those issues altogether. Early in the convention, Walter L. Anderson, a delegate from Lancaster County who had directed wartime conscription in Nebraska, sponsored a proposal that would have written the major provisions of the Siman Act into the constitution.[29] The proposal received vigorous support from the American Legion, whose national and state conventions had voted in favor of the exclusive use of English in the schools.[30] Despite widespread support for the proposal, the convention voted 64 to 28 indefinitely to postpone consideration of the measure.[31] The chairman of the committee that had recommended postponement explained that it was imprudent to "stir up a controversy" by recommending a measure on which where there was "a wide difference" of opinion, especially since the nonpublic schools were abiding by the terms of the Siman Act.[32] Anderson alleged that the enactment of the amendment would diminish public controversy by removing the language issue from politics.[33]

In place of Anderson's proposal, the convention adopted a measure that declared English to be the official language of the state. This provision mandated the use of English in all official proceedings, records, and publications and required that all basic subjects be taught in English in public, private, and parochial schools.[34] At least two delegates who supported the measure acknowledged that the provisions concerning schools already were included in the Siman Act but warned that the same forces that opposed the act might force its repeal in a subsequent session of the legislature.[35] By a margin of one vote, the convention defeated Anderson's proposal for an addition to this measure that would have prohibited the use of any language other than English for instruction in the basic curriculum and in official proceedings and documents. Anderson argued that rejection of this measure would permit ethnic schools to comply with the constitution by teaching in English for a mere five minutes per day.[36] The convention also failed to adopt a proposed addition to the measure that would have prohibited instruction in a foreign language in any school until the student was "able, understandably, to read, write and speak the English language."[37] Nevertheless, the convention failed to still the language controversy, which was beginning to enter its most significant phase.

After the supreme court's decision, counsel for the plaintiffs met and concurred in the view that the decision plainly permitted a teacher to offer German instruction during a recess period without violating any provision of the statute.[38] As a result of the state supreme court's narrow interpretation of the Siman Act, parochial schools throughout Nebraska began to offer instruction in foreign languages during the recess period. As we have seen, the two schools operated by the Zion Lutheran Church in Hampton were among those schools. The church's council voted in January 1920 to change the schools' schedule to offer German during an expanded recess period. Before the court's decision, the Zion schools had conducted classes from 9 until 12 in the morning and from 1 until 4 in the afternoon. Starting in January 1920, Zion extended its recess period until 1:30 and offered German-language instruction from 1 until 1:30. Since the school day continued to begin at 9 and end at 4, Zion offered German during time that previously had been allocated to instruction conducted in the English language.

Despite its narrow reading of the Siman Act, the court's decision to uphold the law and its acknowledgment of the need to encourage Americanization had appeased many of the harshest critics of the use of the German language. The *Lincoln Daily Star,* for example, explained that the Siman Act would make it easier "for children of foreign extraction to understand Americanism."[39] The resumption of German-language instruction by many schools during recess periods, however, vexed proponents of Americanization. After Meyer's arrest, the *Star* denounced this "subterfuge" and declared that the state should not tolerate it.[40] Even after Meyer's indictment, however, many schools continued to offer German during recess periods. Attorneys for the synod advised Pastor Brommer that Meyer had not broken the law as construed by the state supreme court and that teachers should continue to offer German during noon recess or before or after the regular school day.[41]

In his appeal to the state supreme court, Meyer argued that he had com-

The Fight against the Language Laws 105

mitted no offense under the statute as it had been construed by the court, because he had not offered instruction in German during the regular school hours. He also argued that the Siman Act was unconstitutional under the Fourteenth Amendment as an improper deprivation of both property and liberty. He maintained that the law destroyed his vocation as a teacher of foreign languages and also constituted an "invasion of personal liberty." Meyer further contended that the Siman Act violated the Nebraska constitution's guarantees of religious freedom.[42]

The state argued that the statute was within the state's police power inasmuch as its purpose was "to prevent the inoculation [*sic*] of minor children with foreign languages and foreign ideals before they had a chance to appreciate and retain American standards." The state denied that the statute significantly impaired Meyer's livelihood, because he remained free to teach students who were above the eighth grade level. The state also denied that the statute violated religious freedom, contending that "religion is dependent upon no language" and that the "Supreme Being is not a German God, who hears supplications only when addressed to Him in the Teutonic Tongue." The state further held that German-American parents would not need to instruct their offspring in German if they would bother to acquire a better knowledge of English. "What we need is more English in the church, rather than more German in the schools," the state declared. Denying that the supreme court's decision had permitted instruction during recess periods, the state contended that Meyer had tried to evade the law through a subterfuge.[43]

During the pendency of Meyer's appeal, the legislature repealed the Siman Act and replaced it with the more stringent Norval Act. The new statute's namesake, state senator Richard S. Norval of Seward, had sought to help his numerous German-American constituents by amending the Siman Act explicitly to permit parochial schools to offer instruction in foreign languages to elementary school children outside normal school hours. Norval acted, however, without consulting German-American leaders in his district, who correctly perceived that the time was not ripe for repealing restrictions on foreign-language instruction.[44] Brommer reported to Graebner that Norval's proposal raised "a great howl" among opponents of the German language and that Lutheran leaders had not bothered to argue in favor of the Siman Act's repeal at public hearings on the Norval measure because such testimony would have been as futile as speaking "to a vicious steer."[45] In response to pressure from the American Legion and other proponents of

Americanization, the legislature amended the bill to require quite the opposite of what Norval had intended; Norval voted against the measure and unsuccessfully attempted to remove his name from it.[46]

The new statute reiterated the Siman Act's requirement that all subjects in all public, private, and parochial schools must be taught in the English language, and it explicitly extended this requirement to all school instruction held at all times, other than religious instruction offered on the Sabbath.[47] The Norval Act therefore removed the loophole that the state supreme court had created and through which Meyer had attempted to crawl. Like the Siman Act, the Norval Act provided that foreign languages could be taught, as languages only, after a pupil had passed the eighth grade. The Norval Act likewise reiterated the declaration in the new constitutional amendment that English was the official language of the state. Unlike the Siman Act, the Norval Act stated that a parent could offer foreign-language instruction to his own children in his own home.[48] The new act also included a novel section that prohibited "any organization, whether social, religious or commercial," from discriminating against the use of the English language in any meeting, school, or proceeding. Brommer explained to Graebner that this rather cryptic provision was intended to force the use of English by congregations in which advocates of the use of English were unable to bring about the abandonment of German. It was added at the behest of two American Legion members who "went wild," according to Brommer, when the Lutheran parish at Emerald voted over the objection of one-third of its congregation to reduce the number of English-language services and to restore the use of German in the Sunday school.[49]

Like the Siman Act, the Norval Act engendered considerable opposition. Willa Cather declared that "no Nebraska child now growing up will ever have a mastery of a foreign language, because your legislature has made it a crime to teach a foreign language to a child in its early years, the only period when it can really lay a foundation for a thorough understanding of a foreign language."[50] The Missouri Synod wasted no time in moving to enjoin the enforcement of the new act. John Siedlik, the father of four children who attended a Roman Catholic school that taught the Polish language, joined the action.

At the hearing before the district court, Roman Catholic and Lutheran clergy testified that elimination of foreign languages from the curriculum would interfere with the religious education of students by preventing them from participating fully in foreign-language worship at church and devotions at home. A Lutheran pastor explained, for example, that parents had a duty to assist in the preparation of their elementary school age children for their first communion. Parents obviously could not perform this duty if they were unable to communicate fluently with their children about religious subjects. Lutheran clergy explained that parochial instruction in foreign languages would not tend to perpetuate the use of German, since the young people were receiving all their secular instruction in English, and that this new generation would introduce the use of English into the churches.[51] The district court apparently found these arguments to be persuasive, for it enjoined the enforcement of the Norval Act, and the state appealed to the Nebraska Supreme Court while the defendant's appeal in *Meyer* was pending before that court.

In their brief in the case, the churches argued that the Norval Act clearly was unconstitutional because the supreme court had stated in its 1919 decision that the Siman Act would have been unconstitutional if it had prohibited the teaching of German at any time. As in that case, the churches also argued that the statute was unconstitutional because it deprived them of property without due process of law and unduly interfered with religious liberty under both the state and federal constitutions. Once again, the opponents of restrictions on language instruction failed to explain why the federal Constitution would protect religious liberty.

In arguing that the statute unconstitutionally deprived them of liberty and property, however, the churches placed more emphasis on property and less on religious freedom than they had in their challenge to the Siman Act. The Missouri Synod alleged that the Norval Act imperiled the synod's investment of more than a quarter of a million dollars in its parochial schools and that "the right of a person to conduct a lawful enterprise in his own way is a property right." The synod also argued again that the statute interfered with the right of teachers to pursue their vocation.[52]

Like the synod, the state reiterated many of the arguments that it had advanced in the action to enjoin the Siman Act. The state argued that the synod had failed to demonstrate that the statute injured any property right or diminished the value or goodwill of its schools. The state also contended that the statute did not interfere with religious worship, and it pointed out that the federal Constitution did not protect religious freedom. The state further argued that the statute was a valid exercise of the police power, since the presence of unassimilated citizens created a public menace.[53] Similarly, the American Legion stated in an amicus brief, "We must eliminate every influence that tends to perpetuate foreign ideals and foreign allegiances."[54]

The Supreme Court of Nebraska ruled in favor of the state in the *Meyer* case in February 1922.[55] In its decision, the court held that the Siman Act was a valid exercise of the state's police power because the legislature reasonably could have determined that there was a compelling need to ensure that the children of immigrants would not learn any foreign language until they were thoroughly grounded in the English language and American ideals. Although the parties in their briefs had not emphasized the question of religious freedom, the court stated that this was the central issue in the case and concluded that there was no undue interference with religion. Though conceding twice in its opinion that the statute might limit the ability of children to participate in German-language religious services, the court emphasized that the church's doctrines could be adequately imparted in English and that the law did not "interfere with the entire freedom of religious worship." The court also explained that religious freedom did not permit an individual to engage in activities that were inimical to the best interests of the state.

Since the Zion Lutheran Church scrupulously had undertaken to conduct its German classes outside the normal class hours, the court's decision in *Meyer* squarely was at odds with its earlier holding that German-language instruction could be given outside the hours prescribed for study under the state's compulsory education law. Faced with this inconsistency, the court expressly conceded that its earlier decision should be modified to the extent that it had interpreted the Siman Act as applying only to regular school hours. Since neither the Siman Act nor the compulsory education law defined the scope of the normal school day, the court reasoned that the Siman Act was intended to prohibit foreign-language instruction whenever pupils attended school for the purpose of receiving instruction. The court's decision, which made no reference to the enactment of the Norval Act, also concluded that Zion had altered its schedule in order to evade the statute. The court denied Meyer's motion for a rehearing.[56]

The decision in *Meyer* to uphold the broadest possible interpretation of the Siman Act ensured that the court would uphold the Norval Act. In a ruling handed down two months after it rendered its *Meyer* decision, the court declared that the Norval Act was "a reasonable exercise of the police power" and did not deprive any person of life, liberty, or property without due process of law or deprive anyone of the equal protection of the law.[57]

The Supreme Court of Nebraska was not unanimous in its decisions in

Meyer and the case involving the Norval Act. *Meyer* was decided by a vote of four to two and the Norval Act case was decided by a vote of five to one. Taking a position that would form one of the principal bases for the U.S. Supreme Court's reversal of the Nebraska court's decision, Justice Charles B. Letton in his dissent in *Meyer* argued that the legislature could not "interfere with the fundamental right of every American parent to control, in a degree not harmful to the state, the education of his child." Chief Justice Andrew M. Morrisey, dissenting in the Norval Act decision, argued that the Norval Act arbitrarily forbade the acquisition of useful knowledge and that it was discriminatory because it permitted a parent to impart such instruction himself or herself or through a private tutor.[58] Both dissents ignored the question of whether the statutes violated religious freedom. Letton, who no longer was a member of the court by the time the Norval Act case was decided, observed, "It is patent, obvious, and a matter of common knowledge" that the Siman Act "was the result of crowd psychology; that it is a product of passions engendered by the World War, which had not had time to cool."[59]

On April 10, 1919, only one day after Nebraska passed the Siman Act, the state of Iowa enacted a law that likewise was designed to restrict instruction in foreign languages. The Iowa statute, as we saw in Chapter 3, expressly prohibited the use of any language other than English for secular subjects in any public or private school and provided that foreign languages could be taught above the eighth grade level. The statute therefore was substantially identical to Nebraska's Siman and Norval acts, except that Iowa did not impose any restriction on the use of foreign languages in connection with non-secular subjects.

In January 1920, August Bartels was convicted of offering instruction in the German language in a Lutheran elementary school in a rural area of Bremer County, Iowa, in November 1919. Like Meyer, Bartels received the minimum sentence, a fine of twenty-five dollars.[60] In appealing his conviction to the Iowa Supreme Court, Bartels argued that his German-language lessons were not a "secular subject" within the prohibition of the statute since the purpose of the lessons was to enable the students to worship with their German-speaking parents. Bartels contended that any other construction of the statute would render it unconstitutional under the Ninth and Tenth amendments of the U.S. Constitution, analogous provisions of the Iowa constitution, and Iowa's guarantee of the free exercise of religion.

Like Meyer, Bartels emphasized that the state had a legitimate reason to require that all children receive an adequate knowledge of English. Bartels contended, however, that the German instruction did not endanger the state and that "the teaching of reading in German . . . is essential to the religious beliefs of the Church," since it enabled parents and children to "worship at a common altar in a common language."[61]

The state of Iowa emphasized that the statute was designed to facilitate the Americanization of immigrants and their progeny. Nonetheless, the state offered no specific facts in support of its contention that the continued use of German among German Americans hindered the American war effort and fomented "distrust of American institutions and policies." Echoing the nativist prejudices that had precipitated the enactment of the foreign-language laws, the state alleged that "these people are usually clannish; they are well satisfied with themselves and do not care for the society of Americans, and in most instances the barriers are not broken down until the public school educates the second or third generation and gradually instills into them a love of things American."[62]

The state argued that there was "nothing freakish or arbitrary" about the statute because so many other states had enacted similar measures. Although the state acknowledged that religious freedom "is one of the cornerstones of constitutional structure," it contended that Bartels's appeal to religious freedom was a subterfuge to "perpetuate manners, customs and modes of thought that are not in harmony with our political institutions."[63]

In its decision on February 12, 1921, a year before the Nebraska Supreme Court affirmed Meyer's conviction under the Siman Act, the Supreme Court of Iowa affirmed the conviction of Bartels. In contrast to the four-to-two vote in *Meyer,* the *Bartels* case was decided by the even narrower margin of four to three. As the Nebraska Supreme Court had done in *Meyer* and the two injunction cases, the court in *Bartels* concluded that "this statute was a proper and reasonable exercise of the police power of the state, in attempting to prevent an existing evil which the legislature regarded as inimical to the public welfare."[64] The Iowa court explained that the legislature properly had been concerned because many military conscripts during the First World War were not sufficiently familiar with the English language to understand commands or read orders. Accordingly, the legislature had enacted the statute "to meet this situation, to encourage the more complete assimilation of all foreigners into our American life, to expedite the full Americanization of all our citizens."[65]

As the Nebraska Supreme Court would later do in *Meyer,* the Iowa court rejected the defendant's argument that the statute violated religious freedom. Anticipating the arguments of the Nebraska court in *Meyer,* the Iowa court concluded that a prohibition on the teaching of reading in German did not interfere with religious freedom merely because the ability to read German might facilitate religious instruction. Although the court contended that the statute would permit Bartels to "teach his pupils to read the catechism in German in his school . . . as religious instruction, without violating the law," the court's refusal to permit the teaching of reading as a secular subject made it impossible for any teacher to lay the foundation for religious instruction in a foreign language. For all practical purposes, the court therefore eliminated the legislature's dispensation for religious instruction and prescribed a prohibition on the use of German that was no less sweeping than that of the Nebraska statute.[66]

Expressing dismay that the court had obliterated the statute's distinction between secular and religious subjects, Chief Justice William D. Evans entered a vigorous dissent that was joined by two associate justices. Evans pointed out that reading instruction is not a necessarily a secular subject if it is given to facilitate religious instruction. Since Evans believed that it was necessary for students to learn German in order to participate in religious activities, he argued that the secular subject matter of the reading lessons did not transform reading into a secular subject within the meaning of the statute. Accordingly, he concluded that the construction placed on the statute by the majority interfered with religious freedom.[67]

On May 8, 1919, less than one month after the enactment of the Nebraska and Iowa statutes, the Ohio legislature approved the Ake law, which provided that English would be the sole language of instruction in the first eight grades of parochial schools. The statute also expressly prohibited instruction in German in the first eight grades of both private and parochial schools. The statute was signed by Governor James M. Cox four weeks later. The inclusion of the private and parochial schools was made at the behest of Cox, who hinted that he would veto the measure if it were limited to public schools. In a message to the General Assembly, Cox stated, "We do not want a preserve of treason anywhere in Ohio."[68] As in Nebraska, the state officials who were charged with enforcing the language law preferred to give it a liberal reading that would not interfere with religious instruction in parochial schools. In an opinion in August 1919, the attorney general of Ohio stated that the legislature merely had intended to prohibit the teaching of the common subjects in German and that the statute "had no reference to any religious instruction."[69]

Shortly after the enactment of the law, some congregations of the Missouri Synod in Ohio decided to defy it in order to test its constitutionality. Although proponents of a test case believed that Ohio officials would not prosecute subsequent violations of the law during the case's pendency, the deeply ingrained Lutheran obedience to civil authority made many Lutherans reluctant to disobey the law, particularly since a new state law required all teachers to give a written oath to obey the laws of the state.[70] Asked to express his opinion, Graebner stated that it would "be a very hazardous thing to act in open violation of the new statute. . . . The promise of politicians to the effect that there will be no prosecutions until the law has been tested, should be ignored as all promises of politicians are 'writ in water.'"[71]

At the start of the new school year in September 1919, H. H. Bohning, a trustee of St. John Lutheran School in a Cleveland suburb, was arrested for ordering the school's teacher, Emil Pohl, to teach German to elementary school children. Bohning and Pohl were convicted by a jury in the Mayor's Police Court in Garfield Heights, and each was fined twenty-five dollars. Their conviction was upheld by the Court of Common Pleas of Cuyahoga County and that county's court of appeals.[72]

Bohning and Pohl appealed to the Supreme Court of Ohio. Like the defendants in the Nebraska and Iowa cases, Bohning and Pohl argued that the statute was an unreasonable exercise of the state's police power, in violation of the Fourteenth Amendment and analogous provisions of the Ohio constitution. They alleged that the statute was not necessary as a war measure because the war had ended before the statute's enactment and that it was not needed to respond to the postwar danger of subversion since German Americans had eschewed Bolshevism. Like the defendants in the Nebraska and Iowa cases, Bohning and Pohl also argued that the statute therefore interfered with their religious freedom in a "cruel and oppressive manner," in contravention of the state constitution, since Lutheran parents had "desired that the religion of Martin Luther should be taught to their children in Luther's language."[73]

In contrast to the opponents of the Iowa and Nebraska laws, the defendants in the Ohio cases also made appeals to natural rights. These arguments were particularly significant, since they presaged the reasoning of the U.S. Supreme Court's decision. Bohning and Pohl maintained that the word "liberty" as used in the Fourteenth Amendment embraced "all the natural rights incident to existence in a civilized country" and comprehended "the right to teach and to acquire human knowledge in all of its branches, including all languages of the human race, ancient and modern." They likewise contended that the right to teach and to acquire knowledge was a "privilege" under the privileges and immunities clause of the Fourteenth Amendment. Moreover, they argued that parents had a "sacred and natural right" to control the education of their children, as guaranteed by the word "liberty" in the Fourteenth Amendment, the privileges and immunities clause, and the Ohio constitution. Acknowledging that the state had an interest in the education of children, the defendants contended that the constitution did not intend to revert to Sparta or Bolshevist theory that children "are the property of the state." Like the opponents of compulsory public education, they declared that "the child in Ohio still belongs to its parent."[74]

The defendants further suggested that the statute violated the equal protection clause of the Fourteenth Amendment because it arbitrarily and unnecessarily "singled out the German as the only foreign language which may not be taught in the private and parochial schools below the eighth grade."[75]

In a decision on June 7, 1921, the Supreme Court of Ohio summarily rejected the defendants' arguments and affirmed the judgment of the court of appeals. The court based its unanimous decision on a broad theory of judicial deference to the legislature. The court presumed that the legislature had information concerning the effect of the teaching of the German language to elementary school students which justified the statute and explained that it lacked the power to "review the wisdom of legislative acts" even when a statute was unjustified. The court also rejected the defendants' equal protection argument on the ground that the statute applied equally "to every pupil of the state who has not completed a course of study equivalent to that prescribed in the first eight grades of the elementary schools, regardless of nationality, ancestry, or place of birth."[76]

The court's decisions in the Nebraska, Iowa, and Ohio cases demonstrated that the anti-German passions engendered by the war had not yet disappeared by 1922. Throughout the nation, however, there were signs that wartime enmities were cooling. In the disillusionment that followed the war, many Americans began to question whether the nation should have entered the conflict. Although German ethnicity never fully recovered from the war, German-American organizations, including parochial schools, had begun to thrive again. After the dedication of an impressive new school building in 1920 by a Lutheran church in Minnesota to replace one that had been ransacked in 1918, a parishioner was moved to exclaim that the tribulations of the war had been a blessing in disguise that had strengthened his congregation.[77] Despite these and other hopeful signs, however, the most significant challenges to the parochial school system occurred during the 1920s.

6 The Supreme Court's Invalidation of the Language Laws

Undaunted by their defeats in the supreme courts of Nebraska, Ohio, and Iowa, the opponents of the language laws decided to carry their battle to the United States Supreme Court.[1] The decisions in the two Nebraska cases, the Iowa case, and the two Ohio cases all were appealed to the U.S. Supreme Court, which considered the five cases at the same time. In seeking to overturn the rulings of the state courts, the opponents of the language statutes implicitly challenged the constitutionality of the language laws in the nineteen other states that had restricted the teaching of foreign languages. Since all these laws were essentially the same, the Court's invalidation of the Nebraska, Iowa, and Ohio laws would indicate that the laws of the nineteen other states could not survive a legal challenge. The appeals in the five cases therefore had national significance and attracted widespread interest and attention. Although the parties to the cases knew that the Court's decisions would seal the fate of language legislation and also might affect other attempts to restrict the scope of parochial education, they were only dimly aware that the cases involved broad issues of personal freedom that would have a profound impact on the development of American law.

In their arguments before the Supreme Court, the appellants in all five cases argued that the language statutes interfered with certain fundamental liberties, violating the Fourteenth Amendment because the laws could not be justified on the grounds of public necessity under the government's police power. In reaching this conclusion, the appellants employed various forms of reasoning and raised some arguments that differed from those that they had used at the state level. Generally, however, the contentions of the different appellants complemented one another and reinforced points that they had made to the state courts.

In analyzing the scope of the police power, all appellants acknowledged that the state had a legitimate need to ensure that its citizens were fluent in the English language. At oral argument, for example, Mullen agreed with Justice McReynolds's suggestion that it was "a matter of high importance" to the people of Nebraska that "all of its citizens speak English."[2] The appellants argued, however, that the language laws were overly broad because the prohibition on foreign-language instruction in primary schools did not facilitate the legislative purpose of ameliorating ignorance of English. The Missouri Synod denounced the prohibition as "senseless and silly," and Meyer declared that it was impossible to discern how the law could "serve the public welfare." As Bartels pointed out, "the mischief did not consist in children knowing German; the mischief consisted in children . . . not knowing English—an essentially different thing." The appellants agreed that the government could remedy ignorance of English without prohibiting instruction in foreign languages.[3]

These arguments, however, overlooked the fact that the legislative purpose in enacting the statutes was not merely to facilitate knowledge of English, but also to inculcate a thorough "Americanism" in young children by eradicating the "foreign" ideals and disloyalty that legislators perceived to have infested ethnic culture, particularly German-American society. Among the appellants before the Supreme Court, only Bohning and Pohl seriously addressed the question of whether legislative concern for subversion provided any justification for the language laws. In denying that any such justification existed for the Ohio law—the only one of the challenged statutes that barred solely the teaching of German—Bohning and Pohl argued that the law was not justified as a war measure because it was enacted after the armistice. They further maintained that it was not justified under the police power because there was no evidence that German Americans in Ohio were Communists or were hostile to American institutions or that the extirpation of the German language would tend to repress subversion. Contending that Communist organizations drew their members from the ranks of recent immigrants from non-German-speaking countries, Bohning and Pohl may have attempted to exploit the hostility toward southern and eastern European immigrants and fear of Communism which had replaced the animosity toward German Americans and fear of Germany during the early postwar years.[4]

Skirting the issue of German-American loyalty, the appellants in the Norval Act case simply dismissed the Nebraska legislation as the product of wartime xenophobia. Arguing that instruction in German was not inherently harmful and that its suppression would not promote the public welfare, the Missouri Synod observed sardonically that the law aimed to promote patriotism by prohibiting the teaching of music in the language of Bach, Beethoven, Handel, Mozart, and Wagner and that it sought to preserve the public health by prohibiting the teaching of history in the language of Plutarch, Herodotus, or Caesar.[5] Similarly, Meyer's brief warned that "in our desire for the Americanization of our foreign born population we should not overlook the fact that the spirit of America is liberty and toleration—the disposition to allow each person to live his own life in his own way, unhampered by unreasonable and arbitrary restrictions."[6]

Having concluded that there was no compelling need for the legislation, the appellants argued that the statutes violated certain fundamental personal and property rights. The appellants defined personal rights variously as the right of parents to direct the education of their children, the right of citizens to acquire knowledge, the right to teach, and religious freedom. They defined property rights as the right of a parochial school to conduct foreign-language classes and the right of a foreign-language instructor to follow his vocation.[7]

The argument that parents have the fundamental right to direct the education of their children was made by all the appellants, even though only Bohning and Pohl had relied much on that approach at the state level. None of the appellants emphasized this argument, however, and even Bohning and Pohl gave it less attention than they had at the state level. At oral argument, Mullen mentioned this point only in passing.[8] The appellants were somewhat more forceful in their contention that there is a fundamental right to teach and acquire knowledge. For example, the Missouri Synod denounced Nebraska's restrictions on the acquisition of information and knowledge through the medium of a foreign language as "a capricious, unreasonable and arbitrary use of the police power" in contravention of the due process and privileges and immunities clauses of the Fourteenth Amendment.[9]

In contrast to their arguments at the state level, the appellants' Supreme Court briefs devoted little attention to the abridgment of religious freedom. Meyer and Bohning and Pohl virtually ignored the issue, and Bartels spent little time on it.[10] Instead, the Missouri Synod advanced the then-novel proposition that the Fourteenth Amendment protected the free exercise of religion. In contrast to its more oblique assertion of the same proposition in its briefs to the Nebraska Supreme Court in the actions to enjoin the Siman and Norval acts, the Missouri Synod declared in sweeping terms that "state legislation denying religious liberty is a violation of both the letter and spirit of the 14th Amendment; it is a deprivation of a person's liberty without due process of law; it denies persons the equal protection of the laws; it abridges the privileges and immunities of citizens of the United States." The synod further stated that "the 14th Amendment protects the citizen against adverse action by the state of those privileges and immunities that were protected against adverse action by the Federal Government in the first eight amendments of the Constitution of the United States." These arguments, of course, contravened settled case law as set forth by the U.S. Supreme Court. Unable to cite any case authority for these propositions, the Missouri Synod cited only a brief passage from a constitutional treatise in which the nineteenth-century legal scholar Thomas M. Cooley tentatively had suggested that the Fourteenth Amendment might under certain circumstances protect religious freedom.[11]

The Missouri Synod's reference to the first eight amendments to the Constitution is the sole reference in any brief in any of the cases to any possible theory of incorporation of the Bill of Rights into state law. The potential significance of this reference was considerably diluted, however, by the synod's failure to explain or emphasize its theory. Since its brief did not refer specifically to the free exercise clause of the First Amendment, the synod relied on a general theory of substantive due process rather than on any theory of incorporation.

At oral argument before the Supreme Court, Mullen likewise relied on a theory of substantive due process in contending that the statute's interference with religious liberty violated the Fourteenth Amendment. Acknowledging that the Court had not directly addressed the question of whether the Fourteenth Amendment protected religious liberty, Mullen nevertheless contended that this "question seems to be squarely here." Mullen told the Court that "religious freedom, freedom of conscience and freedom of speech come within 'the privileges and immunities' referred to in the fourteenth amendment." In his autobiography, Mullen stated that "there was no use in basing any argument on the First Amendment" inasmuch as the Court's decision in *Permoli* indicated that the Court would apply the First Amendment's protections of freedom of religion, speech, press, assembly, and the right of petition only against congressional action. Accordingly, Mullen explained that he relied on the Fourteenth Amendment. Although he stated in response to a question by Chief Justice William Howard Taft that he would incorporate the free exercise of religion into the due process clause, Mullen's remarks suggest that he was referring not to incorporation of the First Amendment's guarantee of religious freedom, but rather to the protection of a natural right. When Taft asked whether the Fourteenth Amendment protected free speech, Mullen stated that free speech was protected, as was "the right to study, and the right to use the intellect as a man sees fit." Like his answer to Taft's question about freedom of religion, these comments suggest that Mullen's entire argument embraced a broad theory of substantive due process and that a more narrow theory of incorporation was not viewed even as an alternative.[12]

Even if Mullen and the Missouri Synod did not intend seriously to advocate incorporation, their insistence that the Fourteenth Amendment prevents states from infringing religious freedoms was particularly significant because the Court's dictum in *Meyer* expressed agreement with this novel argument. As we shall see, this argument also helped to prepare the way for the Court's incorporation of the Bill of Rights into state law.

Since the Fourteenth Amendment never previously had been construed by the Supreme Court to guarantee any of the "liberties" that the appellants claimed to have been infringed by the language statutes, the appellants' appeal to fundamental rights seemed to promise little hope of success. Accordingly, the appellants also relied on the contention that the statutes infringed their rights to property in violation of the due process clause and created an arbitrary classification in violation of the equal protection clause. An argument based on property rights had the advantage of particularly sturdy precedent, since the Supreme Court for more than thirty years had carefully scrutinized state and federal legislation in order to determine whether it violated property interests. Although the Court always had upheld more legislation than it had struck down and had been especially deferential to legislation during the years immediately preceding the First World War, the doctrine of economic due process had acquired a new vitality beginning with the Court's invalidation of a federal child labor law in 1918. The apparent trend toward solicitude for property rights had been accelerated by the election of Warren G. Harding to the presidency in 1920 and the appointment to the Court of the conservatives William Howard Taft, Pierce Butler, George Sutherland, and Edward T. Sanford.

Although reliance on the doctrine of economic due process ordinarily would have provided a promising means of attacking legislation before the Supreme Court, the appellants in the language cases lacked any substantial basis for alleging that they had suffered economic loss as a result of the legislation. The Missouri Synod and Bohning had presented no evidence that the enrollments of their parochial schools had declined since the enactment of the language laws. Similarly, Meyer, Bartels, and Pohl could not allege that they had suffered any loss as a result of the laws. Since instruction in German was only a small part of their duties as parochial school teachers, the enactment of the laws had not resulted in the termination of their employment or any diminution of their income.

Falling back on generalities, Bartels and Meyer argued that the statutes interfered with their right to pursue a legitimate vocation. Bartels and Bohning and Pohl also contended that the right to impart instruction was at least in part an economic right. Similarly, the Missouri Synod suggested that it had a property right to operate a school without undue state interference. Mullen, who deeply feared state regulation of parochial schools, explained at oral argument that the language legislation deprived churches of "control over those schools and cripples them and makes less valuable their property."[13]

The appellants' equal protection arguments were more cogent than the ones concerning deprivation of property. Several appellants contended that the statutes were discriminatory because they permitted the children of the wealthy to receive foreign-language instruction at home or in classes outside school. Bartels also maintained that the Iowa law created an unreasonable classification because it failed to distinguish "between good schools and bad schools, or between good teachers and bad teachers," and because it condemned the languages of America's wartime allies along with the language of the enemy. Opponents of the Ohio law complained that there was no fair reason "for prohibiting German while permitting instruction in other languages."[14]

In responding to the appellants' arguments, the states of Nebraska, Iowa, and Ohio all attempted to demonstrate that the laws were within the proper scope of the police power[15] because they were needed to ensure that schoolchildren grew into loyal and patriotic citizens.[16] The state of Nebraska in the Norval Act case warned that Nebraska was developing "little Germanys, little Italys and little Hungarys" under the "control of foreign leaders" in which children were "being reared in a foreign atmosphere."[17] But the state vouchsafed no objective evidence in support of its position that the teaching of foreign languages in the elementary schools in which the principal language was English would preclude children from maturing into liberty-loving citizens.

Likewise, the state of Ohio's contention that the statute's objective was the "upholding of an intelligent citizenship"[18] failed to explain why good citizenship and limited instruction in foreign languages were antithetical when English remained the principal medium of instruction in the schools. Although the state of Iowa purported to offer evidence in support of its vehement assertion that the teaching of foreign languages posed an immediate threat to the security of the state, its evidence was hardly convincing. Forgetting that the Iowa statute was enacted six months after the armistice, Iowa declared, "At the time of the enactment of this legislation our whole country was discovered to be infested with German spies; people of German birth . . . were openly sympathetic with the nation . . . that was engaged in ruthless warfare against unoffending people."[19]

In arguing that the statutes were a legitimate exercise of the police power, the states of Nebraska and Iowa equated those laws to economic legislation recently enacted by various states to protect the fundamental health and safety of their citizens. In the Norval Act case, Nebraska argued that the education of the young and the development of citizenship surely involved sufficient public interest to justify state regulation, since the state had regulated more mundane matters involving interest rates, hours of labor, hotel accommodations, banking, and the renting of apartments.[20] If the state could "compel landlords to place windows in their tenements which will enable their tenants to enjoy the sunshine, it is within the police power of the state to compel every resident of Nebraska to so educate his children that the sunshine of American ideals will permeate the life of the future citizens of this republic," Nebraska declared in its brief in *Meyer*. The state added that a "father has no inalienable constitutional right to rear his children in phyhical [sic] moral or intellectual gloom."[21] Similarly, the state of Iowa declared, "We say to vendors of food, you must not mix poison with your wares. We protect the bodies of our people in this way. Are we powerless to protect them against mental poisons?"[22]

The states' briefs devoted more attention to the issue of religious freedom than did the appellants' briefs. All three of the states argued, as they had in the state courts, that the statutes did not abridge religious freedom because children could receive religious instruction in English. Once again, the states brushed aside the argument that the children needed to learn German in order to participate in German-language worship services at home and at church. The state of Nebraska explained that "religion is a matter of faith, not of language" and that "every doctrine of plaintiffs' church can be expressed as well in English as in German."[23]

Similarly, the state of Iowa contended that the statute did not violate religious freedom, since "there is nothing about the teaching of the language that remotely suggests religion." Instructors of German, according to the state, could use religion as a pretext for propaganda about "the greatness of the fatherland and the divine right of Kaisers." Once again, the state failed to produce any objective evidence of any correlation between German instruction and subversion. The state saw no harm, moreover, in allowing parents to instruct their children in the German language so that the children might receive their religious education in the German tongue.[24] Likewise, the state of Ohio argued that "if a parent wishes his child taught Martin Luther's dogma in Martin Luther's language, there is no law against the child being taught that language, unless it takes so much of the child's time and health as to endanger society in that regard."[25]

In denying that the statutes unduly interfered with property rights, the states of Nebraska and Iowa pointed out that the appellants had failed to present any evidence of such interference. Nebraska contended that the value of the Missouri Synod's schools did not depend on whether or not a foreign language was taught to students in those schools. The state of Iowa observed that there was no evidence that Bartels had lost his job or was prevented by the statute from pursuing his calling as a teacher. Similarly, the state of Nebraska in *Meyer* contended that Meyer's "method of livelihood is not seriously impaired." Although Nebraska conceded that the statute might interfere somewhat with his occupation, it contended that such interference was within the state's police power, just as the state could properly prohibit the sale of alcohol or the sale of cigarettes to minors.[26]

The states' responses to the arguments concerning equal protection were less cogent. Ohio simply ignored Bohning and Pohl's claim that the prohibition on the teaching of German was arbitrary, and the state of Iowa did not address Bartel's argument that the statute discriminated against poor persons who could not afford tutors. Nebraska weakly dismissed a similar argument by Meyer by relying on the Nebraska Supreme Court's opinion in the Norval Act case, which stated that private instruction by tutors was rare. In both the Nebraska cases, the state contended that the statute was not arbitrary because it was general in its application and was enacted pursuant to the police power to remedy a known evil. Similarly, Iowa argued that the law was not arbitrary because it applied to all public, private, and parochial schools. The state contended that the statute would have denied equal protection to public school children if, as Bartels had urged, the law had exempted private schools from the operation of the statute.[27]

At the oral argument in February 1923, Mullen emphasized that the state had a limited right to regulate private education and to require all students to study certain basic subjects, but that private schools had a constitutional right to teach any other subject that was not seditious. He contended that this right was primarily premised on religious liberty, which he argued was protected against infringement by a state under the privileges and immunities clause of the Fourteenth Amendment. Mullen also suggested that the Fourteenth Amendment conferred a right on parents to educate their children in any manner that did not infringe on the legitimate needs of the state.

Questions by Justice James C. McReynolds during the argument demonstrated the close connection between the right to teach foreign languages and the right to operate a private school. McReynolds inquired about whether a state could require children to attend public schools. "You will admit that, will you not?" McReynolds asked Mullen. "I do not admit that," Mullen replied. "You do not admit that?" McReynolds inquired with evident surprise. "I do not admit that," Mullen insisted. "I deny that a State can, by a majority of the legislature, require me to send my child to the public schools." Mullen argued that the power to regulate private schools no more gave the state the right to require public education or proscribe the teaching of foreign languages than the right to inspect restaurants gave the government the right to tell people what to eat. "I deny," Mullen stated, "the power of a legislative majority to take the child from the parent and prescribe the mental bill of fare which that child shall follow in its education." Such regulation, Mullen pointed out, had already been tried by the new atheistic government in the Soviet Union.[28] Mullen reported to a Roman Catholic scholar shortly after the argument that it was apparent from the justices' questions "that the right of the state to prohibit private education and to require everybody to attend the public schools was being considered" by the Court in passing on the validity of the language laws.[29]

Since the cases involved many questions of first impression, it was difficult for attorneys for either side to assess how the Court might rule. The Court's recent pioneering decisions on the subject of free speech ostensibly boded badly for the opponents of the language statutes since in those cases the Court had taken a broad view of governmental power to prevent subversion. In four decisions early in 1919, the Court had upheld convictions under the Espionage Act on the ground that the antiwar statements of the defendants presented a "clear and present danger" to the national security.[30] Although this new "clear and present danger" test seemed to confine treasonous speech to a narrow range of cases, the Court in all four cases applied the test to sustain convictions for speech that hardly seemed likely to incite defiance of the law or pose any imminent threat to the national security. Although an antiwar activist who had published leaflets that urged potential draftees to resist conscription had at least advocated unlawful behavior, the other three defendants had not counseled civil disobedience. The publisher of a German-language newspaper had merely editorialized against the draft and challenged the constitutionality of the war, the Socialist Eugene V. Debs had given an antiwar speech that sizzled in its rhetoric but was cold in its proposals for action, and opponents of American intervention in the Russian civil war had done no more than distribute pamphlets criticizing Wilson for sending troops to Russia. The Court nevertheless found in all four cases that the defendants' words might have caused disruption of the war and that this was sufficient to sustain convictions under the "clear and present danger" test. In two later cases, the Court adopted an even broader test when it upheld the convictions of defendants whose activities were determined to have a "bad tendency" to interfere with the war effort.[31] In another case, *Gilbert v. Minnesota*, the Court in 1921 upheld a conviction under a Minnesota sedition law prohibiting speech that discouraged enlistment in the armed forces.[32]

Although these decisions seemed to suggest that the Court would take a very broad view of the need to protect national security and favor a narrow view of the scope of countervailing constitutional liberties, it would take far more imagination to demonstrate that German instruction threatened the national security. Moreover, the language laws, enacted and enforced during peacetime, could not be sustained as wartime measures. The nation no longer faced the crisis that had loomed when the defendants in the cases arising under Espionage and Sedition acts had criticized the war.

Recent decisions by the Court on economic regulations also offered mixed signals about how it might rule in the language cases. Although the states correctly pointed out that the courts had sustained a wide range of economic legislation as constituting proper uses of the police power, the Supreme Court during the past five years had demonstrated an increasing so-licitude for the rights of private property in decisions in which it had ruled that federal and state legislation violated the Constitution. This growing impatience with social and regulatory laws suggested that the Court would not blindly defer to legislative determinations that the language statutes were needed to protect the public interest.

The personal predilections of the members of the Court also clouded any prediction of the outcome of the language cases. Adhering to a strict con-structionist view of the Constitution, Chief Justice Taft during his two years on the Court had not hesitated to vote to strike down popular legislation that he believed was violative of the language or intent of the nation's char-ter. Although Taft ardently had supported the war and loathed political rad-icals, his very conservatism may have inspired sympathy toward the mid-western farming folk who asked only to teach their ancestral language to their offspring.

Moreover, Taft could have been expected to sympathize with the special needs of Roman Catholics and Lutherans. A Unitarian, Taft was known for his tolerance in religious matters. Catholics esteemed him for treating their church in an enlightened manner when he was governor of the Philippines and for appointing many of their coreligionists to federal office when he was president. Taft believed that the Roman Catholic church was "one of the bulwarks against socialism and anarchy in this country."[33] Taft had learned his toleration at the knee of his father, Judge Alphonso Taft of the Ohio Su-perior Court. In 1870, the elder Taft had written a dissent supporting the constitutionality of a Catholic-sponsored resolution of the Cincinnati School Board to prohibit the reading of the Bible and other religious books in the public schools. Judge Taft emphatically declared in his dissent that the board had properly protected the religious freedom of Roman Catholics under the Ohio constitution.[34]

In addition to respecting Catholics, Taft thought highly of Lutherans. Sending greetings to a Lutheran youth convention shortly after his defeat for reelection to the presidency in 1912, Taft observed, "It has been my privi-lege to know your people in an intimate way, my home city of Cincinnati be-ing a Lutheran center. The Lutherans have been a power for righteousness in that community." In words that were prophetic in view of the *Meyer* deci-sion, Taft declared that "no church shows more clearly than the Lutheran Church the advantages of religious freedom secured by our constitution, and the strength and growth of religion under a system where there is an absence of state interference or control."[35] Taft expressed similar sentiments in a 1912 letter to the president of the Missouri Synod's principal seminary.[36]

Justice Louis D. Brandeis also was likely to be favorably disposed toward invalidation of the language laws. Brandeis had dissented in several of the Espionage Act decisions and had contended in his dissent in *Gilbert* that the liberty guaranteed by the Fourteenth Amendment went beyond property rights and also included personal freedoms. Brandeis's dissent in *Gilbert* was particularly relevant to the *Meyer* case, because Brandeis had stated that the statute's prohibition on the teaching of pacifism "invades the privacy and freedom of the home" and precluded parents from following "the promptings of religious belief, of conscience or of conviction."[37] As a Jew, Brandeis also might have been expected to scrutinize carefully any legislation that discriminated against minority ethnic and religious groups.

Justice Oliver Wendell Holmes also had taken a broad view of personal liberties in dissents in some of the Espionage Act decisions, but his devotion to the ideal of judicial restraint suggested that he might defer to the legislatures in the language cases. Opponents of the language laws could not have been unmindful that Holmes had voted with the majority in *Gilbert*. Moreover, as we shall see, Holmes tended to have a jaundiced view of Catholicism.

Justice Edward Terry Sanford might also have been expected to take a dim view of the language laws. Although Sanford had served on the Court only since January 1923, he had established a record as a moderate during his fifteen years as a federal district judge in Tennessee. An urbane and highly educated man, Sanford had done postgraduate study in languages in France and Germany[38] and had demonstrated considerable solicitude for academic freedom during his service as a member of the board of regents of the University of Tennessee. Writing in the wake of Sanford's appointment to the Court, a Tennessee editor explained that Sanford "is not a professional patrioteer, 'hundred per center,' nor labor baiter. Americanism is dear to his heart—the true type of Americanism, of love for the Constitution, including the Bill of Rights."[39]

Justices Joseph McKenna and Pierce Butler would seem likely to have been sympathetic to the needs of parochial schools since both were practicing Roman Catholics. The son of Irish immigrants, McKenna had been an infant in Philadelphia during the bloody riots that erupted there during the 1844 controversy over the use of the Bible in the public schools. For four years, the future justice had attended a struggling parochial school that suffered the antagonism of Philadelphia's nativists, until his father moved his family to California to escape religious discrimination and economic frustration.[40]

Since Butler, also the son of Irish immigrants, maintained close ties to the Roman Catholic hierarchy, he surely was aware that the church regarded the language laws as part of a broader assault on parochial education. Moreover, Butler could not have been oblivious to the persistence of anti-Catholic prejudice, for his nomination to the Court less than one year before the *Meyer* decision had encountered opposition among nativists. Butler might also have been expected to think carefully before joining in a ruling that offended the Catholic hierarchy, since several prominent Roman Catholic leaders had urged Harding to nominate Butler to the Court. Although Butler had remarked then that he would not accept a place on the Court "as a representative of any creed, class, party, or group,"[41] consideration of the anti-Catholic motivations of the framers of the language laws and recognition of their deleterious impact on Catholicism was not inconsistent with judicial objectivity. Before leaving Minnesota to take his place on the bench, Butler had assured an old acquaintance, Theodore Buenger, a German-American Lutheran, that he would protect the rights of parochial schools. Later, at a dinner in honor of Butler's appointment, Buenger sat with Butler's son, who discussed the nativistic opposition to his father's appointment and expressed eagerness for a final judicial ruling on the question of whether parents had a right to educate their children in parochial schools. Buenger shared this information with Missouri Synod officials, who presumably felt reassured by it.[42]

Other factors, however, cast doubt on whether Butler would be disposed to oppose the language laws. Butler was of Irish rather than German extraction, and he had attended and taught public school in the rural Minnesota community in which he was raised and had graduated from Carleton College, then a Congregationalist institution.[43] Moreover, Butler's closest friend in the Catholic hierarchy was Archbishop Ireland of St. Paul, whose ambivalence toward parochial education had led him to work for closer ties between the parochial schools and the public schools. Then, too, Butler during the war had shown no tolerance for coolness toward the war effort. As a member of the Board of Regents of the University of Minnesota, he had insisted on the summary dismissal of a tenured political science professor who refused to support the war actively.[44]

Justice McReynolds likewise was a problematical vote. At first glance,

McReynolds would not have seemed favorably disposed toward invalidating the language laws. Although he was one of the Court's most vociferous defenders of property rights, he was not known as a civil libertarian. A man of vehement personal hatreds, he was blatantly hostile toward Jews and had revealed a prejudice against German Americans in his dissent in a 1921 decision. In that case, the Court had held that a judge who had admitted his distaste for German Americans should not have presided over the trial of German Americans who were charged with violating the Espionage Act. In explaining in his dissent that there was no evidence that the judge was biased, McReynolds had observed that it was only natural that the judge had been prejudiced against "malevolents from Germany,—a country then engaged in Hunnish warfare, and notoriously encouraged by many of its natives, who, unhappily, had obtained citizenship here."[45]

McReynolds's devotion to property rights, however, could have been expected to make him sympathetic to the economic arguments of the opponents of the school laws, and his antagonism toward statism also suggested that he might be suspicious of laws that infringed on liberties of persons who were not demonstrably radical in their political beliefs. McReynolds's father, who opposed public education and resented taxes to support public schools,[46] had sent his son to private schools and passed on an elitism and individualism that might have disposed McReynolds to favor the rights of private schools.

The views of Justices Willis Van Devanter and George Sutherland also were difficult to predict, although their intense desire to protect property rights against government encroachments suggested that they would be inclined to agree with the economic arguments of the parochial schools. Their fervent individualism and antistatism further indicated that they would be favorably disposed toward the personal liberties involving private education. Sutherland, who had lived in Utah during much of his youth, admired the self-sufficiency of the early pioneer Mormons, who had established their own schools.[47]

In two separate opinions announced on June 4, 1923, the Supreme Court, by a margin of seven to two, reversed the state court decisions upholding the language statutes.[48] Both opinions were written by McReynolds, who read them aloud with great vigor in a sarcastic tone that seemed to ridicule legislative efforts to deprive citizens of their basic rights.[49] In its opinion in *Meyer,* the Court held that the Siman Act deprived language teachers, pupils, and parents of liberty in violation of the Fourteenth Amendment. Although the Court stated that "the desire of the legislature to foster a homo-geneous people with American ideals . . . is easy to appreciate," it held that "the means adopted . . . exceed the limitations upon the power of the State" inasmuch as "mere knowledge of the German language cannot reasonably be regarded as harmful."[50] Accordingly, the Court determined that the Siman Act was in conflict with rights assured to Meyer under the United States Constitution.

In discussing the character of those rights, the Court explained that though it was not necessary "to define with exactness" the liberty guaran-teed by the fourteenth amendment, it could state "without doubt" that the amendment

> denotes not merely freedom from bodily restraint but also the right of the individual to contract, to engage in any of the common occupa-tions of life, to acquire useful knowledge, to marry, establish a home and bring up children, to worship God according to the dictates of his own conscience, and generally to enjoy those privileges long recog-nized at common law as essential to the orderly pursuit of happiness by free men.[51]

Pointing out that "the American people have always regarded education and acquisition of knowledge as matters of supreme importance which should be diligently promoted" and that parents have a duty to give their children an appropriate education, the Court concluded that Meyer's right to teach and the right of parents to engage Meyer to instruct their children were "within the liberty of the Amendment."[52] The Court found that the Siman Act's prohibition on the teaching of all modern languages could "in-terfere with the calling of modern language teachers, with the opportunities of pupils to acquire knowledge, and with the power of parents to control the education of their own." The Court observed that Plato's proposal for com-munal rearing of children and other similar ideas that "men of great genius" had advocated were wholly at odds with the ideals on which American insti-tutions rest.[53]

Although the Court acknowledged that "the state may do much, go very far, indeed, in order to improve the quality of its citizens, physically, men-tally and morally," it declared that "the individual has certain fundamental rights which must be respected." The Court explained, "The protection of the Constitution extends to all, to those who speak other languages as well as to those born with English on the tongue." The Court observed that "perhaps it would be highly advantageous if all had ready understanding of our ordinary speech, but this cannot be coerced by methods which conflict with the Constitution—a desirable end cannot be promoted by prohibited means."[54] Since "no emergency has arisen which renders knowledge by a child of some language other than English so clearly harmful as to justify its inhibition with the consequent infringement of rights long freely enjoyed," the Court concluded that "the statute as applied is arbitrary and without reasonable relation to any end within the competency of the state."[55]

The Court invalidated the language laws only to the extent that they applied to private and parochial schools. Although it did not explicitly say that public schools could prohibit the teaching of German, the Court stated that no one had challenged the "state's power to prescribe a curriculum for institutions which it supports" and this issue was not under adjudication.[56] In a letter to Professor George Fox of Yale, Taft confirmed that the decision "does not prevent the Legislature from excluding German or any other subject from the curriculum of a public school, and it does not prevent the Legislature from requiring the study of English and the study of the fundamental branches in English in every private school, but it does prevent the Legislature from forbidding a parent to employ a private school or a private school teacher to teach his child any subject matter which is not itself vicious."[57] Taft explained to his daughter that "we are engaged in correcting the constitutional errors of some of the State Legislatures."[58]

The Court's second opinion, also written by Justice McReynolds, in the other four cases relied solely on the authority of the Court's decision in *Meyer* in reversing the state supreme court decisions in those cases.

Holmes and Sutherland were the only dissenters. In a short opinion joined by Sutherland, Holmes argued that the statutes did not unduly restrict the liberty of either teachers or students, since the laws were a reasonable and perhaps necessary method of achieving a common language, a goal that all members of the Court seemed to agree was desirable. Holmes acknowledged that he dissented "with hesitation and unwillingness," but he explained that "youth is the time when familiarity with a language is established and if there are sections in the State where a child would hear only Polish or French or German spoken at home I am not prepared to say that it is unreasonable to provide that in his early years he shall hear and speak only English at school." Holmes pointed out that "no one would doubt that a teacher might be forbidden to teach many things." Quoting a 1912 decision that upheld a Mississippi statute prohibiting the sale of malt liquor, Holmes stated that the constitutionality of the statute should be measured by asking "whether, considering the end in view, the statute passes the bounds of reason and assumes the character of merely arbitrary fiat." Holmes concluded, "I think I appreciate the objection to the law but it appears to me to present a question upon which men reasonably might differ and therefore I am unable to say that the Constitution . . . prevents the experiment being tried." Holmes and Sutherland agreed with the Court only to the extent that it invalidated the provision in the Ohio statute that singled out the teaching of the German language for special prohibition.[59]

It may seem ironic that Holmes, who is widely remembered and revered as a great civil libertarian, dissented in the language cases while the arch-conservative McReynolds wrote the majority opinion. The opinions are not surprising, however, insofar as Holmes's represented his ideal of judicial restraint and McReynolds's reflected the same broad concept of judicial review that had made the justice one of the Court's most inexorable critics of social and economic legislation.

Mullen believed that his point that the state had no right to require all children to attend public school won over a previously hostile McReynolds, apparently because this argument demonstrated that the Nebraska law could lead to the sort of untrammeled state power that prevailed in the Soviet Union.[60] Although the decisions of the Court in the recent cases involving free speech showed that McReynolds and other conservatives on the Supreme Court had no desire to expand the liberties of political radicals, the members of the Court could perceive no threat to government from the parochial schools, which did not present any danger to the existing social or political order. Indeed, McReynolds and other conservatives on the Court may have perceived that the traditional moral and religious values that were propounded by these schools helped to discourage the economic, political, and social radicalism that they so feared. They may have prized the schools as bastions of stability in an increasingly turbulent society.

As in previous opinions, however, Holmes was less concerned about the wisdom of the legislation than about the issue of whether the Court should interfere with a legislative determination about the need for a law. While Holmes may have abhorred the nativism that motivated the statute and questioned whether the law would actually achieve the goal of promoting a common language, his dissent in the language cases was based on the same deference to legislative findings that had motivated his dissents in many other cases. In *Lochner* and the first child labor case, for example, the Court had invalidated economic and social welfare legislation that Holmes may personally have disliked. Holmes's characterization of the language laws as an experiment echoed his dissent in *Abrams,* in which he observed that the Constitution's protection of free speech is an experiment, "as all life is an experiment."[61] Holmes's dissent in the language cases was inconsistent with his dissent in *Abrams* and the other recent free speech cases, however, insofar as it discouraged the freedom of expression that Holmes professed to cherish. If Holmes did not believe that Congress had the right to punish criticism of the war that did not demonstrably harm the government, it is difficult to understand how he could conclude that the state legislatures could ban the teaching of foreign languages in the absence of any real evidence that such instruction constituted the sort of "clear and present danger" that he had required in *Abrams* and other free speech cases.

Although, as Fred Rodell once pointed out, Holmes's dissent in the language cases often is regarded as "his most illiberal view and vote,"[62] many of Holmes's opinions in support of illiberal legislation vie for that dubious honor. In addition to concurring in the Court's decision in *Gilbert v. Minnesota,* Holmes later wrote the Court's opinion sustaining a Virginia law that permitted sterilization of inmates in institutions for the mentally retarded,[63] and in 1911 he had dissented in the Court's decision invalidating an Alabama peonage statute.[64]

Moreover, Holmes may not have seen any need to be particularly solicitous of the liberties of ethnic Americans; perhaps he did not believe that they had been oppressed in the same way as racial minorities and unpopular political groups. He also lacked any innate sympathy for parochial education. An agnostic, Holmes viewed organized religion with bemused contempt. His private correspondence betrayed an anti-Catholicism that was not unusual for a Boston Brahmin of his time, and he often expressed alarm over what he regarded as the baneful effects of a religious education. In a 1917 letter to Harold Laski, for example, Holmes remarked that he had been "sick at heart" to read a book in which a "puke in an apron" warned Roman Catholic youth about the perils of hell. Holmes stated, "I don't believe men who took an active part in ordinary life could or at any rate would have invented such mean and dirty spiritual tortures."[65]

Despite Holmes's insistence that the legislatures had a rational basis for enacting the language laws, the history and background of those statutes demonstrate that the Court correctly concluded that the laws were not reasonably calculated to achieve the ends for which they were supposed to be intended and that they therefore did not justify the abridgment of the liberty of teachers, parents, and students. Contrary to Holmes's contention, it is clear that the legislation was not reasonably calculated to facilitate the alleged legislative purposes of promoting literacy in the English language, encouraging the "Americanization" of second-generation Americans, or discouraging subversion. Since the core curriculum of the parochial schools was taught in English, supplementary foreign-language instruction did not inhibit literacy in English. Likewise, it is difficult to discern how limited instruction in foreign languages discouraged students from absorbing American ideals. The Nebraska district judge who enjoined the enforcement of the Norval Act made a telling joke at trial: after the state's attorney asked a pastor whether parochial school graduates could recite the national anthem, the judge remarked that the bilingual children "probably beat us in that. They can repeat it in two languages."[66] The failure of the states to make any serious attempt to demonstrate that large numbers of German Americans were disloyal or subversive or that there was any significant nexus between isolated instances of subversion and instruction in the German language also indicates that it was impossible for the state to show that the use of German encouraged subversion. In view of these considerations, it is clear that Holmes should have scrutinized the statutes with the same discernment that he had employed in the free speech cases in which he recently had dissented.

The Supreme Court's invalidation of the language laws was propitiously timed, for it occurred just when the assault on parochial education was reaching its zenith in campaigns for compulsory public education. Although, as we shall see, the Court's opinion in *Meyer* has had far-reaching constitutional consequences, its most immediate impact was to warn the foes of the parochial schools that the Court would closely examine the constitutionality of any law that interfered with the operation of parochial schools. The decision also struck a blow at nativistic legislation in general. Mullen accurately predicted shortly after *Meyer* was decided that the "whole brood of laws that are aimed at the citizen because of his religion, his nationality and his condition in life has received a set-back."[67]

7   The Michigan and Washington State School Bills

At the same time that parochial schools were challenging the constitutionality of the language laws, the schools were fighting in some states for their very existence. Nativists attempted to destroy parochial education by advocating laws to require all elementary school children to attend public school. Although Oregon was the only state in which voters approved a compulsory public education initiative, nativists sponsored major campaigns in support of similar measures in Michigan and Washington. An examination of those campaigns offers insights into the social and legal controversies surrounding parochial education during the early 1920s.

The movement for compulsory education in Michigan reflected the growing social tensions of a state that had rapidly industrialized during the first two decades of the twentieth century. Michigan's transformation from a predominantly agricultural state into the automobile capital of the world produced demographic changes on a vast scale. The migration of large numbers of ethnic Americans, mostly Roman Catholic, to the state to work in the factories caused unease among many Anglo-American Protestants. The migration of southern African Americans to the state's large industrial cities during and after the First World War exacerbated racial tensions, and the arrival of poor southern whites in the same areas swelled the ranks of persons who were receptive to nativist appeals. Meanwhile the state's most prominent citizen, Henry Ford, stoked the fires of bigotry during the early 1920s by publishing in his *Dearborn Independent* a series of viciously anti-Semitic screeds.[1]

Although Michigan's German-American population was somewhat smaller than that of most other middle western states, it had attracted considerable animus during the war. A Lutheran church in Flint, for example, suspended its German-language services in 1918 after the Council of Defense warned that the congregation's continued use of German would create trouble.[2] A Lutheran pastor told Theodore Graebner five weeks before the armistice that "sentiment is very strong in our State against everything German," and he predicted that the legislature would enact a law prohibiting the teaching of German in the lower grades of public and parochial schools.[3] Although Michigan never prohibited foreign-language instruction, the state in 1919 adopted a law that required all instruction in the first eight grades of all schools to be given in the English language. The statute specifically provided that it did not prohibit private and parochial schools from offering religious instruction in any language in addition to the regular course of study.[4]

This statute failed to satisfy nativists, who had begun to agitate for a more extreme measure before the end of the war. In 1918, the Wayne County Civic League advocated a constitutional amendment that would have required all children between the ages of five and sixteen to attend public schools in their respective school districts.[5] The league, which had been formed two years earlier in Detroit by a group of obscure citizens for the avowed purpose of promoting "good government,"[6] was dominated by James Hamilton, a Canadian native who had worked as a miner, longshoreman, restaurateur, and contractor before becoming active in right-wing politics.[7] The state legislature failed to enact the amendment, and its proponents were unable during 1918 to gather enough signatures to place the matter before the voters.[8]

In 1919, the league again collected signatures for a compulsory public education initiative, but the state supreme court rejected the petition because of technical deficiencies.[9] Undaunted, the league collected more signatures to place the proposed amendment on the ballot at the general election of 1920. In a letter sent to Michigan voters, the league insinuated that virtually all the residents of homes for wayward girls and unwed mothers in the state had attended parochial schools.[10] By February, the league had collected enough signatures to place the initiative on the ballot and began a vigorous campaign to promote the amendment.

Alarmed by the proposal, Roman Catholics and Missouri Synod Lutherans organized an extensive campaign of opposition to it. Since only about 26 percent of the state's population were members of the Roman Catholic or Lutheran churches,[11] it was necessary for leaders of those churches to persuade many persons of other faiths to oppose the amendment. The struggle against the language laws had honed the political skills of the Missouri Synod, which conducted a highly sophisticated and well-organized campaign against the proposed amendment. The synod, which maintained 94 schools that enrolled 6,844 pupils in Michigan in 1920,[12] retained the services of a state campaign manager and established local committees in each of the state's eighty-three counties and in every parish. The Lutherans adopted a slogan, "Whose Is the Child?," which was emblazoned on fifty thousand campaign buttons and discussed in a widely distributed pamphlet in which Professor W. H. T. Dau of the Concordia Seminary in St. Louis insisted that parental rights over children were superior to the rights of the state. Lutherans also organized mass meetings that featured prominent speakers.[13] Ten thousand volunteers disseminated more than four million handbills and pamphlets, together with 125,000 posters and placards. In addition, the Lutheran Schools Committee placed advertisements in newspapers throughout the state.[14]

Although some Roman Catholic leaders worried that vocal opposition to the amendment would enhance fears of Catholic political power, Bishop Michael Gallagher of Detroit publicly denounced the measure as early as February and Bishop Edward D. Kelly of Grand Rapids castigated it in a letter that was read at masses throughout his diocese on Easter Sunday. The Knights of Columbus appropriated funds late in the spring to oppose the measure.[15] In August, Gallagher organized a committee that had branches in every parish in Wayne County.[16] Kelly and the two other Roman Catholic bishops in Michigan refused, however, to accept assistance from the National Catholic Welfare Conference. In rebuffing the NCWC's assistance, Kelly told the Bishop of Baltimore in May 1920, "Some of our priests and people are quite indignant that they should be considered incapable of handling the situation."[17] Kelly's rebuff to the conference also may have reflected the fears of many bishops that the newly organized council would intrude on episcopal prerogatives.[18]

Opponents of the measure based their arguments on moral, legal, and practical grounds. They contended that the initiative was morally flawed because it was founded on ethnic and religious prejudices and deprived parents of control over the education of their children. It was illegal because parents had a constitutional right to educate their children privately. And it was impractical because parochial schools offered a sound education and the amendment would foist a crushing strain on an already overburdened public school system.

Pointing out that Roman Catholics believed that "religious education confined to Sunday schools is insufficient," the Educational Liberty League, a Catholic organization, stated in a pamphlet that denial of educational freedom would constitute a "substantial privation" of religious liberties.[19] In his Easter Sunday letter, Bishop Kelly alleged that the amendment was virtually "an act to proscribe the Catholic religion" and would permit "the assumption on the part of the state of parental duties which, before God, cannot be yielded."[20] The *Detroit Journal* denounced the measure as "the foul offspring of religious bigotry" and contended that its sole purpose was to close parochial schools.[21]

Proponents of the measure emphasized throughout the campaign that the amendment was needed in order to ensure a higher degree of social cohesion. Denying that the amendment would exacerbate religious animosities, Hamilton contended that the measure "would eliminate much of the suspicion and bitterness between peoples of different religious beliefs and do more than any one thing to help our people to grow up together."[22] A handbill distributed by the Wayne County Civic League stated that parochial schools existed "only to perpetuate some foreign language, custom or creed." Advocates of compulsory public education also argued that the discovery of a high rate of illiteracy in English among recruits during the war demonstrated the need for public schooling.[23]

Despite their protestations, Hamilton and many of the amendment's proponents scarcely attempted to conceal their anti-Catholicism.[24] Comparing the high literacy rates of predominantly Protestant nations with the low rates of heavily Roman Catholic countries, one advertisement depicted Uncle Sam telling a group of Roman Catholic prelates that they would never be permitted to "control the schools . . . while the figures stand like that."[25] A rally in favor of the amendment at a rural Methodist church turned violent when shots were fired into the air after Roman Catholics began to protest outside the church. Although investigators could not determine who fired the first shot, a deputy sheriff who fired from the church killed two Catholic men who were passing by in an automobile.[26]

In arguing that the amendment was impractical, its opponents pointed out that it would force the state's already congested public schools to absorb at least 115,000 more pupils, an increase in enrollment of about 15 percent.[27] In April, Bishop Kelly estimated that the measure would cost taxpayers between 70 and 100 million dollars to replace the land, buildings, and equipment of the parochial schools.[28] Warnings about the overcrowding of the schools gained more credence in August, when Detroit's school superintendent announced that 25,000 students would be attending half-day sessions during the coming school year, an increase of 5,000 from the previous year.[29] Roman Catholics pointed out that it would be impossible to find enough teachers for so many new students.[30]

In response to these arguments, proponents of the measure contended that the amendment would save the state money because the parochial schools had produced so many criminals. They further contended that opponents of the measure could demonstrate their patriotism by loaning some of their buildings to the state until it had sufficient schools of its own. Supporters of the measure emphasized that the amendment would not prohibit parents from sending their children to parochial schools during the many hours when the public schools were not in session.[31]

In addition to the organized opposition by Roman Catholics and Lutherans, the measure was actively opposed by leaders of other religious denominations that maintained parochial schools, including the Seventh Day Adventists and the Christian Reformed church, which operated many schools in Michigan's numerous Dutch-American communities.[32] Episcopal churchmen were vocal in opposing the measure, perhaps in part because many Episcopalians sent their children to private schools.[33] Sensitive to ethnic and religious bigotry, several prominent Jewish leaders also denounced the amendment.[34]

Many prominent educators attacked the amendment, including the president emeritus of the University of Michigan and several members of the Board of Regents. The Lutheran Schools Committee solicited a letter from Philander P. Claxton, U.S. Commissioner of Public Education, in opposition to the amendment. Political figures, businessmen, and candidates for public office joined the rising chorus of opposition.[35] The measure also was opposed by Franklin Moore, a member of the Michigan House of Representatives and coauthor of the 1919 statute that required parochial schools to give instruction in the English language. Moore contended that the amendment was not needed because parochial schools had complied with the 1919 law.

As in the fight against the language laws, Roman Catholics and Protestants coordinated their efforts in opposition to the amendment, breaking down barriers that had separated members of the different churches. Such unaccustomed cooperation bothered some Protestants and Catholics. One Lutheran minister wrote to Graebner in 1921 to urge that the Lutheran churches declare that "the schools of Rome are a menace to America" but that "Hamilton and his crowd are equally dangerous in their principles." Although Graebner disparaged the idea that Catholic schools were subversive, he emphasized that Lutherans should make clear that their common cause with the Catholics was political rather than spiritual.[36] Other Lutherans expressed uneasiness over the political activism of their traditionally apolitical church.[37]

Lutherans tried to prevent the amendment from being placed on the ballot, contending that the measure would be unconstitutional. In July, Attorney General Alex J. Groesbeck, a nonpracticing Catholic, issued an opinion that the amendment would violate the due process and privileges and immunities clauses of the Fourteenth Amendment because it exceeded the scope of the police power. Analyzing the issue in terms of property rights rather than personal rights, Groesbeck concluded that the state could not destroy or diminish the value of the private and parochial schools and interfere with the vocations of the teachers in those schools, since neither the schools nor the teachers were "antagonistic or inimical to the general welfare."[38] In accordance with Groesbeck's opinion, the secretary of state refused to place the amendment on the ballot, and Hamilton commenced a mandamus action in July to compel the secretary to submit the amendment to the voters. On October 1, the state supreme court ruled by a vote of five to three that the secretary of state was compelled to place the amendment on the ballot since he was not authorized by law to determine its constitutionality. The court also held that it lacked the power to determine the constitutionality of the amendment in advance of its enactment.[39]

The dissenting judges contended that the court could prevent balloting on an initiative that plainly would be unconstitutional. Submission of the amendment to the people, the judges believed, would precipitate "a bitter religious warfare" that would bring Protestants into conflict with both Catholics and other Protestants. Echoing Groesbeck's opinion, the dissenting judges contended that the amendment exceeded the state's police power because it bore no reasonable relation to the health, morals, safety, or welfare of the public. The judges also pointed out that the statute would interfere with the property rights of the schools since it would take from them without compensation property that was valued at seventy million dollars. Finally, the judges indicated that the amendment was unconstitutional because it would affect personal liberties by interfering with the right of parents to exercise control of the education of their children.[40]

On the Sunday before the election, one hundred thousand Roman Catholics marched through Detroit in opposition to the proposed amendment. The Catholics, including ten thousand former servicemen in uniform and fifty thousand parochial school children who carried American flags and sang patriotic songs, proceeded to Navin Field, where a chaplain of the Michigan National Guard celebrated mass and Bishop Gallagher once more denounced the proposal as a product of bigotry.[41]

When the electorate went to the polls on November 2, it defeated the amendment by a vote of 610,699 to 353,818. Supporters of the amendment prevailed in only seven of Michigan's eighty-three counties. Despite the size of the majority by which the amendment was defeated, many of its opponents were distressed that so many voters would have supported such a radical and dangerous measure. Writing to Theodore Graebner shortly after the election, Rudolph H. C. Meyer of the Lutheran Schools Committee declared that he was "very much disappointed at the outcome" since he had anticipated a vote of at least three to one against the amendment.[42] Similarly, the Jesuit publication *America* observed, "It is sad to reflect that notwithstanding the splendid record of the Catholic parish schools before, during, and since the war, this amendment was so vigorously supported by a horde of anti-Catholic fanatics as to render the result, for a time, gravely uncertain." Although the editors warned that "it would be perilous to believe that bigotry and bureaucracy are on their death-bed," they felt that the Michigan victory would retard the compulsory public education movement.[43] The large vote in favor of the amendment encouraged proponents of the measure to place it again before the voters. Hamilton claimed a moral victory and began to gear up for another initiative within weeks of the 1920 election.[44]

Supporters of parochial education hoped to discourage any new campaigns against private schools by promoting legislation to require closer state supervision of nonpublic schools. Although church leaders previously had opposed state supervision of parochial schools, they conceded that regulation was preferable to annihilation. Indeed, the parochial schools may have helped to secure support for the amendment's defeat by promising to submit to more extensive regulation by the state.[45] Some church leaders also may have welcomed regulatory legislation because it encouraged improvements in the standards of parochial schools. Even though church leaders had publicly defended the quality of their schools during the 1920 campaign, they admitted among themselves that some schools needed to raise their standards. The Roman Catholic schools had no superintendent until 1918, and administration continued to be weak for many years thereafter since the superintendent had no office or staff and served also as a parish priest.[46] Some Lutheran schools also suffered from significant deficiencies. A pastor in Saginaw informed Graebner in 1918 that one local teacher, nearly seventy years old, was very deficient in his grasp of the English language and was preoccupied with the management of his farm. Complaining that "such conditions are abominable and should not be tolerated in our midst," the pastor remarked that it was "small wonder" that public school officials were "not always friendly towards our school system."[47]

After the election, Roman Catholic, Lutheran, Dutch Reformed, and Seventh Day Adventist clergy met among themselves and with lawmakers and other state officials to discuss such legislation. Henry Frincke, a leader of the Lutheran campaign against the 1920 school amendment, explained, "It was our purpose to frame a law that would take all arguments against the parochial schools away from our antagonists and still would jealously guard the principles upon which our republic is founded." As enacted, the so-called Dacey Inspection Law allowed the superintendent of public instruction to supervise and to inspect private and parochial schools. The law required those schools to conform to the same courses of study, teacher qualifications, and sanitary conditions that were prescribed by the state's general school law. The statute also required parochial school teachers to obtain state certification. The framers of the statute purposely omitted any provision that would have prohibited parochial schools from teaching religion in any foreign language. Supporters of the school amendment generally opposed enactment of the law, contending that it failed to regulate the schools effectively.[48]

After the enactment of the Dacey Law, the Lutheran and Roman Catholic churches continued to try to ameliorate public hostility toward their schools. Most Lutheran parochial schools eliminated instruction in German during regular school hours, and many dropped it altogether.[49] Meanwhile, the use of English became more prevalent in church services, although the language transition engendered considerable discord within the Michigan District of the Missouri Synod.[50] Lutherans also worked to improve the quality of their schools by increasing their financial support and constructing modern brick buildings to replace the dilapidated frame structures that had exposed Lutheran parochial education to much criticism. Although several Lutheran schools in Michigan closed during the early 1920s, most emerged from the school controversy with renewed strength.[51]

Meanwhile, within a year of the 1920 election, the Lutheran Schools Committee had resumed vigorous activities to generate public tolerance of parochial education, opening a new headquarters in Detroit and reengaging on a half-time basis the services of the pastor who had coordinated the 1920 campaign. By November 1922, the committee had mailed out 350,000 pieces of literature.[52] In a widely circulated pamphlet, Theodore Graebner argued that natural law conferred on parents the right to direct the education of their children and that the amendment would contravene the Anglo-American ideal of limited government. Graebner also contended that the amendment would violate the religious freedom guaranteed by the federal and state constitutions, and he indignantly rejected suggestions that Lutherans were insufficiently "Americanized."[53]

Predicting that a court probably would strike down any law that required all children to attend public schools, the committee nevertheless warned that the church could not have absolute confidence in a judicial victory and that the church therefore would need to sustain its public activities on behalf of its schools. The committee reminded the clergy and educators that parental rights were "not clearly and specifically" safeguarded by the state and federal constitutions and that the so-called police power that would be invoked to close the parochial schools aptly had been called the "dark continent of American jurisprudence." The committee also shrewdly pointed out that the results of future ballots might influence judicial decisions.[54]

Even though Hamilton's forces failed to collect enough signatures to place the school amendment on the ballot again in 1922 and 1923,[55] opponents of the amendment warned against complacency. The success of the Oregon initiative provided a sharp reminder of the vitality of opposition to the parochial schools. Movements for similar measures in California, Texas, Oklahoma, Ohio, Wyoming, Arkansas, and Nebraska likewise demonstrated that opposition to parochial schools was widespread.[56] The executive secretary of the Lutheran Schools Committee predicted in September 1922 that "the fight for the existence of our schools will be national in scope in a very short time."[57]

Meanwhile, Hamilton and other opponents of nonpublic education carried on their crusade. Arguments against nonpublic schools continued to be tinged with anti-Catholicism, fanned by a resurgent Ku Klux Klan. The

Klan had increased its membership in Michigan from a few thousand in 1921 to perhaps 75,000 in 1924,[58] and Hamilton became its King Kleagle. As in other northern states, the Klan tapped ancient reservoirs of local nativism, but its popularity in Michigan also is attributable to the influx of southern whites who had migrated to the state during the First World War to work in war industries.[59] After Hiram Evans became the national head of the Klan in 1922, he urged members to provide more vigorous support for public schools "as a means of subverting private and parochial schools."[60] The campaign for compulsory public education was the major activity of the Klan in Michigan.[61] Although many of the outspoken opponents of parochial education were ill-educated clergymen, the movement received some support from more elite sources. During the spring of 1923, H. Dallas Sharp, a Boston University professor and *Atlantic Monthly* editor, urged compulsory public education because only the public schools could provide the type of education that a democracy needed.[62] Sharp's view demonstrated the resiliency of the old Protestant ideal of public schooling among sundry Anglo-American educators, social reformers, and progressives.

In 1923, opponents of compulsory public education persuaded the legislature to enact a statute that increased the technical requirements for the filing of petitions to initiate legislation. Since Hamilton refused to comply with the requirements of this law, the secretary of state would not accept petitions to place a school amendment on the 1924 ballot.[63] Hamilton once again commenced a mandamus action and finally won a court battle when the state supreme court in a five-to-three decision in May 1924 ordered the secretary to submit the amendment to the voters.[64] Justice Grant Fellows, who had written the dissenting opinion in the 1920 case concerning the amendment, reiterated his belief that the amendment was unconstitutional and therefore should not be placed on the ballot. He relied on *Meyer* and the recent decision of the Oregon District Court in *Pierce* in support of his contention that the measure clearly was unconstitutional.[65]

The campaigns both for and against the proposed amendment in 1924 were quieter than they had been in 1920. Roman Catholic leaders apparently feared that public rallies and other dramatic activities might inflame fears of Catholic political power.[66] Opposition to the measure, however, was no less intense than it had been four years earlier. Once more, Roman Catholics and Lutherans carefully organized a highly effective assault on the amendment, which again was denounced by a broad spectrum of prominent educators and other community leaders.[67] This time the Roman Catholic hierarchy, jarred perhaps by Oregon's enactment of a compulsory school law, was willing to accept some help from the National Catholic Welfare Conference.[68] The Lutheran Schools Committee raised $26,000 and distributed one million copies of a broadside, as well as several thousand copies of a four-page pamphlet. In addition to working through the committee, Lutherans helped to form a nondenominational association that represented private schools and the parochial schools of several Protestant groups.[69]

As in 1920, opponents of the amendment emphasized that it would abridge religious freedom, interfere with parental rights, and cast a huge burden on the taxpayers. A pamphlet published by Roman Catholics declared that the addition of an estimated 125,000 children "would swamp the public schools in most localities, creating a hopeless confusion which would handicap the public schools for years to come."[70] Opponents of the amendment estimated once again that new buildings and equipment would cost the taxpayers tens of millions of dollars and that additional millions would be needed each year for maintenance.[71] Since the amendment was scheduled to take effect at the beginning of the 1925–26 school year, the state would have had almost no time to prepare for the influx of new students. The *Detroit Free Press* denounced the amendment as "an autocratic invasion of the rights of parents,"[72] and a Roman Catholic pamphlet declared that it "attempts a direct usurpation of the natural right of parents to direct the education of their children in schools of their choice and of teachers to teach in the schools of their choice."[73] Opponents of the measure also emphasized that nonpublic schools maintained high academic standards and instilled patriotism in their students. Moreover, they pointed out that public education had continued to flourish in Michigan despite the presence of a strong alternative system of education.[74]

The amendment was defeated in November by a vote of 760,571 to 421,472. Despite this wide margin, the results of the poll demonstrated that anti–parochial school sentiment was persistent and that it was growing in many areas. The proportion of voters supporting the amendment decreased only slightly, from 37 percent in 1920 to 35 percent in 1924, and it increased in approximately half the counties. The number of counties in which a majority of the voters supported the amendment grew from seven in 1920 to eighteen in 1924, probably a reflection of Klan influence in rural areas.[75] Outside Detroit, the percentage of persons supporting the amendment increased from 38 percent to 40 percent. The results of the poll nevertheless encouraged the Lutheran School Defense Committee, which had feared that the Klan might significantly erode opposition to the amendment.[76]

On the same day that Michigan defeated the second compulsory public education initiative, voters in Washington state rejected a similar measure that would have required every child between the ages of seven and sixteen to attend a public school.[77] As in Oregon, the Ku Klux Klan and the Masonic lodges were instrumental in the campaign to place the compulsory school bill on the ballot. Opponents of the Washington measure, like their counterparts in Michigan and Oregon, contended that many voters and signers of the initiative petition had been deceived into believing that the measure provided for compulsory education rather than for compulsory public education. Opponents of the bill tirelessly pointed out that elementary education had been compulsory in Washington for many years.[78]

Spirited opposition to the measure was undertaken by Seventh Day Adventist clergy, the nonsectarian Friends of Educational Freedom, and Lutheran groups. In a pamphlet that was distributed to more than four hundred thousand persons, the Seventh Day Adventists declared that a person "who shouts for the Stars and Stripes and makes great outward demonstrations but who does not respect the equal rights of his neighbor is not a true American."[79]

The Roman Catholic church also actively opposed the measure. As early as January 1924, when the petition for the initiative was still circulating, John J. Burke wrote to the bishop of Spokane to offer the assistance of the National Catholic Welfare Conference. Burke explained that the defense of parochial schools in Washington was "a defense of all the parochial schools of the nation." The struggle, he averred, was "a national one" that extended even into Congress, where Catholics were fighting against extension of federal control over education.[80] Roman Catholics in Washington state were grateful for the assistance of the conference, which sent tens of thousands of copies of pamphlets into the state during the autumn campaign.[81]

Like their counterparts in Michigan and Oregon, proponents of compulsory public education insisted that they were promoting egalitarianism and that universal public schooling would safeguard democracy. One attorney who favored the measure contended that proponents of parochial schools who had withdrawn their children from public schools "because of religious prejudice" were the real bigots. He also declared that "parochial schools recognize the authority of the greatest autocracy the world has today. It is absurd to think that such an autocracy can teach fidelity to the ideals of democracy."[82] Similarly, the former Grand Cyclops of the Seattle Klan publicly declared that the school bill was needed because the pope insisted on extending temporal power over members of the Roman Catholic church.[83] A Methodist minister who was a member of the Klan declared that public schools enabled "the children of the rich and the poor, of every race and creed learn the true democracy of citizenship together." He insisted that no religion had reason to fear compulsory public education, since nothing taught in the public schools would "steal away the faith of any child," and that any teacher who attempted to proselytize for a particular dogma "is admittedly unfit to teach in the public schools."[84]

In response to these arguments, defenders of the nonpublic schools insisted that private schools were more egalitarian than public schools because they mixed students from different social and economic classes, in contrast to public schools, which were segregated by neighborhood.[85] Like opponents of compulsory public education in Michigan, they warned that the measure would add to the burden of the taxpayers since it would require millions of dollars for the expansion of public school facilities and substantial additional sums for annual maintenance. The *Seattle Post-Intelligencer* predicted that many districts would find it impossible to handle the large enrollment increases.[86]

Opponents of compulsory public education further argued that the law would be unconstitutional, as evidenced by a federal court's invalidation of Oregon's statute in March 1924, because it unduly interfered with parental rights.[87] Opponents also warned that enactment of the bill would discourage immigration into Washington and would lead to the exodus of parents to states in which they would be free to enroll their children in private schools.[88]

As in Michigan, the compulsory public education initiative was opposed by most of the newspapers and by prominent educators and businesspersons. The *Seattle Daily Times* declared on the Sunday before the election that there was no room in the state "for the bigotry, the intolerance and the injustice which are the very essence of that un-American measure!"[89] The *Seattle Post-Intelligencer* warned that the initiative "threatens injury to the public school system, the wiping out of private schools, increased taxes and an era of ill will," and the *Tacoma Daily Ledger* maintained that it was "subversive of the fundamental principles of Americanism."[90] Stephen J. Chadwick, former chief justice of the state supreme court and a non-Catholic who had sent his children to public schools, declared, "There could be no more un-American sentiment than to destroy existing institutions that have in no way offended and which have contributed so much to the development of our youth."[91] The chorus against the bill also was joined by labor leaders, the lieutenant governor, and the educational committee of the Spokane Chamber of Commerce.[92] In New York, Columbia University president Nicholas Murray Butler denounced the measure as "un-American in principle and in purpose," since it would promote "a uniform government-made paganism."[93]

Opponents of the measure expressed confidence that voters would defeat it. In early October, the executive secretary of the Roman Catholic Educational Committee reported to James H. Ryan, executive secretary of the National Catholic Welfare conference, "We should win; however, we are far from over-confident." He explained that the "hooded order is quite generally discredited in the larger cities, but is firmly entrenched in many small towns."[94]

These optimistic predictions proved to be well founded, for the voters of Washington rejected the initiative by a vote of 221,500 (58.2 percent) to 158,922 (41.8 percent). Opponents of the measure carried thirty of the state's thirty-nine counties.[95] Although the margin of the initiative's defeat was narrower than it had been in either of the Michigan votes, it was sufficiently decisive to demoralize further the movement for compulsory public education, which had been in disarray since March, when the district court in Oregon had held that Oregon's compulsory public education law was unconstitutional. The final defeat of the movement would come in the following June, when the U.S. Supreme Court nullified the Oregon law.

8   The Oregon School Law

The nativist crusade to purge allegedly alien influences from the education of all elementary school children reached its culmination in Oregon in 1922. Adopting the extreme remedy that Michigan voters twice rejected, Oregon was the only state that ever enacted legislation to require compulsory attendance at public schools. The nativist triumph in Oregon was ephemeral, however, since it provoked the U.S. Supreme Court decision that upheld the right of parents to educate their children in nonpublic institutions.

Oregon ostensibly was an unlikely venue for a controversy over parochial education. In contrast to other states that spawned significant nativist legislation during the late nineteenth and early twentieth centuries, Oregon had a highly homogeneous population. The ethnic population was far too small to challenge the dominance of native-born Protestants, many of whom traced their roots to the Mississippi Valley or to the New England towns whose names dot the maps of the Pacific Northwest. In 1920, only 13 percent of the population was foreign born. Nearly 95 percent of the children between the ages of seven and thirteen attended school, and more than 93 percent of them attended public school. The state's illiteracy rate of 1.5 percent was one of the lowest in the nation.[1] About 7 percent of the population was Roman Catholic, and Lutherans and Jews each comprised only about 1.5 percent of the population.[2]

Although nativism and racism never had flourished in Oregon, ethnic strife was not unknown. Tensions between Protestant and Roman Catholic missionaries had marked the territorial period, when the initial success of Protestant missionaries in converting Indians had been retarded when Indians began to be attracted to the more ritualistic Catholic worship. In attempting to explain the enactment of the school law, Edwin V. O'Hara, the superintendent of Roman Catholic schools in Oregon, observed with only some exaggeration in 1923 that Oregon was "settled as a Protestant missionary enterprise." He maintained that "the wild charge of Catholic complicity" in the 1847 massacre of white settlers by Indians at the mission established by the Congregational minister and physician Marcus Whitman was "a household heirloom in the great Protestant tradition of Oregon history."[3] There was some agitation against parochial education during the 1870s and 1880s, and the nativistic American Protective Association was active in the state during the 1890s.[4] Many early Oregon settlers had imbibed the prejudices of the nativistic strongholds of the rural areas of New England and the Mississippi Valley from which they had migrated. Moreover, many pioneers settled "in narrow and shut-in valleys where social traditions tended to remain unchallenged."[5]

During the early twentieth century, nativism grew somewhat more pronounced. In 1917, nativists formed the Oregon Federation of Patriotic Societies, which was dedicated in part to increasing the strength of the public schools and decreasing the influence of the Roman Catholic hierarchy.[6] Postwar Oregon was ripe for nativistic appeals, for the state had been swept during and after the war by the same nativistic fervor that had infected so much of the rest of the nation. In 1919, the legislature passed laws to prohibit public or private schools from teaching any subject, other than foreign languages, in any language other than English.[7] Some anti-Catholic measures were introduced in the legislature during 1921, including bills to forbid the state from recognizing private schools as teacher-training institutions and to prohibit nuns who taught in public schools from wearing their habits.[8] A tong war in Portland's Chinatown in 1921 exacerbated hostility toward Asian Americans and immigrants in general.[9] In the same year, a slate supported by the federation won a landslide victory in Portland's municipal elections. The victors vowed to maintain the integrity of the public schools against the alleged assaults of Catholics.[10]

During this same period, the Ku Klux Klan began to gather strength, and by the summer of 1922 it claimed fourteen thousand members. Since the African-American population of Oregon was only 0.3 percent, the Klan's wrath was directed principally against aliens and ethnics.[11] Inasmuch as even aliens and ethnics comprised only a small part of the population, one study aptly has concluded that the impetus behind the Oregon Klan "apparently was not the desire to make the state American but to keep it American."[12] As in other parts of the nation, the Klan sought to stem what it perceived as the growth of corruption and the erosion of traditional community values.[13] By May 1922, the Klan had grown so strong that Governor Ben W. Olcott denounced it and called on law enforcement officers to guard against Klan lawlessness.[14]

Oregon's progressive tradition also may have stoked nativistic fires. Before the war, progressivism had been more successful in Oregon than in any state other than Wisconsin. Oregonians were particularly amenable to the progressive ideal of direct democracy, which was more practicable in this homogeneous and sparsely populated state than it was in most other states. During the decade before the war, Oregon had instituted primary elections for the nomination of candidates for public office, adopted legislation that permitted voters to recall elected officials, and enacted laws to enable the electorate to vote on legislation initiated by public petition or referred to the voters by the legislature.[15] Conservatives who opposed the recall, initiative, and referendum had warned that these devices could generate majoritarian tyranny. The adoption of the compulsory public education law by a narrow vote in an election initiated by public petition was precisely the sort of popular tyranny that opponents of direct democracy had prophesied. Proponents of compulsory public education may have used the initiative because Catholics were a significant force in the legislature.[16]

Organized agitation in favor of compulsory public education had started in 1920, when the Masonic Grand Lodge of Oregon adopted the resolution of the Scottish Rite's Supreme Council for the Southern Jurisdiction calling for compulsory public education. Meanwhile, the Oregon Klan had responded enthusiastically to an appeal by Hiram Evans, the national Imperial Wizard, for greater support of the public schools, and Oregon's Grand Dragon had organized a committee on Americanization of the public schools which objected to the hiring of nuns by public schools in western Oregon.[17]

During the spring of 1922, Masons circulated a petition for an initiative to require all children between the ages of eight and sixteen who had not completed the eighth grade to attend public school. Robert F. Smith, a right-wing activist who organized the petition campaign, explained that he had acted at the behest of the supreme council, which believed that Oregon would provide a receptive environment for the initiative and that it could set an "example for the rest of the country."[18] Proponents of the measure had no difficulty obtaining the requisite 13,000 signatures that were needed to place

the initiative on the ballot, although opponents contended that many sig-
natories mistakenly believed they were merely signing a petition for a compulsory education bill.[19] The measure exempted children who were physically or mentally disabled, who lived a long distance from public schools, or
who obtained the permission of the county school superintendent to receive
instruction from a parent or tutor.

The school bill emerged as a significant issue during the 1922 primary and
general election campaigns. Charles Hall, a candidate for the Republican
gubernatorial nomination, won the endorsement of the Klan because he
strongly supported the school bill. Although Hall was defeated by Olcott in
the primary in May, his strong showing encouraged proponents of the initiative. The Klan urged Walter M. Pierce, the Democratic nominee, to support the measure. Pierce at first privately declined, predicting that the school
bill would be defeated and that his promotion of it would ensure his own
defeat. After the Klan endorsed Hall as a third-party candidate, however,
Pierce publicly supported the bill, explaining that "we would have a better
generation of Americans, free from snobbery and bigotry, if all children . . .
were educated in free public schools."[20] Although Pierce's endorsement of
the measure was no doubt in part inspired by political considerations, it also
may have reflected his nostalgia for his happy years as a young public school
teacher and county school superintendent during the 1880s. Pierce's stand
on the school bill was consistent with his politics, a populistic and progressive blend of support for social reform, economic regulation, prohibition,
and nativism.

After Pierce's endorsement of the school bill, Hall withdrew from the
race and endorsed Pierce.[21] Although Pierce continued throughout the campaign to pledge his support for the school bill, he preferred to emphasize his
less controversial support for tax reduction, and many of his most prominent supporters opposed the bill.[22] Despite his failure to emphasize the
school issue, Pierce continued to court the Klan vote. Although his biogra-
pher insisted that Pierce was not actually a member of the Klan,[23] minutes of
meetings of the Klonclave in his hometown of LaGrande refer to him as an
honorary Klansman. Pierce addressed the LaGrande Klonclave shortly after
his election as governor to express his thanks for the Klan's support.[24]

Pierce's reluctance to endorse the school initiative reflected the narrowness of its support. The Ku Klux Klan, the Federation of Patriotic Societies,
and the Scottish Rite Masons were the only groups that aggressively
worked for its enactment. The measure also had the backing of the Odd Fel-

lows and the Knights of Pythias.[25] Since the Klan tried to infiltrate Oregon lodges during the 1920s, Masonic support for the initiative may in part be traced to Klan influence.[26] Despite the Masons' role in promoting the measure, many Masons opposed the school amendment.[27] Several prominent Masons actively worked to defeat it, and a former Grand Master alleged that Klansmen had packed a special meeting at which the amendment was endorsed.[28] Far from working together to ensure the success of the school bill, the Klan and the Masons seem to have been at odds. Prominent Oregon Masons opposed the Klan, and the national Masonic organization threatened to expel any known Klansman.[29]

In contrast to anti–parochial school measures of the nineteenth century, the Oregon initiative, like the Michigan initiatives of 1920 and 1924, received the endorsement of no major religious denomination and few newspapers. Public school teachers and administrators likewise were not active supporters of the measure.[30] Although the bill had the backing of the *Oregon Teachers Monthly,* the president of Oregon State University, and a convention of 133 teachers in Columbia County, most public educators remained silent.[31] Despite Pierce's endorsement, the initiative lacked the widespread partisan support that earlier anti–parochial school measures had enjoyed. The failure of the Oregon and Michigan initiatives to attract broader support may be attributed in part to the radicalism of these measures, which exceeded the scope of earlier efforts to restrict parochial education. Moreover, the growing sophistication of clergy and educators may have diminished their anti-Catholicism, despite the upsurge in popular anti-Catholicism during the 1920s. As Roman Catholics increased their numbers and moved into the mainstream of American life, blatant anti-Catholicism became more déclassé in polite circles, even though the growth of Catholic power contributed toward the virulence of anti-Catholicism among lower-class Protestants.

Proponents of the Oregon initiative contended that compulsory public education was needed to ensure the assimilation and education of foreign-born citizens and their children. They argued that nonpublic schools exacerbated social conflict and bigotry by perpetuating religious, ethnic, and economic divisions. As the Scottish Rite Masons explained in their statement on the ballot, children should not "be divided into antagonistic groups" based on "money, creed or social status," since such divisions would separate the nation into "cliques, cults and factions" that would strive "for the supremacy of themselves" rather than for "the good of the whole." The Masons warned that a "divided school can no more succeed than a divided nation."[32] Similarly, the *Oregon Teachers Monthly* declared that the measure would expose all children to the "nationalizing influence" of the public school and would ameliorate "class consciousness" and the "snobbish private school attitude."[33] The paucity of African Americans and other racial and religious minorities in Oregon may help to explain why the xenophobic and racist Klan favored the mixing of races and nationalities in the common school.[34] Like the nativists of the mid-nineteenth century, the Klan apparently failed to see any contradiction between its belief in innate Nordic superiority and its belief that non-Nordic groups could benefit from public schooling. Proponents of the plan also contended that the nonpublic schools undermined support for the public schools. Only compulsory public education, the Masons explained, would ensure "united interest in the growth and higher efficiency of our public schools."[35] The Masonic journal *New Age* alleged that the Roman Catholic hierarchy favored the abolition of public schools.[36]

As in Michigan, proponents of compulsory public education contended that a disproportionate number of criminals were parochial school alumni and that children could receive ample sectarian religious instruction when the public schools were not in session.[37] Proponents of the school bill further professed outrage because Roman Catholic nuns in heavily Catholic communities taught in public schools, where they wore their habits. The Klan's wide distribution of a postcard that bore a photograph of a nun surrounded by children in front of a public school may have been an especially effective instrument of propaganda. As the superintendent of Catholic schools in Oregon observed, "the picture served as a symbol of the Catholic encroachments on the public school system, and fanned the embers of bigotry to a lively flame."[38] Similarly, an official of the National Catholic Welfare Conference believed that the success of the school initiative was largely the result of fear that instruction by nuns in public schools might enable Catholics to control public education, even though the measure would not have prohibited nuns from teaching in public schools.[39]

Like their counterparts in Michigan and Washington, proponents of compulsory public education often referred to their proposal as "the compulsory education bill," thereby suggesting that it merely would require all children to attend school. Despite persistent efforts by opponents of the measure to explain to voters that Oregon already had compulsory education, misunderstanding about the measure may have significantly inflated the vote in its favor. It is not surprising that many Oregonians were unaware that the state already had a compulsory education law, since Oregon had passed its first attendance law only in 1889 and the state had not seriously tried to enforce the law until 1907.[40] Lingering hostility toward state compulsion may actually have cost the 1922 measure support among some anti-Catholic voters who mistakenly assumed that the school bill simply was a compulsory education measure.

Despite the contention of proponents of the measure that it was designed to promote high-minded social and educational objectives, the unabashed anti-Catholic appeals demonstrated that the bill was motivated in large part by a recrudescent nativism. As an article in *The Survey* pointed out shortly after the Supreme Court struck down the law in 1925, the law "was inspired not so much by high scientific and educational considerations as by a determination to use the schools as artillery in a religious controversy which dates back to the Middle Ages and which persists as a political issue in spite of the Constitution and the courts."[41] Like many other manifestations of nativism during American history, support for the school bill reflected the fears of agrarian, proletarian, and lower-middle-class persons who felt threatened by the rapid changes of an increasingly sophisticated and pluralistic society. The school bill embodied the yearning for the supposedly simpler and sounder prewar world which pervaded the American spirit during the early 1920s. Following the example of Warren Harding, who had won votes in 1920 by promising a return to a chimerical "normalcy," politicians throughout the nation attempted to exploit the anomie and tension that afflicted postwar America. The public school provided an ideal symbol for this appeal to nostalgia, for many voters remembered their school days as a time of an innocence that seemed to have vanished in the wake of a perplexing postwar age of Prohibition, sexual license, automobiles, motion pictures, and corrosive cynicism that reacted to the unfulfilled promises of wartime idealism.

The public school was a particularly potent symbol in Oregon, where the disappearance of the frontier during the early twentieth century had threatened the values of a pioneer people. Many Oregonians wistfully recalled their education in one-room rural schoolhouses, where they had absorbed simple verities that were mocked and challenged by their experiences as adults in a more complex world. With time having softened the memories of childhood hardships, these aging rustics may have recalled a frontier Eden in which they desired to take refuge from a world that they no longer understood. While this Eden of rugged individualism and pure democracy never really existed, it was not entirely mythical. Although class tensions never were far from the surface of frontier life, distinctions of rank and wealth were mitigated by the common struggle for survival, the absence of any entrenched hierarchy, and the paucity of consumer goods. As society became more stable and more commercial, class distinctions were increasingly apparent and many people felt that they had less control over their destinies.

The psychology of these displaced pioneers was poignantly reflected in *The Old Cedar School,* a Klan tract in defense of compulsory public education that was published immediately after the adoption of the initiative.[42] As David B. Tyack aptly has observed, the pamphlet was a bizarre brew of "nostalgia, paranoia, anticlericalism, Populist egalitarianism, anti-intellectualism, and bitter fantasy."[43] It presented a dialogue between an elderly farmer and his four children, all of whom had attended the Old Cedar School, a one-room public school near Portland that dated from territorial times. Prodded by their social-climbing spouses, the farmer's affluent and sophisticated children believed that the Old Cedar School was not good enough for their own children, whom they were planning to send to fashionable parochial schools.

The farmer's eldest child, Jim, under the influence of "a 'Piscopalyun wife" and the Hon. Ab. Squealright, a snobbish local Episcopalian, had selected Oxford Towers, where "there's a hull lot of big bishops an' fellers that wear their collars an' vests buttoned in the back" who "couldn't ketch a fish 'less they had a jointed pole an' a spring reel which would cost mor'n all the fish they'd ever catch 'ud be worth." The next child, Sally, married to a Seventh Day Adventist, wanted to send her children to the Saturday Sanctuary, "where it 'ud take all the money she could carry in a wheel-barrow to pay for their keep, an' they'd be learnin' . . . 'bout which day of the week you goin' to rest on, [although] it seems to me a great deal more necessary to find out which day you're goin' to work on." The farmer's second daughter, Ryar, the wife of a Methodist, planned to send her offspring to Stanhope Hall, "where everything is meek an' lowly at $100 per month for each of them three kids." And his son John, having married a Roman Catholic, intended to send his children to the Academy of St. Gregory's Holy Toe Nail, where they would "trace the original authority and ecclesiastical record of Peter's Pence, together with the Beatification of Saint Caviar," but would fail to learn "to repeat the multiplication table or milk old Cherry-picker."[44]

The farmer's contempt for pompous clerics, ritualism, and religious dogma reflected the attitudes of many Protestants who had championed the public schools. Although these rustic prejudices were in part the product of ignorance, envy, and xenophobia, they also evinced more admirable qualities of pragmatism, egalitarianism, and individualism that are deeply ingrained in the American character. The farmer acknowledged that religion had been the source of much good, but he pointed out that much wrong had been done in the name of religion, including the recent massacres of Christian Armenians by Moslem Turks.[45] Like many Oregonians who supported the school bill, the fictional farmer believed that the real bigots were the clerics and parents who wished to segregate children in schools where they would be taught that their own religious beliefs were superior to those of their neighbors and where they would submit to an authoritarianism that was antithetical to the libertarian spirit of the American frontier.

As in Michigan, opposition to compulsory public schooling was persistent and vigorous. The *Oregon Voter* contended that competition with the private schools prevented the public schools "from falling into a rut."[46] Similarly, a Roman Catholic publication explained that the nonpublic schools were "a valuable aid to the development and progress of educational methods" because they were more free to conduct educational experiments.[47] Opponents of the law also contended that it was superfluous because Oregon had few illiterates or hyphenated Americans.[48]

Like opponents of the language laws in the Middle West, opponents of the compulsory public education law pointed out that its philosophy was distressingly similar to some of the alien ideologies against which it was designed to guard.[49] A leaflet published by the Seventh Day Adventists denounced the bill as Prussianistic and Communistic since the kaiser and Lenin had suppressed private education.[50] And a Roman Catholic pamphlet warned that true Americanism could not be attained through the Bolshevik practice of a "flat-pattern, rigid, autocratic system of State monopoly of education, which will obliterate the talents and capabilities of the different races and classes."[51]

The *Oregon Voter* estimated that the new law would require the state's taxpayers to spend 3.6 million dollars to construct new schools and that the annual cost of educating the twelve thousand new pupils would exceed one million dollars.[52] Roman Catholics alleged that the cost of building new schools would be six million dollars.[53] Estimates of the amount of additional taxes needed to finance the new burdens ranged between a half million and a million dollars.[54]

One opponent of the measures composed a ditty called "School Bills, School Bills," apparently to be sung to the tune of the popular "School Days, School Days," which included the chorus:

> School bills, school bills,
> Dear old freak and fool bills.
> Make it "compulsory" that's the plan,
> Teachers are scarce but of course we can
> Help things along by cutting short
> All private schools of every sort.
> Will that make things nice? Well, we should snort!
> Though it would make trouble for kids.[55]

As in the Michigan school fight, a broad coalition of citizens and organizations opposed compulsory public education. The most active opponents of the measure were Roman Catholic groups, particularly the Catholic Civic Rights Association of Oregon, which was formed by Oregon's archbishop to fight the school bill. The committee sponsored lectures, paid for newspaper advertisements, distributed more than a half million copies of a pamphlet opposing the measure, and tried to contact every voter through committees that were organized in every parish in the state.[56] In contrast to the Roman Catholic hierarchy in Michigan in 1920, Archbishop Alexander Christie of Oregon City solicited assistance from the National Catholic Welfare Conference. Catholics had "a fair chance to defeat" the measure, Christie told Burke in July, if the conference and other Catholic organizations would offer "proper financial aid."[57] Beset by troubled relations with Rome and financial difficulties, the conference regretfully was unable to offer financial assistance, although John J. Burke assured Christie that Catholics throughout the nation should help defeat the Oregon law, since "your fight is not only for your own diocese but for every diocese in the United States."[58] Prominent educators, including the presidents of Yale, Columbia, and the University of Texas, denounced the bill. It also was unpopular among many businesspersons, who noticed that vocal supporters of the measure lost the patronage of Roman Catholics.[59] Although most of the press did not take a position, the *Portland Telegram* and *The Oregonian*, two of the state's largest papers, opposed the measure.[60]

No significant religious organization endorsed the school initiative, and Christian opposition to the measure spread far beyond the denominations that maintained parochial schools. A group of Presbyterian ministers, for example, declared that the bill "violates what we conceive to be the spirit of . . . brotherly love taught by our Master."[61] Widespread support for the measure among Protestants, however, made many clergy reluctant to oppose the school initiative actively. The state's largest organization of clergy refused to take a stand on the initiative, partly on the ground that Protestant lay opinion was divided.[62] The principal Christian opposition to the measure therefore fell to the denominations that would be adversely affected by the law.

Jews also were vocal opponents of compulsory public education. Even though Jews maintained no full-time schools in Oregon and most Jewish children attended public schools, Jews correctly perceived that the school amendment represented forces of bigotry that threatened all minority groups. *The Scribe* urged its readers to "defend Oregon from an invasion of bigotry,"[63] and a prominent rabbi pointed out that the bill embodied the spirit of intolerance that had found expression in the Inquisition. The Jewish League for the Preservation of American Ideals purchased advertisements in opposition to the bill.[64] African Americans similarly recognized that the measure reflected an intolerance that would hurt even minorities, such as the blacks, that did not maintain schools.[65]

Ultimately, the largest number of voters who opposed the bill were Protestants who had no direct personal interest in the perpetuation of private education. For example, Stephen A. Lowell, a Pendleton attorney who was a Mason and a Congregationalist, opposed the bill for both moral and economic reasons. In correspondence to a local editor and the Lutheran Schools Committee, Lowell declared that the bill offended the spirit of tolerance that pervaded Masonry and the freedom of conscience on which Protestantism rested. Lowell also declared that the law was "Prussian and not American" because it would undermine "free speech, free press, free worship and freedom of opportunity." Lowell believed, moreover, that the measure would erode parental authority, "the only sure bulwark against ultimate anarchy." He also feared that the law would deter migration to Oregon and would necessitate a huge increase in taxes.[66]

Unfortunately, there were not quite enough Stephen Lowells in Oregon to defeat the initiative. At the election in November, voters approved it by a vote of 115,506 to 103,685.[67] The enactment of the law surprised political pundits, who had predicted its defeat.[68] Rudolph Messerli, an official of the Lutheran Schools Committee, stated that the outcome was "entirely unexpected," although Lutherans had not dared "to hope for a victory by more than a very small majority."[69]

The school law embarrassed many Oregonians, as well as fair-minded persons in other parts of the country. The *Oregon Voter* denounced the measure as "a disgrace to the state,"[70] and the *Baltimore Sun* declared that it was "a reproach to this country that a single State in the American Union should have yielded to this degrading and shameful spirit of bigotry."[71] Writing in 1923, O'Hara expressed his belief that the law had discouraged immigration into Oregon and had accelerated the departure of persons "to regions less given to intolerance."[72] Not all mainstream opinion, however, entirely disapproved the measure. Although the *Journal of Education* regretted the law because it believed that Oregonians were unduly alarmed about the threat to public education, it acknowledged that Oregon voters may correctly have discerned that compulsory public education was necessary to protect the public schools from hostile forces.[73]

Despite their dismay over the statute, opponents of compulsory public education were encouraged because so many persons who had no personal interest in the perpetuation of private education had voted against the measure. Since Catholics, Missouri Synod Lutherans, Seventh Day Adventists, and the parents of nondenominational private school children constituted no more than 10 percent of the voters, it is possible to hypothesize that approximately 40 percent of other voters opposed the measure. Dudley G. Wooten, executive director of the Catholic Civil Rights Association, observed that "never before was there such wide-spread sympathy and understanding towards Catholics by the Protestant and non-Catholic population."[74] Likewise, the Jewish *Scribe* remarked on the eve of the election that opposition to the measure among Protestants who had no interest in parochial education was "the most hopeful activity in the whole disagreeable rumpus."[75] Roman Catholic leaders believed that the law had intensified Catholic support for parochial schools and inspired solidarity among Catholics.[76]

Of course, nativists who supported the school measure regarded the enactment of the statute as an unqualified triumph and an augury of future success in their efforts to "Americanize" Oregon and other states. Buoyed by the school bill's passage, the newly elected Oregon legislature considered a parcel of other nativistic legislation. Anti-Catholic measures generally did not fare well, however. Although the legislature overwhelmingly approved a measure to ban public school teachers from wearing religious garb, it defeated measures to eliminate Columbus Day as a state holiday, to ban the importation of wine used for sacramental purposes, and to tax church property. A bill to provide free textbooks to public school children, which was intended in part to discourage enrollment in parochial schools, was defeated because it would have required a tax increase. Racist and antialien measures were more successful. The state prohibited aliens of Asiatic descent from owning or leasing real estate and enacted a literacy test that required voters to read a passage from the state constitution and to write at least ten words in the English language. Another bill, passed by the house but defeated by the senate, required all foreign owners of business establishments to post conspicuous notices of their nationality.[77]

The national significance of the enactment of the Oregon school law was apparent to both its friends and its foes. Oregon's Grand Dragon predicted at a Klan meeting in January 1923 that a national compulsory education law would be enacted in the near future.[78] In order to avert further assaults on parochial education, opponents of the law girded for a challenge to the statute. The *Oregon Voter* predicted that the law would be repealed by new legislation, for it inflicted "a hideous wrong." The editors contended that it would be better for the state to repeal the law than to "place the onus for killing the law upon the courts," since an "adverse court decision would simply invite application of the recall, and would keep the flames of religious warfare fanned to white heat."[79]

Most opponents of the school measure, however, had little hope that the law could be repealed through the legislative process, and they looked to the courts for relief. A Lutheran Schools Committee official who believed that the U.S. Supreme Court would nullify the law regarded it as "a God-sent blessing in disguise" because it provided "an ideal case to test out the constitutionality" of compulsory public education.[80] Justin McGrath, director of the NCWC, believed that a judicial decision in favor of the law would result in proposals for similar laws in sixteen states in every part of the nation.[81] Although Burke believed that another estimate of action in twenty-four states was "a very great exaggeration," he acknowledged that the affirmation of the Oregon law "would give a strong impetus" to anti–parochial school measures.[82]

Two weeks after the election, Oregon's Roman Catholic bishops agreed that they would test the constitutionality of the statute as soon as possible.[83] At the request of Archbishop Christie, the Administrative Committee of the National Catholic Welfare Conference agreed early in 1923 to coordinate opposition to the law and to raise funds from Catholic bishops throughout the nation.[84] As one official of the conference observed, this "attack on the Constitution" affected the entire nation and provided an opportunity to demonstrate "that the Catholics of this country will not stand for any infringement upon their rights."[85]

In addition to the conference, the Knights of Columbus assisted in the struggle and helped to pay the legal expenses of the Hill Military Academy, a nonsectarian school for boys which filed a separate action to enjoin the statute. The Oregon state deputy of the Knights of Columbus believed that the academy was "a very necessary auxiliary" to the Roman Catholic action "in order to show that the fight was not an exclusively Catholic one."[86] After bitter wrangling over the selection of counsel, the church divided responsibilities among several Oregon attorneys, led by J. P. Kavanaugh, and a nationally renowned attorney, William D. Guthrie. Guthrie, who had taught constitutional law at Columbia and served as president of the New York State Bar Association, was well suited to oppose the Oregon law: his long career was characterized by opposition to the expansion of governmental power and an ardent championship of Roman Catholic causes. He had helped to argue the cases that led to the Court's nullification of the federal income tax law in 1895, and he had long advocated the reimbursement of parochial schools for the funds that they saved local governments.[87] Guthrie applied himself diligently to the Oregon case and personally discussed it with Peter Cardinal Gasparri, the secretary of state to the pope.[88] The selection of Guthrie rankled Arthur Mullen, who later insisted that Guthrie had failed to give proper credit to Mullen for sowing in the language cases the seeds of Guthrie's victory in the Oregon case.[89]

Unlike the opponents of the language laws, who filed their actions in state court, the foes of the Oregon law commenced their action in federal court. They believed that federal courts would be more sympathetic toward their claims, especially since the U.S. Supreme Court had upheld the rights of private schools in *Meyer,* which was decided one month before the Oregon lawsuit was begun. One Roman Catholic attorney who was helping to prepare the challenge to the Oregon law believed that the *Meyer* decision "practically settles" the Oregon controversy.[90]

The Society of the Sisters of the Holy Names of Jesus and Mary, which maintained some parochial schools in Oregon, was selected by the Roman Catholic church to act as plaintiff in an action to enjoin the enforcement of the school law. The Society and the Hill Academy alleged that the law violated the Fourteenth Amendment because it deprived them of their property without due process of law by interfering with investments and a useful business. They also argued that the law impaired the obligations of their contracts, in violation of Section 10 of Article I of the Constitution, which prohibits states from impairing any obligation arising under a contract. The Sisters further contended that the statute violated due process because it infringed personal rights by depriving parents of the right to direct their children's education, by depriving children of the right to acquire useful knowledge in private schools, and by attempting to control the free exercise of religious opinions.[91]

In correspondence with Kavanaugh, Guthrie stated that "in the broader aspect of the litigation, we must stand on the Fourteenth Amendment and its guaranty that no person shall be deprived of *liberty* without due process of law." Guthrie believed that *Meyer* would be "ample for our purposes," for that decision should make the court receptive to the argument that "it is the very essence of political liberty" that parents have a right to send their children to any school that maintains the minimum requirements prescribed by the state.[92] He feared that a decision based solely on property rights "might not adequately protect the Catholic Church in the future."[93]

Guthrie believed, however, that the action should be brought only in the name of institutions rather than in the name of parents or teachers who were affected by the law, since the joinder of pupils, parents, or teachers might create the impression that the Roman Catholic church was betraying a fear that the state had broad powers to regulate incorporated educational institutions.[94] Observing the case from Nebraska, Mullen publicly complained that the failure to join pupils or teachers as plaintiffs would invite a decision that was based wholly or arguably on corporate property rights. "The inherent and inalienable right belongs . . . to the people the Lord made, not the people the state made," Mullen declared.[95]

Despite their confidence that the federal district court would base its decision in part on personal liberties, the plaintiffs apparently anticipated that the court would find economic due process arguments to be more persuasive. Accordingly, the complaint by the Society took pains to recite the value of various properties it owned and maintained.[96] The Society further alleged that the law violated the contract clause because it impaired the corporate charter by which Oregon had permitted private schools to conduct their educational missions.

In oral argument before the court in January 1924, attorneys for the schools contended that the state had failed to demonstrate that any public necessity justified such an extreme measure. Although counsel for the schools emphasized that the state had the right to enact compulsory education laws and to regulate private schools, they argued that the statute was prohibitory rather than regulatory and that it would destroy the private schools. "How absurd it is to say," Dan Malarkey declared, "that after these children have gone to one school they are going to have the capacity or the time, or their parents are going to impose upon them . . . the burden of doubling up and going to another school." Malarkey disparaged "this talk about the melting pot," pointing out that the public schools were rigidly stratified along economic and class lines because children attended schools in their neighborhoods. Attorneys for the schools also contended that the *Meyer* decision demonstrated that the Oregon law was invalid since the Court's ruling that a private school had the right to teach German implied that private schools had the right to exist.[97]

Attorneys for the state, however, contended that *Meyer* was inapposite because Oregon's need to require public education was much more compelling than was Nebraska's need to prohibit the teaching of German. They pointed out that the Court in *Meyer* had conceded that a state could "compel attendance at some school" and "could make reasonable regulations for all schools." Although the state had undertaken to regulate the private schools, Wallace McCamant, one of the state's attorneys, told the court that "there will be a certain percentage of cases where the supervision will be a farce" and that the statute was designed to combat class hatred by enabling children from all walks of life to "meet in the common schools, which are the great American melting pot." Attorneys for the state contended that the plaintiffs lacked standing to sue for violation of personal liberties, because no parent, child, or teacher was a party to the lawsuit, and that the schools did not suffer property damage, because the statute did not actually prohibit their operation. Ignoring the long line of cases in which state and federal courts had invoked due process to protect economic liberties, attorneys further contended that the plaintiffs' reliance on due process was misplaced, because the Fourteenth Amendment was enacted primarily to protect the rights of African Americans.[98]

In a decision on March 31, 1924, a three-judge panel of the district court ruled that the statute was unconstitutional. After explaining that the lawsuits were not premature, because the impending requirement of compulsory public education already had caused the schools to lose patronage and suffer irremediable harm, the court noted that the statute exceeded the appropriate scope of the state's police power. Although it acknowledged that the state had the right to require universal schooling and to regulate both public and nonpublic schools, the court explained that the statute was not designed to facilitate any of the state's legitimate aims in promoting education. Brushing aside the contention that the law did not actually ban nonpublic schools, the court pointed out that the statute "could not be more effective for utterly destroying" those schools. Nonpublic schools, the court declared, had a "natural and inherent" right to teach the elementary grades. Relying on *Meyer,* the court stated that the right of the schools to offer instruction and the right of parents to engage the schools to instruct their children were within the liberty protected by the Fourteenth Amendment.[99]

The court explained that proponents of the law had failed to demonstrate that the nonpublic schools presented a menace to the state and that there was "no plausible or sound reason why they should be eliminated from taking part in the primary education of the youth." The court also rejected as "an extravagance in simile" the argument that the schools should serve as a "melting pot." Pointing out that very few children who were foreign born or of foreign-born parentage attended nonpublic schools, the court declared that "the assimilation problem could afford no reasonable basis for the adoption of the measure."[100]

Although the court's ruling against the law had been widely predicted, civil libertarians and proponents of private education hailed the decision as a landmark victory. The decision was greeted with what *The Literary Digest* described as a "salvo of commendation" from newspapers in all corners of the nation. *The Oregonian* declared, "It is firm and prompt action such as this, that justifies continued confidence in the high purposes and lofty character of the Federal judiciary."[101] The *Oregon Voter* was more circumspect. It warned that "anti-Catholic prejudice, anti-alien prejudice and anti-snob prejudice was neither reduced nor wiped out by the decision. It is not inconceivable that they will continue to feed on each other and bring about some other form of drastic legislation."[102] Similarly, *America* cautioned that "it would be unwise to assume that the battle is at an end. The motives which prompted the attack still exist and the enemies of the private school are but awaiting a favorable opportunity to renew the struggle."[103]

Within a week after the district court rendered its decision, Oregon officials decided to appeal to the United States Supreme Court. As in the lower court proceedings, the state relied heavily on the legal services of politically prominent Oregon attorneys whose work was financed by the Scottish Rite Masons.[104] The Masons had expressed interest in hiring John W. Davis, the renowned New York corporate attorney who became the Democratic presidential nominee later in 1924. They decided not to hire him, however, after he advised them that the law was unconstitutional. Although such a view was hardly surprising, the Masons believed that Davis may have been influenced by political aspirations.[105]

During the pendency of the appeal, the legislature enacted a law that was designed to discredit arguments that the statute interfered with freedom of religion. The new statute provided that a parent could request that a child be excused from public school for up to two hours per week in order to attend weekday schools that provided instruction in religion.[106] Even though the district court had not expressly addressed the question of religious freedom, the legislature apparently recognized that the compulsory public education law was vulnerable because of its obvious potential for interference with religious instruction.

In its appeal to the Supreme Court, the state argued that the statute was within its police power because it was designed to facilitate social cohesion, as well as ameliorate political subversion and juvenile crime, since the law would stem "the rising tide of religious suspicions." The state also contended that the religious segregation of parochial school students during their formative years created a baneful "distrust and suspicion of those from whom they were so carefully guarded." Arguing that "bolshevists, syndicalists, and communists" would organize schools if the state were not permitted to require compulsory public education, the state declared, "Within a few years . . . our country will be dotted with elementary schools which instead of being red on the outside will be red on the inside."[107]

The state offered no evidence for these propositions and failed to provide any empirical justification for its further contention that the proliferation of parochial schools threatened the existence of public schools.[108] The state urged the Court to defer to the wisdom of the Oregon voters, who presumably had investigated the need for the legislation and concluded that there were sound reasons for its enactment.

The state contended that the statute would not impose any undue burden on parents, schools, teachers, or children.[109] The state explained that "there would remain an abundance of time and opportunity for supplementary instruction either in religion or in the language, history and traditions of the land of their ancestors." At oral argument, however, counsel for the state admitted in response to a question by Justice McReynolds that the law would have the effect of shutting down every parochial school.[110]

The state also contended that the law would not interfere with the rights of teachers, because a properly qualified teacher could "easily secure a position as one of the additional teachers who would be required by the public schools." And children under the age of sixteen had no liberty of choice regarding their education.[111] Brushing aside the issue of religious freedom, the state pointed out that the Fourteenth Amendment had not been interpreted to incorporate the Bill of Rights and that parents had no right to provide sectarian instruction in private schools during normal school hours since public school children were denied religious instruction in school.[112]

Although the state conceded that "the inherent right of parents to the custody and control of their minor children is recognized and protected in every civilized nation," it declared that parental rights were subject to the "paramount right of the state to exercise control over such minors" in matters that affected the welfare of children and the general public.[113] The state contended that the due process clause did not accord parents the right to control the education of their children.[114] The due process clause, the state argued, safeguarded only procedural rights, not substantive rights. The state held that the many decisions in which the Court had appeared to rely on the Fourteenth Amendment in striking down economic legislation were actually based on rights conferred by other constitutional provisions, statutes, or common law.[115] Though many constitutional scholars today would agree that the due process clause does not create substantive rights, the state's argument was clearly at odds with the Court's use of due process to protect substantive economic rights during the late nineteenth and early twentieth centuries. The state further contended that the statute did not violate the equal protection clause, because it applied equally to all children and ensured that all children would receive the benefits of a public education. Citing *Permoli*, the state flatly denied that a federal court could intervene in any state controversy regarding religious freedom; it also contended that the federal government lacked any power over state regulations involving education or domestic relations. The state held that the dicta to the contrary in *Meyer* was "broader than can be supported" by earlier Supreme Court decisions and that "if the states are to be deprived of their power over education and domestic relations it is hard to see what powers can be logically left to them."[116]

The state further argued that the statute did not violate due process, since the Supreme Court had upheld many statutes, including liquor-prohibition laws, that had caused aggrieved parties to lose business. The state failed to point out, however, that few if any of those decisions resulted in the destruction of the businesses of the parties who had complained about state regulation. The state cited *Meyer* in support of its contention that a state had the power to regulate education.[117]

Opponents of the statute argued that the law exceeded the police power because there was no demonstrated need for so drastic a measure. Although they emphasized that the state could regulate private schools, they contended that the statute was prohibitory rather than regulatory and that it would have the practical effect of abolishing private schools. The Hill Academy observed that a "public danger cannot be very great or a public necessity cannot be very pressing if learned counsel, after a long and painstaking effort, cannot locate it." Similarly, the Sisters observed that "it requires nimble dexterity . . . to discover some slender pretext to sustain this law" and that its proponents were forced to "indulge in pessimistic predictions, and speculations" in their efforts to justify the law.[118]

In particular, opponents of the statute argued that it failed to promote its proponents' goals of encouraging assimilation of immigrants and discouraging juvenile crime and religious suspicions. The Sisters contended that nonpublic schools assimilated foreigners as quickly as public schools, and an amicus brief submitted by the American Jewish Committee argued that nonpublic schools "advanced rather than retarded" the assimilation of foreign-born children. The Hill Academy contended that "Oregon is not confronted with any serious problem of assimilation," since 85 percent of the population was native white. Ever zealous in his defense of parochial education, Guthrie even suggested to the Court during oral argument that the public schools were inferior to the private schools.[119]

Opponents of the statute also denied that the nonpublic schools threatened the public schools. The Hill Academy pointed out that enrollment in Oregon's public schools had increased by nearly 50 percent between 1910 and 1920, while enrollment in private schools had slightly declined. The Sisters explained to the Court that "Oregon is not choosing between two competing liberties which cannot co-exist." Some of the briefs in opposition to the law pointed out that private schools were more free to engage in forms of experimentation that ultimately could encourage innovations in public schools. The existence of multiple schools also was said to encourage a healthy diversity. "If the children of the country are to be educated upon a dead level of uniformity and by a single method," the American Jewish Committee argued, "then eventually our nation would consist of mechanical Robots and standardized Babbitts."[120] Although the statute applied only to elementary schools, opponents warned that later enactments might prohibit private secondary schools and colleges.[121]

Since there was no real need for the statute, its opponents argued that it violated due process[122] by unduly infringing both personal rights and property rights. They compared the law to recent Soviet attempts to crush religion and make education a monopoly of the state.[123] Like the opponents of the language laws, the opponents of the Oregon statute relied in part on judicial decisions striking down social and economic legislation that the courts had found to exceed the police power of the state. The Hill Military Academy, for example, invoked the Supreme Court's notorious *Lochner* decision, in which the court struck down a New York law that regulated the hours of bakers, holding that the law violated due process by interfering with the substantive right of employees and employers to enter into contracts without undue interference by the state.[124] The academy likewise invoked the Court's 1923 decision invalidating a minimum wage law for women in the District of Columbia, which had inspired passionate denunciations of the Court among social reformers and other liberals. Both the academy and the Sisters also relied on the Court's 1917 decision that struck down a Washington law prohibiting employment agencies from collecting fees from persons seeking employment.[125]

In arguing that the statute infringed property rights, the Society reiterated statements concerning the value of its property which it first had recited in its complaint. Its buildings had "small value for anything but school purposes," and the equipment would be "a total loss" if the buildings were abandoned. An amicus brief submitted by the Episcopal church argued that the statute would adversely affect the value of a school that it operated in Portland and pointed out that the church had invested a substantial amount of money in its schools in other states. The Hill Academy did not discuss the value of its property, although it informed the Court that it was "engaged in the business of conducting a private school for profit and is particularly concerned with its right to continue that business."[126]

In arguing that the statute also contravened due process by violating personal liberties, the opponents of the law contended that it infringed what Guthrie called the "sacred right and duty" of parents to educate their children. Echoing the slogan of the opponents of the Michigan school measure, the American Jewish Committee declared, "Our children do not belong to the State." Although the Society of Sisters conceded that no parent was a party to the lawsuit, the Sisters explained that parental rights were an issue in the case because the ability of the private schools to remain in operation hinged on the question of whether parents had the right to send their children to private schools. Appealing to a theory of natural law, the Sisters asserted that parents enjoyed a fundamental right to "direct and control" the education of their children. The Sisters alleged that the "Oregon Law is more truly Spartan" than the Nebraska law because it interfered even more profoundly with the rights of parents that McReynolds had recognized in *Meyer*.[127]

Opponents of the law also raised the issue of religious freedom. The Sisters insisted that the law violated religious liberty since the Catholic schools were intended to provide religious instruction that could not be offered in the public schools. The Society cited *Meyer* in support of the argument that the First Amendment's guarantee of the free exercise of religion is among the liberties protected by the Fourteenth Amendment. The Society further explained that Roman Catholic parents believed that religious and moral training should be offered every day and should "underlie and influence" instruction in all subjects. At oral argument, Guthrie stated that the paramount issues in the case were "religious liberty, freedom of conscience, freedom of education, and the right of parents to bring up their children in the faith of their fathers."[128] The *Literary Digest* reported that the religious elements of the case had attracted widespread public interest.[129] Concern for religious liberty was the factor that motivated most Roman Catholic opposition toward the law and infused Guthrie, Mullen, and other prominent Catholic attorneys with their passionate hostility toward the statute.

Despite their concern for religious liberty, however, lawyers for the schools did not emphasize the religious aspects of the case, and they tended to discuss religion in connection with their argument that the statute served no useful purpose instead of as part of their due process argument. The appellees emphasized that the suppression of religious instruction would adversely affect the common good of society rather than the constitutional rights of the schools or the students, since religious training encouraged decent morality and good citizenship. The Sisters pointed out that "social order and civilized society have always rested upon religion." Similarly, the Episcopal church's amicus brief stated that the church's schools helped to combat "the evil tendencies of our time," particularly juvenile crime.[130]

Guthrie explained to Burke that it would be useful to demonstrate that many private schools "were and are more or less religious," since he detected "a growing conviction on the part of Protestant and Jewish parents . . . that religious instruction is essential as part of the primary instruction of children, and that the public schools are defective in this aspect."[131]

Although the Episcopal schools, as we have seen, were primarily concerned with the inculcation of civic virtue rather than religious dogma, one of the principal missions of the Catholic schools was to provide doctrinal instruction. The fact that the Catholic briefs nevertheless emphasized the secular rather than the spiritual benefits of religious education suggests that the Catholics were aware that most members of the Court viewed religion in functional terms. At least three justices—McReynolds, Van Devanter, and Sanford—were schooled in an Anglo-American Protestant tradition that elevated morality over dogma. Other members of the Court who were not affiliated with mainstream American Protestantism also were likely to be more sympathetic to functional arguments. The Unitarian tradition of Holmes and Taft eschewed doctrine and emphasized morality. The form of non-Orthodox Judaism espoused by Brandeis likewise was more a religion of morality than a religion of doctrine. And even the Roman Catholic Butler appears to have viewed religion in highly functional terms. The Catholics therefore may have believed that it was in their interest to emphasize that religious instruction instilled morality and patriotism rather than to argue that it helped to propagate the Catholic faith. Wariness of latent anti-Catholic prejudice on the Court caused Guthrie to omit from his brief any references to the phenomenal growth of the Roman Catholic school system in the United States.[132] Moreover, the church's failure to emphasize the religious freedom issue may have reflected its recognition that the Court in *Meyer* had virtually ignored the religious implications of the language laws.

In addition to arguing that the statute infringed the Fourteenth Amendment's due process clause, the Society of Sisters held that the statute violated Section 10 of Article I of the U.S. Constitution, which prohibits a state from enacting any law that impairs the obligation of contracts. The Society likewise contended that the statute violated a similar provision of the Oregon constitution which prohibited the state from impairing vested corporate rights.[133]

Opponents of the law remained optimistic that the Court would strike it down. Although fair consideration was presumably given to the arguments advanced by proponents of the law, members of the Court do not ever seem to have been seriously in doubt about how they would rule. When the case was argued before the Court in March 1925 and Guthrie asked Taft for more time to present his oral argument, Taft replied, "I don't see why you want any more time. In principle, this case is simply the Meyer case over again."[134] Roman Catholics nevertheless feared that the Court's opinion in striking down the law might define the power of states to regulate schools so broadly as to invite future intrusions on the autonomy of parochial schools.[135]

In a short opinion upholding the district court's decision, Justice McReynolds held that the statute would unduly interfere with the property rights of the schools or the liberty of the parents to direct the upbringing and education of their children. In examining the property interests of the schools, the Court pointed out that they had acquired the valuable goodwill of many parents and that they owned valuable buildings, which were especially constructed and equipped for school purposes. The Court determined that "enforcement of the statute would seriously impair, perhaps destroy, the profitable features of appellees' business and greatly diminish the value of their property."[136] According to the Court, the state had failed to demonstrate any circumstances that would justify such a drastic interference with the schools' property interests. Although the Court acknowledged that the state could reasonably regulate all schools, the Court explained that they were "engaged in a kind of undertaking not inherently harmful, but long regarded as useful and meritorious," and the state had presented no evidence "that they have failed to discharge their obligations to patrons, students or the State." Moreover, the Court averred that "there are no peculiar circumstances or present emergencies which demand extraordinary measures relative to primary education."[137]

In holding that the statute unduly interfered with the liberties of parents, the Court relied on *Meyer*. As in *Meyer,* the Court emphasized that parents have the right to control the education of their children unless the state could demonstrate some need to abridge that right. A "fundamental theory of liberty," the Court explained, "excludes any general power of the state to standardize its children by forcing them to accept instruction from public teachers only." The Court then provided a forceful answer to the question, "Whose is the child?" which opponents of compulsory education had asked so often: "The child is not the mere creature of the State; those who nurture him and direct his destiny have the right, coupled with the high duty, to recognize and prepare him for additional obligations."[138]

As Taft had predicted before oral argument, *Pierce* added little to *Meyer*.

Since *Pierce* squarely established the constitutional foundation for parochial education at which the Court had only hinted in *Meyer,* however, *Pierce* represented a more substantial victory for nonpublic schools. The attention accorded to *Pierce* irritated Mullen, who with only slight exaggeration" contended that the "right to maintain private education was squarely presented in the language cases" and that the Court in *Meyer* for the first time had given "constitutional protection to the maintenance of private schools."[139] As late as 1937, Mullen alleged that "there has been a conspiracy of silence about the language cases" and that the Oregon decision "was merely a development of the doctrine announced in the Meyer case."[140] Guthrie himself publicly acknowledged that the principle of the language cases "ultimately controlled the decision of the Oregon cases," and he privately assured Mullen that *Meyer* "was most helpful, if not decisive, in the Oregon cases."[141]

Like the district court ruling of the previous year, the Supreme Court's decision received widespread praise and little public criticism. The decision was generally viewed as creating a significant precedent for the protection of fundamental civil liberties.[142] The *Journal of Education* expressed satisfaction that the decision had repudiated the "theory that the individual is a chattel of the ruling authorities," and an article in *The Survey* noted approvingly that the "effect of the decision is to check the use of the public schools as a partisan weapon in a political controversy."[143]

Some Roman Catholics who had participated in the parochial struggles, however, were less sanguine. Shortly after he argued the *Pierce* case, Guthrie told Burke, "The subject of religious prejudice is altogether too profitable a field for the agitators of the Ku Klux Klan and others to abandon."[144] Although Burke believed that the portion of the decision concerning parental rights was "epoch-making," he feared that the decision might invite undue governmental regulation of Catholic schools. Burke, who had unsuccessfully urged Guthrie and Kavanaugh to revise their oral arguments to raise this issue, believed that the Court's remarks on regulation suggested that the Court would uphold a law that prohibited parochial schools in which the teachers were not patriotic or where good citizenship was not taught. The possibility of intrusive supervision or abolition of schools under the guise of 'reasonable' regulation, Burke contended, "should sober those who are inclined to be drunk with enthusiasm over this decision."[145] A Roman Catholic attorney who had worked on the case expressed a prevailing view, however, when he assured Burke that the decision "forever bars the abolition of the private school" because it was predicated on the natural rights of children and parents.[146] And the editors of *America* contended that the decision was more than a victory for the Roman Catholic school. "In a larger sense," they declared, "it is a victory over the forces which would make every American the abject creature of an omnipotent state."[147]

9   The Hawaiian Case

The territory of Hawaii, which suppressed part-time schools that offered instruction in Asiatic languages and culture, was the final scene of conflict involving the legal rights of private schools. As in the states of the mainland, hostility toward ethnic minorities led to the enactment of legislation designed to interfere with the rights of parents to inculcate in their children the language and culture of their forebears. Once again, the U.S. Supreme Court vindicated the rights of the parents.

The ethnic tensions that led to the suppression of Asiatic schools in Hawaii were presaged by intense wartime hostility toward its sizable German-American community. Although Hawaiian Germans had enthusiastically supported the German war effort, they quickly transferred their support to the Allied cause after the United States declared war on Germany. Many Anglo-Americans, however, questioned the patriotism of their German neighbors. Numerous Germans suffered indignities ranging from petty harassment to loss of employment, criminal prosecution, and confiscation of property. Despite these pressures, Germans were loath to abandon their use of the German language. Although the Lutheran parish in Honolulu began to conduct regular services in English, it retained German-language services and continued to offer instruction in German. The school's decision to reduce the scale of its German instruction apparently appeased superpatriots in Honolulu. The Lutheran school on Kauai, however, closed its doors at the behest of the superintendent of public instruction following a controversy over its teaching of the German language and the alleged German sympathies of its teacher. By the end of the war, anti-German hostility had destroyed the fabric of the German community in Hawaii to an extent that occurred in few German communities on the mainland. In the words of one scholar, "the German community simply ceased to exist."[1]

After the war, nativist anxiety in Hawaii shifted from the German community to the much larger and more exotic Asiatic community. Even before the war, there had been a noticeable increase in hostility toward Japanese Americans, both in Hawaii and on the Mainland. Agitation for restriction of Japanese immigration had grown so great by 1907 that the United States government entered into the so-called Gentleman's Agreement, whereby Japan informally promised to restrict emigration to American lands, including Hawaii. In response to concern about the growth of landownership by Japanese, California in 1913 enacted a statute that limited the rights of aliens to own real property. After the war, California enacted an even more stringent alien land law aimed against Japanese; some other states enacted similar statutes.[2] In 1922, the U.S. Supreme Court ruled that Japanese persons could be excluded from naturalization because they were not "white" persons within the meaning of the naturalization law.[3] The restrictive immigration law enacted in 1924 was intended in part to reduce further immigration from Japan.

As in other parts of the nation, schools that provided foreign-language instruction became a special target of nativist agitation in Hawaii after the First World War. Since the late nineteenth century, various Asian groups in Hawaii had operated special schools that were devoted to propagating their language and culture. By 1927, some twenty thousand students attended 163 foreign-language schools in Hawaii. Of these schools, all were Japanese except for 9 Korean and 7 Chinese.[4] Foreign-language schools first had been established in the territory during a period of heavy Asian immigration during the late nineteenth century. Like the German-language schools, they were intended in part to bridge the linguistic and cultural gap between immigrants, who spoke little or no English, and their offspring, who were exposed to the English language in public schools and among their peers. Many parents were particularly eager for their children to study Japanese language and culture because they planned for their families to return to Japan.[5] By 1917, the majority of Japanese-American school-age children attended Japanese-language schools during the late afternoon and on weekends. Although the first schools were connected with Buddhist or Christian organizations, most schools by the 1920s were nondenominational. Anglo-Americans expressed little anxiety about the schools until the recrudescence of nativism during the late 1910s.

Early in 1919, bills were introduced in the legislature to require teachers at all territorial schools to have a knowledge of the English language, a standard that many teachers in the language schools were unable to meet. Other bills introduced during the 1919 session of the legislature called for the complete abolition of the schools. Swift and sharp Japanese-American opposition to these measures ensured their defeat. Many Anglo-Americans, however, remained resolute in their conviction that the language schools were a menace to social unity and economic progress. The superintendent of public instruction denounced Japanese supporters of the language schools as "troublemakers and agitators,"[6] and the Aloha Chapter of the Daughters of the American Revolution adopted a resolution denouncing the schools as "subversive to the peace and order of our nation and the undivided allegiance of our people."[7]

Hostilities toward the Japanese community were exacerbated by sugar plantation strikes in 1920. Even though the strikes were broken, they reminded the Anglo community of the threats posed by the sort of cultural and political solidarity that the language schools were designed to inculcate. The strikes also might have convinced some Anglo-Americans that the language schools were desirable to the extent that assimilation of the Japanese would threaten the cultural and economic hegemony of the Caucasians.[8] Generally, however, support for the regulation or abolition of the language schools remained strong in the Anglo-American community. This hostility received a potent impetus from a 1920 survey conducted by a federal commission appointed by the U.S. Commissioner of Education. The survey concluded that the Hawaiian language schools were "centers of influence which, if not distinctly anti-American, are certainly un-American."[9]

During the autumn of 1920, opponents of the language schools introduced legislation in Hawaii's house of representatives that would have prohibited foreign-language instruction to children under the age of fourteen. The Speaker of the house and leading officials of the local branches of the American Legion and the Chamber of Commerce expressed support for legislation that would either immediately abolish the schools or provide for their gradual elimination. An American Legion representative declared, for example, that "the foreign language schools must be abolished entirely" because the Japanese would find a way to evade regulations.[10] Abolition of foreign-language instruction to elementary school pupils encountered intense resistance within the Japanese community and among some Anglo-Americans. During public hearings on the measures, prominent Anglo-Americans warned that the house bill would needlessly antagonize the Japanese community and, in the words of one speaker, mark "a fatal step toward helping the trouble makers." Opponents of the house bill emphasized that the measure would have the practical effect of abolishing the foreign-language schools.[11]

Since Japanese opposition to the legislation made abolition of the schools impracticable, Anglo-American political, business, and educational leaders were willing to settle for a compromise senate bill that provided for regulation rather than prohibition of the foreign-language schools. The house agreed to the senate measure by a vote of 25 to 2 in late November.[12] The extensive regulations prescribed by the statute were designed to effect the act's stated purpose of encouraging the Americanization of students who attended foreign-language schools. Although most language schools already conducted classes for only one hour per day, the law provided that no student could attend a foreign-language school for more than one hour per day or six hours per week. The statute also required the schools to obtain a license from the state and required teachers to obtain certification. Applicants for certification had to demonstrate that they could read, write, and speak the English language, that they appreciated the ideals of democracy, and that they were familiar with American history and institutions. The law further authorized the territorial Department of Public Instruction to prescribe textbooks and courses of study.

In 1922, a joint committee of Japanese and Anglos was formed to make recommendations to the Department of Public Instruction concerning the curriculum and textbooks to be used in the language schools. Some Anglo members of the committee proposed that the study of Japanese be postponed until the third grade because they believed that the simultaneous study of Japanese and English would tax the minds of small children. Japanese members of the committee objected to this proposal and issued a statement arguing that the Japanese language should be taught to children "when their minds are in a receptive and imitative state" and that eight-year-old children would "be uninterested in the simple and easy subjects they have to begin studying with." They also expressed fear that children would be "turned loose on streets, mountains and fields" and subjected to unwholesome influences if they were not occupied in the language schools between the end of the public school day and the time that their parents returned from work in the sugar fields. As a compromise, they suggested simplification of the first-year Japanese curriculum. The American members of the committee, however, rejected this proposal and recommended the elimination of the kindergartens and first and second grades of the language schools. Although the Japanese members of the committee strongly objected to this recommendation, they acquiesced because they feared that the alternative would be even more drastic legislation against the schools.[13]

The Anglo members of the committee declared in a public statement that it would be "unjust" to allow American citizens of Japanese ancestry "to be surrounded by preventable alien influence, and forced . . . to enter the competitive American life under the resulting handicap." They explained, "In the interests of social harmony and good will, it is inexpedient that we should have, as a permanent institution, a system of schools managed and taught by aliens, even with the best of intentions on their part." Accordingly, the language schools must be regarded as "a temporary expedient."[14] At the behest of the committee, the Hawaiian Sugar Planters' Association agreed to try to provide after-school facilities for children who would be too young to attend the language schools.[15]

The Japanese Society of Hawaii vigorously objected to the recommendation and urged the Department of Public Instruction to reject the committee's proposal. Although the society emphasized that it wished for Japanese-American children to obtain an appreciation of democracy and American institutions and that Japanese teachers had made "painstaking and anxious efforts" to comply with the law, it contended that the new regulations were "too far reaching." According to the society, the elimination of the first two grades of the language schools would cause "financial disaster" to the schools and many would be forced to close. The society's petition suggested that the regulation would disrupt intercultural harmony in the territory.[16] Despite protests from the Japanese community, the commissioners of public instruction in August 1922 accepted the recommendations of the committee. In response to this decision, Anglo-American attorneys for the Japanese Society of Hawaii presented a formal petition to Governor Wallace R. Farrington on September 19 to urge him not to sign the recommendation. The attorneys argued that the recommendations violated the 1920 statute, which was merely intended to regulate the foreign-language schools, rather than abolish any part of their operation. The attorneys obtained from the territorial attorney general an opinion that any "regulation" of the schools that operated as a practical prohibition would be contrary to the intent of the statute. The attorneys further argued that the abolition of any part of the language schools would be unconstitutional: because there was no compelling state interest in curtailing the schools, it would exceed the scope of the police power. Pointing out that the "Japanese had attained quite a high degree of civilization when our ancestors were living in caves," the attorneys stated that Japanese parents ought to be allowed to make their children familiar with their ancestral language so they could "read of the great and noble things in Japanese history."[17]

Like the Japanese members of the joint committee, the attorneys argued that the schools were needed to occupy the attention of small children while their parents worked long hours in the fields to sustain the territory's industries. Neither the state nor the plantation owners, they argued, were likely to be able to establish a complete network of kindergartens at any time in the near future. Finally, the attorneys warned that the vast majority of Japanese parents opposed the regulation and that the abolition of the schools would "cause a feeling of distrust on the part of those parents" which would impair interracial harmony.[18]

The society's efforts were unavailing, and Governor Farrington signed the recommendation into law on November 18, 1922. As enacted, the regulations provided that no child could enroll in a foreign language school after September 1, 1923, if he or she had not completed the first and second grades of a public school. After signing the measure, the governor declared that Hawaii was amicable toward "alien races," but he warned that "we have no thought of allowing our friendship and tolerance to be abused so that there shall be established here alien principalities that foster a spirit of opposition to American institutions and defiance of those who support them." He vowed that this "thoroughly American territory" would "continue to go forward on American lines."[19] At the same time, the Department of Public Instruction issued a statement declaring that the new regulations were needed because the "great majority of Hawaiian-born children of alien parents enter the public schools deficient in, or wholly ignorant of English." The department further contended that the attendance of young children at academic studies "after the prescribed public school hours is detrimental to the health of the children."[20] Supporting the regulation, the *Honolulu Star-Bulletin* urged Asian Americans to accept it and declared, "There can be no compromise in Hawaii on the principle of Americanism *first*."[21]

On taking effect, the regulation would have removed more than two thousand children from the Japanese schools.[22] Although many members of the Japanese community favored litigation to challenge the new regulation, others opposed a test case. When representatives of thirteen schools in Honolulu met on December 11, eight schools opposed litigation, four favored it, and one abstained. Sixteen leaders of the Japanese community, many of whom had vigorously opposed the enactment of the regulation, issued a statement opposing a test case. They averred that a legal contest "would work to the disadvantage of the Japanese language schools and handicap the future of children attending these schools" and "would injure the feeling between Americans and Japanese in Hawaii."[23]

Despite widespread opposition to legal action, one Japanese language school in Honolulu brought a lawsuit to enjoin the enforcement of the regulation and to challenge the constitutionality of the 1920 statute that regulated the schools. Several other schools later joined the litigation. On December 28, 1922, the circuit court granted a temporary injunction against enforcement of the regulations.[24] On February 3, after a full hearing, Judge James J. Banks upheld the constitutionality of the 1920 statute but declared that it did not authorize the regulation to prohibit attendance until the third grade. Banks explained that the statute was a valid exercise of the police power because there was an "imperative" need to inculcate the English language and American ideals in children whose parents were "unfamiliar with the genius and spirit of our institutions and unable to speak the language in which our laws are written and our government conducted." He concluded, however, that the statute was not intended to divest the schools of the right to enroll any pupil.[25]

In response to this decision, the Hawaiian legislature in 1923 enacted a statute that codified most of the department's regulations, including a provision that prohibited attendance at language schools until a child had completed the second grade of a public school, unless the Department of Public Instruction provided otherwise. The statute also called for the appointment of inspectors of the foreign-language schools, required the schools to make annual reports to the department, and imposed on all schools an annual fee of one dollar per student. After the department had difficulty collecting fees, lawmakers in April 1925 enacted legislation to facilitate collection. The threat of rigid enforcement of the fees provision caused many schools to close their doors and provoked a renewal of the constitutional challenge to the school laws. During the pendency of proceedings on the injunction, the department exercised its right to modify the prohibitions of the 1923 statute to permit all grade school children to attend language schools. Although the department's regulations therefore retained only the ban on kindergarten instruction in language schools, the schools protested even against this restriction and also continued to allege that the head tax was unduly burden-some. In a decision on July 21, 1925, Judge John T. DeBolt of the U.S. District Court enjoined the territory from enforcing any provisions of the 1923 and 1925 amendments to the 1920 statute.

The U.S. Court of Appeals sustained the injunction in March 1926 after concluding that the statute exceeded the scope of the territory's police power and contravened the Supreme Court's decision in *Meyer v. Nebraska*. The court warned that the government "cannot make good citizens by op-pression, or by a denial of constitutional rights." One of the judges on the three-judge panel disagreed that the law was wholly invalid, but even he conceded that the state could not bar the attendance of any child at the lan-guage schools or prescribe textbooks.[26]

The territory of Hawaii persuaded the U.S. Supreme Court to hear the case. In its briefs to the Court, the territory insisted that the statutes and reg-ulations were a proper exercise of the police power, for otherwise aliens could educate their children in a subversive manner. In support of their con-tention that the schools taught Asian-American students "loyalty to a for-eign country and disloyalty to their own country" and hindered their ability to learn English, the territory relied heavily on the 1920 survey of the federal commission.[27]

The territorial briefs were replete with scarcely disguised efforts to ex-ploit racial prejudice and the widespread fear that Anglo-Americans and their culture in Hawaii would be overwhelmed by the rapidly growing Asian population. Lawyers for Hawaii warned that some of the territory's foreign-born citizens displayed an "aloofness and racial assertiveness not only on their own part but in their aggressive efforts to lead or force the na-tive-born in the same direction." Denying that the Hawaiian law was prompted by the "mob psychology" that had inspired the Oregon law, the territory argued that the statute arose "naturally from an extremely difficult situation presented by the numerical dominance of alien races in Hawaii." Surely the increasingly beleaguered Anglo-American community could not be expected to "stand by impotently" and "watch its foreign-born guests conduct a vast system of schools" that inculcated alien ideals.[28]

The territorial attorneys made a valiant but unconvincing effort to distin-guish the hostile precedents of *Pierce* and *Meyer*. The laws that were nullified in those decisions, they insisted, were prohibitory, whereas the Hawaiian enactments were merely regulatory. The territory suggested that the Court should sustain the provisions regarding textbooks and inspections even if it invalidated the restrictions on attendance.[29]

Relying on *Meyer* and *Pierce,* the attorneys for the schools insisted that the statute was prohibitory rather than regulatory, because its effect was "to make all these private schools in fact public schools in all but the name, though the public contributes not one cent to their support." The schools argued that such drastic legislation "by a paternalistic government" exceeded the scope of the territory's police power, since "the Americanism of the pupils is advanced, not retarded in these schools." The schools further contended that the law did not facilitate enforcement of the territory's public school policy since the hours of the school did not interfere with the attendance of the pupils at the public schools. Like the schools in the midwestern language cases, the Hawaiian schools relied in part on *Lochner* in arguing that the statute exceeded the scope of the police power. Generally, however, they were content to rely on *Meyer* and *Pierce* rather than on economic due process decisions. Although in their bills of complaint the schools had duly recited the economic losses that they would incur as a result of the enforcement of the legislation, in their briefs they emphasized personal freedom rather than economic freedom. The briefs for the schools did not delve deeply into the doctrinal bases of *Meyer* and *Pierce* but primarily cited those decisions as standing for the right of parents freely to control the education of their children rather than as sustaining economic liberties.[30]

The schools contended that kindergarten, the only remaining grade in which attendance at the language schools was proscribed by the Department of Education, was "an essential grade in the system." The schools also warned that the statute permitted the department to prescribe regulations that would prohibit the teaching of languages in all grades, and they predicted that the department would adopt such a draconian regulation if the Court upheld the statute. In response to the territory's insistence that Hawaii's unique cultural diversity justified the statutes, the attorneys for the schools stated that "if there are peculiar circumstances in Hawaii relating to our foreign born population, there were similar circumstances in Nebraska and Ohio which were urged in support of the constitutionality of the acts relating to education in those states."[31]

In an opinion handed down on February 21, 1927, the United States Supreme Court affirmed the circuit court's decree enjoining the enforcement of the 1920 statute and its amendments. Relying on the *Meyer* and *Pierce* decisions, the Court found that the regulation of the schools far exceeded any legitimate governmental interest. In a terse opinion, Justice McReynolds explained that the Hawaiian government had failed to justify any need for a statute that gave "affirmative direction concerning the intimate and essential details" of the schools, "intrust[ed] their control to public officers, and den[ied] both owners and patrons reasonable choice and discretion in respect of teachers, curriculum and text-books." Accordingly, the Court held that the statute violated the Fifth Amendment of the Constitution, which imposes on the federal government the same due process requirements that act as checks against state power in the Fourteenth Amendment. The Court declared, "The Japanese parent has the right to direct the education of his own child without unreasonable restrictions; the Constitution protects him as well as those who speak another tongue."[32] McReynolds stated that the Court would refuse to undertake an analysis of the validity of the various provisions of the statute, since "all are parts of a deliberate plan to bring foreign language schools under a strict governmental control for which the record discloses no adequate reason." McReynolds observed that the regulations probably would destroy most, if not all, of the schools and "would deprive parents of fair opportunity to procure for their children instruction which they think important and we cannot say is harmful." Although he acknowledged that the Court appreciated "the grave problems incident to the large alien population of the Hawaiian Islands" and conceded that these problems "should be given due weight whenever the validity of any governmental regulation of private schools is under consideration," McReynolds explained that "the limitations of the Constitution must not be transcended."[33]

Many Anglo-Americans in Hawaii acquiesced to the Court's decision only grudgingly. The *Honolulu Advertiser* declared, "United popular sentiment in Hawaii still holds that the double educational system is not good for the children" because "[i]t will tend to keep them alien and oriental in a community which is becoming more occidental." Insisting that rapid assimilation was necessary in order to preserve democracy and promote commercial growth in Hawaii, the *Advertiser* expressed hope that Asian Americans would abandon their schools. "Citizens have many rights which they never think of exercising. We trust that the oriental population will remember this."[34] Despite continuing public hostility toward the schools, the Hawaiian legislature voted in April 1927 to repay the language schools the full amount that the territory had collected in fees under the 1925 statute. Meanwhile, Japanese language schools reopened, and Japanese-American educational leaders met to develop ways of cooperating more closely with the Department of Public Instruction and of encouraging Americanism among students in the language schools.[35]

The Supreme Court's decision in *Farrington v. Tokushige* marked the practical end of the parochial school controversies of the 1920s. Although proponents of Americanization of the immigrant continued for a few more years to campaign for a comprehensive federal education statute, the Supreme Court's trilogy of decisions in 1923, 1925, and 1927 had demonstrated the futility of any effort to try to impose crippling restraints on parochial education. Those decisions, however, continue to have an important practical significance: they established significant new legal doctrines that have profoundly affected the development of American law in matters that extend far beyond education. In the final chapter, we examine the enduring legacy of those decisions.

10 The Constitutional Legacy of the School Decisions

Shortly after he defied the Siman Act, Robert T. Meyer left his position at the South School, perhaps because of controversy in the Zion congregation over whether he should have obeyed the law.[1] Meyer continued to teach in southeastern Nebraska until he retired in 1942. He died in 1972 at the age of ninety-four. Meyer was proud of his role in the case that he had provoked. "It is indeed very gratifying to know," he wrote to Arthur Mullen in 1938, "how that case had a happy termination, and of what far reaching effect it has for the present and for the future. The rights of parents over their children have been safeguarded by that decision."[2] Seventy years after he recited in German for the Hamilton County attorney, Raymond Parpart likewise remained keenly aware of the importance of the *Meyer* decision. As an active eighty-one-year-old farmer in 1990, Parpart remarked that the *Meyer* decision demonstrated that legislatures "can't just make up laws to tell people that they can't do what they want to do. It shows how valuable the Constitution really is."[3]

Both Meyer and Parpart comprehended the essential spirit of the *Meyer* decision. That decision, however, has had far broader consequences than anyone could have foreseen. The Court's decisions in *Meyer* and *Pierce* were a turning point in American constitutional history, presaging the emergence of the Supreme Court as a persistent guardian of personal liberties. Although the Court had long since established itself as the balance wheel of the federal system and a staunch defender of property rights, the Court before *Meyer* had not yet assumed its modern role as a palladium of human liberties. Until the parochial school decisions, the Court seldom had checked infringements of personal liberties by the federal government and almost never had interfered with such infringements by states. Although the Court occasionally had invoked the equal protection clause of the Fourteenth Amendment to prevent extreme forms of racial discrimination, *Meyer* was the first decision in which it construed the amendment to protect personal liberties against infringement by states in cases not involving race. The decision therefore serves as the cornerstone for federal judicial protection of personal liberties against infringements by states. In addition to inaugurating a new era of civil liberties, *Meyer* and *Pierce* started a profound revolution in federalism by anticipating the long process by which the Court gradually incorporated most of the guarantees of the Bill of Rights into state law.

Despite the broad language of the Court about human liberties, its opinion in *Meyer* suggests that it based its precise holding on the narrow ground that the statute interfered with the economic right of Meyer "to teach and the right of parents to engage him to so instruct their children." This economic right presumably was the right to contract, which the Court had consistently found to be a liberty that was protected by the Fourteenth Amendment. Liberty of contract had been the basis for *Adkins v. Children's Hospital,* a controversial decision two months before *Meyer* in which the Court had invalidated a federal statute providing for a minimum wage for women workers in the District of Columbia.[4] The Court in that decision had reasoned that the statute interfered with the right of women workers and their employers to enter freely into contracts for the sale and hire of labor. Closely related to the liberty of contract was the liberty to pursue a useful vocation, which the Court also had invoked in many of its economic due process decisions.

Inasmuch as the precise language of the decision's holding refers only to economic rights, it is not surprising that many scholars and commentators have contended that the Court's decisions were premised solely on the grounds that the statutes interfered with economic rights.[5] This interpretation, however, is at odds with the sweeping language of the decision. Although the Court's references to Meyer's right to teach and the right of parents to engage him to teach indicate that the decision was based partly on economic grounds, the magisterial dicta about the fundamental rights of citizens indicates that the Court also was invoking the Fourteenth Amendment to protect personal liberties that transcended economic considerations—liberties that embraced activities that are not tied to the "property" to which the Fourteenth Amendment refers.

The facts and arguments presented by the appellants demonstrate that

the Court easily could have based its decisions solely on economic due process without discussing personal liberty. The Court surely has been known
to base decisions upon less ingenuous and more ingenious grounds. Although the property rights of the parents in the five language cases were not
particularly compelling, the Court could have limited its holding to its contention that the statutes interfered with the rights of language teachers to
pursue an economic livelihood. The Court could have made even a stronger
case for deprivation of economic rights if it had held that the statutes diminished the value of the property owned by the parochial schools. If the decision is to be interpreted primarily in economic terms, it is difficult to explain
why the Court omitted any reference to the economic impact of the statutes
upon the schools, a subject that the appellants had taken pains to discuss in
their briefs. Likewise, if the grounds for the decision were primarily economic, it is strange that the Court's dicta so strenuously emphasized the
protection of personal rights while saying so little about economic rights.
Even if the basis for the *Meyer* decision were wholly economic, however, the
decision nevertheless broke new constitutional ground in its dictum that the
Fourteenth Amendment "without doubt" denotes various personal freedoms, including the right to learn, to marry, to worship freely, to establish a
home, and to bring up children.

As in *Meyer,* the technical holding in *Pierce* appears to have been based
partly and perhaps entirely on economic liberties, for the Court held that enforcement of the statute would destroy the business and property of the
schools by depriving them of patronage. By declaring that the statute violated parental rights, however, the Court appears to have rendered a decision that transcended economic grounds to protect personal freedom. Although those parental rights might have been no more than the liberty to
enter into contracts for the education of children, the broad language of the
Court suggests that it was referring to personal rights rather than economic
rights. If the Court in *Pierce* had wished to base its decision solely on economic rights, it could have based its decision entirely on the rights of the
corporations that were the only parties to the case and need not have said
anything about parental rights.

In view of its solicitude for the economic rights of corporations, it is
hardly surprising that the Court would have based its decisions in *Meyer* and
Pierce partly on economic grounds. The Court's bold and seemingly gratuitous pronouncements concerning human freedom in both cases are more
difficult to explain. Rather than making an oblique reference to the right of

Meyer to teach and the right of parents to engage him to teach, the Court in *Meyer* could specifically have discussed the economic loss that parochial schools and their teachers would suffer if the statute were sustained. The Court could have provided a similar discussion in *Pierce*. Since the briefs and pleadings in the language cases and the Oregon cases were replete with recitations of the economic value of the parochial schools that were alleged to have been harmed by the statutes, the Court surely had plenty of data on which to base such a discussion. The Court also might have analyzed the character of the contractual rights with which the statute interfered.

Taken together, the Court's vagueness about the economic liberties that it was protecting and its robust language concerning human freedoms indicate that *Meyer* and *Pierce* represent the application of a doctrine of substantive due process to personal liberties that go beyond economic rights. In effect, the Court was announcing that the ambiguous contours of due process under the Fourteenth Amendment would henceforth be invoked to protect human rights as well as the economic rights that the Court had protected under that amendment for the past several decades.

Moreover, it is clear that at least Justice Brandeis believed that *Meyer* embraced noneconomic rights. In a conversation about the language cases at Brandeis's summer home six weeks after *Meyer* was handed down, Brandeis and Harvard law professor Felix Frankfurter agreed that the due process clause should be extended to substantive laws that affected fundamental noneconomic liberties. Brandeis and Frankfurter defined those fundamental liberties as the right of speech, education, choice of profession, and locomotion, which they believed "are such fundamental rights [so as] not to be impaired or withdrawn except as judged by the 'clear and present danger' test."[6] While Brandeis and Frankfurter agreed that due process ideally should be restricted to procedural regularity and that the due process clause of the Fourteenth Amendment should be repealed, they believed that due process meanwhile should be applied to those personal liberties that they had identified as being fundamental. Although Holmes apparently had told Brandeis that he did not want to extend the scope of the Fourteenth Amendment, Brandeis appears to have pointed out the anomaly of allowing the amendment to be used to strike down regulatons of property but not to protect individual freedom. Anticipating the course of the Supreme Court after 1937, Brandeis and Frankfurter suggested that laws that impinged on personal liberties ought to be subjected to more intensive judicial scrutiny than laws that affected property.[7]

Although the Court would continue to use substantive due process to scrutinize the validity of state economic legislation until the so-called Judicial Revolution of 1937, the Court almost immediately after its decision in *Pierce* virtually abandoned the use of substantive due process in personal liberties decisions in preference to the application of specific provisions of the Bill of Rights. In its landmark decision in *Gitlow v. New York,* handed down only seven days after *Pierce,* the Court asserted for the first time that the "freedom of speech and of the press—which are protected by the First Amendment from abridgement by Congress—are among the fundamental personal rights and 'Liberties' protected by the due process clause of the Fourteenth Amendment from impairment by the States."[8] Although this language was only dictum, the Court in a series of decisions during the next few years incorporated the First Amendment freedom of speech and freedom of the press into state law.[9] The Court's decisions in *Meyer* and *Pierce* therefore may be said to have augured its later decisions incorporating most of the provisions of the Bill of Rights into state law. Accordingly, it is useful to ask why the Court did not begin the process of incorporation in *Meyer* or *Pierce.*

The most obvious explanation is that the use of substantive due process was more consistent with the precedent that was available to the Court. The decision in *Meyer* expressed essentially the same theory of natural law on which the Court had based its economic due process decisions. Indeed, as we have seen, the opponents of the language laws were not ashamed to rely on the natural law theories espoused by the Supreme Court in *Lochner v. New York* and other notorious economic due process decisions.

Incorporation, moreover, would have been inconsistent with existing precedent. Although a court today might strike down similar laws as violative of the First Amendment's rights of free exercise of religion, free speech, or freedom of assembly, the Court before *Meyer,* as we have seen, had repeatedly refused to incorporate any of the explicit liberties of the Bill of Rights into state law. The most recent refusal had occurred only one year before *Meyer,* when the Court had affirmed that neither the Fourteenth Amendment nor any other provision of the federal Constitution imposed on the states any restrictions concerning freedom of speech.[10] Under the influence of Brandeis and perhaps Holmes, however, the Court had shown signs of growing receptivity toward protection of personal liberties. In a 1921 decision, *Gilbert v. Minnesota,* the Court had conceded that freedom of speech is "natural and inherent," although it had emphasized that such free-

dom is not absolute and did not protect the plaintiff in that case from prosecution under a state law prohibiting pacifist speeches. In a dissent in *Gilbert*, Justice Brandeis had argued in favor of incorporation.[11]

In view of the Court's nascent protection of personal liberties against
state infringement in *Gilbert* and its tentative acceptance of incorporation in
Gitlow, the decision in *Meyer* should furnish clues about the process that led
to incorporation, even though *Meyer* does not mention the First Amendment. The Court's failure to couch its *Meyer* and *Pierce* decisions in First
Amendment terms is particularly intriguing, since the facts of the cases
would have enabled the Court to base their decisions on free exercise of religion, freedom of speech, or even freedom of assembly if it had been willing
to incorporate these First Amendment protections into state law.

Freedom of religion would seem to have presented the strongest First
Amendment argument in both *Meyer* and *Pierce*. The Court's opinions,
however, did not even mention freedom of religion, except for *Meyer*'s list-
ing of it among the fundamental freedoms protected by the Fourteenth
Amendment. As Mark DeWolfe Howe observed, "McReynolds seems to
have made a studied effort to play down the religious aspects of the [*Meyer*]
case."[12] Informed of the *Pierce* decision by a French lawyer in Cairo, the
Grand Mufti of Egypt indicated that an Islamic court would have based the
decision squarely on the right of a parent to provide any religious education
for his child that did not endanger the state. "It is a matter of money with
you," he declared. "God's wishes you have not consulted." When the lawyer
pointed out that the Supreme Court had based its decision in part on a theory of the natural rights of parents, the Grand Mufti replied, "Then why talk
so much about money and law ruining the business of the teacher?"[13]

Despite the failure of the Court to discuss the religious implications of
the laws that it struck down, the reference in *Meyer* to religious freedom was
highly significant: the Court had never before explicitly stated that the
Fourteenth Amendment protects religious freedom. Writing shortly after
the Court decided *Meyer*, Professor Carl Zollmann, an authority on church-
state relations, declared that *Meyer* had "most far reaching importance,"
since it would allow the Supreme Court henceforth to protect religious freedom from interference by the states.[14] But the clear implication of the
Court's opinion was that religious freedom is guaranteed by substantive
due process rather than by the First Amendment.

Although the right of Meyer to teach and the right of Nebraska pupils to
learn could perhaps also be characterized as rights that are related to free-

dom of speech, the opponents of the statutes had largely ignored the issue of free speech,[15] and the Court did not base its decision on any such explicit right. The Court's recent decisions concerning freedom of speech, however, may have informed its decision in *Meyer*. In finding that "no emergency has arisen which renders knowledge by a child of some language other than English so clearly harmful as to justify its inhibition," the Court in *Meyer* appears to have applied the reasoning of the "clear and present danger" test.

Moreover, the Court might also have held that the First Amendment embraced a theory of freedom of education. Stephen Arons concluded that the Court today might decide *Pierce* under the First Amendment, since "*Pierce* could be seen as having for its central principle the preservation of individual consciousness from governmental coercion." Arons explained that "the specific application of this principle to education is that any state-constructed school system must maintain a neutral position toward parents' educational choice whenever values or beliefs are at stake."[16] Indeed, some justices of the Supreme Court have used *Meyer* and *Pierce* as First Amendment precedents in this manner. In 1965, Justice William O. Douglas cited *Meyer* for the proposition that the First Amendment prohibits a state from restricting the scope of available knowledge.[17] Similarly, Justice Abe Fortas in 1969 cited *Meyer* as a First Amendment precedent in a decision that held that a high school could not prohibit students from wearing black armbands to protest American participation in the Vietnam War.[18] As Philip Bobbitt has pointed out, *Meyer* "may now be seen as the decisive first step in the development of a First Amendment doctrine of freedom of ideas"; its transformation into a First Amendment precedent therefore is not inappropriate.[19]

Inasmuch as *Meyer* and *Pierce* contained elements of freedom of religion and speech and other values protected by the First Amendment, the Court's failure to consider those issues in a First Amendment context is surprising: incorporation would seem to have constituted a more conservative course by confining the scope of those liberties to the specific limitations of the Bill of Rights. In contrast, protection of civil liberties by invocation of the amorphous due process clause provides judges with greater discretion in defining constitutional rights.

In large measure, it is this very ambiguity that ultimately led the Court to abnegate the doctrine of economic due process; this same ambiguity has made many scholars uncomfortable about the new substantive due process that has emerged since 1965 to protect privacy and sexual freedoms. Although most constitutional scholars today agree that the Fourteenth

Amendment prohibits states from denying most of the rights that are enumerated in the Bill of Rights, many scholars deny that the due process clauses of the Fifth and Fourteenth amendments protect rights that are not spelled out in the Bill of Rights. In contrast to Arthur F. Mullen, who rejoiced that *Meyer* had established a "fenceless land of liberty,"[20] these scholars worry that the creation of rights that are not specifically mentioned in the Constitution accords undue latitude to judges to define the rights of Americans and to accord rights that were not envisioned by the Framers of the Constitution. The use of substantive due process to protect personal freedoms, they believe, is as pernicious as was the Court's use of substantive due process to strike down economic legislation during the late nineteenth and early twentieth centuries.[21]

From the viewpoint of the Court in 1923 and 1925, however, substantive due process provided a more circumspect option than did incorporation. Although the Court's use of substantive due process to protect personal rights was novel, the use itself naturally flowed from its affinity for economic due process. By relying in part on traditional economic due process theory and basing the remainder of its opinion on the right of parental autonomy and the right of students to learn, the Court was able to avoid altogether the vexing issue of incorporation. Reliance on the freedoms of religion or speech would have forced the Court to grapple with the issue of incorporation—a subject that it was not yet ready, willing, or able to face.

Nevertheless, the Court could not have been unaware of the fecund implications of its holdings and dicta in the decisions. The breadth of the *Meyer* opinion led Howe to conclude that the Court played down the religious aspects of the case because it "was consciously endeavoring, for one reason or another, to find a ground for what it conceived to be a liberating decision that would do something more than set religion free."[22] Although Howe may have exaggerated the liberalism of what was, after all, a very conservative Court, the magisterial language of the *Meyer* opinion permits no doubt that the Court consciously articulated a broad view of personal freedom. A desire to emphasize the importance of such secular liberties as the right of parents to control their children's education may indeed in part have led the Court to minimize the religious aspects of the case. Mullen, for example, believed that McReynolds was persuaded to reverse the lower court rulings in *Meyer* only because Mullen had contended at oral argument, in response to McReynolds's query, that the state has no power to require parents to send their children to public schools. Mullen thought that the prospect of such untrammeled state power, rather than any threat to parochial schools, alarmed McReynolds.[23]

Moreover, the Court might also have regarded substantive due process as a more conservative option than incorporation because the specific rights that the Court recognized—the rights of teachers to teach and students to learn—did not seem likely to protect social or political radicals or to set a precedent that such persons or groups easily could exploit. The Court may have feared that recognition of any right to free speech would open a left-wing Pandora's box and that recognition of any right to religious freedom under the First Amendment would have set a precedent for incorporation of freedom of speech.

The Court's failure to rely on a theory of incorporation also may be attributed in part to the failure of any of the parties to make any distinct argument in favor of incorporation. The protracted litigation of the parochial cases yielded only one instance in which opponents of the anti–parochial school statutes argued that the First Amendment protected religious freedom: the single paragraph of a Roman Catholic brief in *Pierce* that cited *Meyer* as incorporating the First Amendment's right to free exercise of religion. The Missouri Synod's abrupt and stunted remarks about federal protection of religious freedom in its brief in the Nebraska injunction case and Mullen's similarly ambiguous remarks during oral argument in *Meyer* suggest, as we have seen, more of a substantive due process theory of religious freedom than an explicit theory of incorporation. The record otherwise is barren of any attempt to persuade the Court to invoke specifically by incorporation the free exercise clause or free speech clause of the First Amendment. In contrast, the briefs and oral arguments of all the opponents of the anti–parochial school statutes were replete with advocacy of substantive due process.

The Court's reliance on general due process also may have been intended as a means of enhancing public support for judicial activism in decisions in which the Court invoked substantive due process to strike down economic legislation. During the year before the *Meyer* decision, the Court had been subjected to fierce criticism by labor unions and leaders of the waning progressive movement for a recent series of decisions invalidating various state and federal social and economic regulations.[24] In June 1922, Senator Robert M. La Follette and the American Federation of Labor had endorsed a plan permitting Congress to reenact by a two-thirds vote any statute that the Supreme Court had invalidated.[25] Early in 1923, Senator William E. Borah had introduced a bill that would have required the concurrence of seven out of nine justices in any decision striking down federal legislation.[26] Other critics of the Court proposed similar measures to curb federal judicial power. Hostility against the Court had reached new levels of intensity less than two months before *Meyer*, when the Court in *Adkins* invalidated the D.C. minimum wage law. Meanwhile, the Hearst press and the Socialist party had begun an attack on Chief Justice Taft for his acceptance of a legacy under Andrew Carnegie's will.[27] The criticism of the Court sufficiently troubled Taft that he tacitly chided the Court's detractors in a public speech less than one month before the announcement of the *Meyer* decision. Speaking at the dedication of a monument to Chief Justice Salmon P. Chase, Taft recounted attempts during Chase's tenure to limit the Court's powers and asserted, "The people now are glad that the guarantees of personal liberty were maintained by the court against the partisan zeal of the then majority."[28] Taft's defense of the Court as a guardian of "personal liberty" against majoritarian tyranny foreshadowed the imminent announcement of the *Meyer* decision and suggests that Taft might have hoped that *Meyer* would discourage efforts to curb the Court's jurisdiction. Although the political climate of the day favored the Court's probusiness decisions and the Court-curbing bills enjoyed little support in the conservative Congress that sat during 1923, Taft and his colleagues hardly could have been unaware that the tides of political opinion and congressional power could abruptly turn against the Court. The *Meyer* decision enabled the Court to demonstrate that the power of judicial review and the doctrine of substantive due process that could strike down a "progressive" minimum wage law also could be used to invalidate "reactionary" language laws.

In attempting to bolster public support for the Court, defenders of judicial review frequently pointed to *Meyer* and later to *Pierce* as examples of the salutary exercise of judicial review. During the 1924 presidential campaign, relentless and vigorous Republican attacks on LaFollette for his proposal to restrict judicial power may have drained votes from the Wisconsin senator; at the same time, the Republicans deliberately used the *Meyer* decision as a means of winning votes among the ethnic electorate. Taft himself encouraged Republicans to use *Meyer* as an example of the Court's role as a palladium of personal liberties.[29] Recognizing that his proposal to curb the Court's power had become a political albatross, LaFollette took pains to explain to voters that his plan extended only to judicial review of federal legislation and would not have prevented the Court from striking down the state statutes in the language cases.[30] The Republican party's deft use of the Court issue appears to have cut deeply into La Follette's core constituencies among German and Scandinavian Lutherans in the Midwest and Roman Catholic voters in the major cities of the East and Midwest; it also hurt La Follette among other voters who feared diminution of federal judicial power.[31]

The Court's decisions in *Meyer* and *Pierce* also helped to turn Roman Catholic opinion against President Franklin Roosevelt's Court-packing plan in 1937. Roman Catholic leaders tended to oppose the plan, as did many lay Catholics.[32] In commending Senator Borah for his opposition to the Court plan, one of Borah's Catholic constituents explained that he could not forget Oregon's mandatory public education law and that "it was only the Supreme Court . . . that stood as a bulwark against this attempt of a majority to bend a minority to its will."[33]

Although Congress did not curtail the power of the Court and its decisions in *Meyer* and *Pierce* won it some political support, the Court's decisions in those cases did not silence its critics. The Court's reliance on substantive due process in *Meyer* and *Pierce* troubled many opponents of economic due process, who recognized that the use of substantive due process in the two decisions reinforced the doctrine of economic due process. Although *The Survey* observed with satisfaction after *Meyer* that the "Supreme Court is once more committed to the defense of the freedom of the individual," it remarked with frustration that "the decision really rests back upon the main political and economic tenet . . . of the present court, that the right of the freedom of contract is never to be lightly infringed." Refering to *Adkins*, *The Survey* pointed out that "the very same reasoning that insisted that Willie Lyons should be permitted to work at any wage she could freely exact from her employer, comes in to permit Robert T. Meyer to teach German to any one in Nebraska, or elsewhere, who will employ him."[34] Two years later, during the pendency of *Pierce*, *The Survey* predicted with some prescience that "the determining argument for the unconstitutionality of the intolerant law will not be found in the right of the people to have the kind of education they want, but in the right of owners of property to have the use of that property for their own purposes. . . . So, property rights may, once again, prove to be the substantial support of threatened human rights."[35]

Similarly, Felix Frankfurter acknowledged in 1925 that the results in *Meyer* and *Pierce* were "cause for rejoicing," but he warned that "a heavy price must be paid for these occasional services to liberalism" since the very doctrine that had served in *Meyer* and *Pierce* as a shield against socially repressive legislation could continue to be used as a sword against what Frankfurter viewed as economically progressive legislation. Frankfurter believed that the benefits of using the doctrine of substantive due process to invalidate socially intolerant legislation were not worth the price of allowing the same doctrine to be used against economic legislation. Frankfurter further cautioned that *Meyer* and *Pierce* did not even provide unalloyed protection for personal liberties. *Pierce*'s acknowledgment of the need for the schools to inculcate values of good citizenship might provide "ample room for the patrioteers to roll in their Trojan horses." Frankfurter explained that liberals should remain mindful that "the real battles of liberalism are not won in the Supreme Court." Since the Court ultimately reflected general public opinion, Frankfurter concluded, "Only a persistent, positive translation of the liberal faith into the thoughts and acts of the community is the real reliance against the unabated temptation to straightjacket the human mind."[36]

Recognizing the fragility of federal judicial protection of the rights of parochial schools, many Roman Catholics preferred to seek their ultimate protection at the state level, even though it was the states that had enacted the hostile legislation. Despite their belief that *Meyer* had struck a fatal blow at compulsory public education laws, some Roman Catholics called for a campaign to amend state constitutions to include provisions that would forever protect the rights of parents to send their children to parochial schools.[37] The Supreme Court's emergence as the principal guardian of personal liberties during the mid-twentieth century may have made these efforts to seek refuge in state law seem odd in retrospect. In the 1980s and 1990s, however, the Court's retreat from its earlier civil libertarianism has prompted renewed recognition of the possibilities of using state law to protect human rights.[38] Even the result of the Court's decision in *Meyer* was not universally acclaimed by liberal opinion. Labor and progressive journals that had so often assailed the Court for its invalidation of social and economic legislation were largely silent about *Meyer*. The ruling was condemned by some prominent educators who contended that it would inhibit the development of a uniform American culture and would retard the spread of republican virtue and democratic values.[39]

Although *Meyer* and *Pierce* seem to form a missing link between substantive due process and incorporation, it is not clear to what extent the Court relied on those decisions in the line of cases, beginning with *Gitlow*, in which it began to incorporate into state law the specific guarantees of the Bill of

Rights.[40] In *Gitlow*, the Court did not cite *Meyer* or *Pierce* or any other decision in support of its famous declaration that it would assume that freedoms of press and speech are among the liberties that the Fourteenth Amendment protects against state infringement. The Court did, however, cite *Meyer* and several other decisions, including *Gilbert*, in support of its statement that its "incidental statement" to the contrary in *Prudential* was not determinative of the question of whether the Fourteenth Amendment protects free speech from infringement by states.[41]

The Court did not even mention *Meyer* and *Pierce* in later decisions between 1927 and 1931 that confirmed that freedoms of speech and the press are within the liberties protected by the Fourteenth Amendment. During this period, however, the Court cited *Meyer* in several other decisions as a precedent in support of economic due process.[42] Despite the dearth of citations to *Meyer* in the Court's early incorporation decisions, *Meyer* provided an impetus for the emergence of incorporation: the Court recognized that it could use the Fourteenth Amendment as a means of vindicating personal rights, and the decision contained language and reasoning that supported the incorporation of the First Amendment into state law. *Meyer* therefore may be seen as a Janus-faced decision that uses concepts borrowed from the old doctrine of economic due process to create a new theory of personal freedoms. Although the Court in the years immediately following *Meyer* and *Pierce* did not explicitly acknowledge the importance of those decisions in moving it toward a more civil libertarian position, it began to use the education decisions as civil liberties precedents shortly after the demise of substantive economic due process in 1937. In his fecund *Carolene Products* footnote in 1938, Justice Harlan Fiske Stone cited *Meyer, Bartels*, and *Farrington* in support of his suggestion that the Court might exercise a high level of scrutiny in reviewing statutes directed at particular national groups, and he cited *Pierce* as an example of the way in which the Court might specially scrutinize legislation that was directed at a particular religion.[43] Stone's footnote presaged the emergence of the federal judiciary's modern role in protecting "discrete and insular" minorities that are unable to protect themselves through the normal political process.

The Court in recent decades has continued to cite those decisions as wellsprings of constitutional theory. As Laurence H. Tribe has observed, *Meyer* and *Pierce* "have remained durable and fertile sources of constitutional doctrine concerning the nature of liberty, the respective rights of social institutions, and the limits of governmental power to homogenize the beliefs and attitudes of the populace."[44]

In most of their civil liberties decisions since *Meyer* and *Pierce,* the courts have not needed to cite the parochial school decisions because they have been able to find that most rights are protected by specific provisions of the Bill of Rights. Similarly, in cases involving race relations, courts generally have been able to rely on the equal protection clause of the Fourteenth Amendment in invalidating racial discrimination. Even in decisions in which the Supreme Court has protected rights that are not specifically enumerated in the Bill of Rights, the Court until 1965 did not cite the school cases inasmuch as it was able to find various analogous provisions in the Bill of Rights on which to base those rights.

In 1965, however, the Supreme Court cited *Meyer* in its landmark decision in *Griswold v. Connecticut,* which overturned the conviction of a physician and a Planned Parenthood official who had recommended contraceptives to married persons in Connecticut, where a statute prohibited the use of contraceptives.[45] Unable to find any specific provision in the Bill of Rights that protected the dissemination of birth control information, the Court resurrected substantive due process to strike down the conviction under the Fourteenth Amendment. Explaining that the specific provisions of the Bill of Rights cast shadows that protect other more general rights, Justice Douglas's opinion cited *Meyer* in support of his proposition that a state may not restrict the spectrum of available knowledge. Without peripheral rights that are incident to the specific rights of the Bill of Rights, Douglas declared, "the specific rights would be less secure. And so we reaffirm the principle of the *Pierce* and the *Meyer* cases."[46]

The *Griswold* decision presaged the Supreme Court's decision eight years later in *Roe v. Wade,* which declared that a state could not prohibit abortion prior to viability. In *Roe,* the Court cited *Meyer* in support of its contention that a right to privacy may be inferred from the concept of liberty guaranteed in the Fourteenth Amendment. *Roe v. Wade* marked the high-water mark of judicial reliance on *Meyer,* since the Court based its decision explicitly on the doctrine of substantive due process and relied heavily on *Meyer* and *Pierce*. The Court also cited *Meyer* as a substantive due process precedent in *Carey v. Population Services,* its later decision limiting restrictions on the sale and advertising of contraceptives.[47] As recently as 1986, the Court cited *Meyer* and *Pierce* in striking down a state statute that restricted the availability of abortion.[48] The use of those decisions as precedents in that instance troubled Justice Byron White, who noted in dissent that abortion involves a unique moral issue, "different in kind from the others that the Court has protected under the rubric of personal or family privacy and autonomy."[49]

Similarly, legal scholars have questioned the extent to which *Meyer* and *Pierce* should serve as precedents in cases involving questions that stray far beyond the rights that the Court protected in those decisions. John Hart Ely has complained, for example, that the Court "has offered little assistance to one's understanding of what it is that makes all this a unit." Ely points out that "there's no trick to finding some connections" among the subjects of marriage, procreation, contraception, family relationships, childrearing, and education, since the *Meyer* and *Pierce* decisions about where to send one's children to school "do bear some faint resemblance to decisions whether to have children at all, and that has something to do with marriage . . . and so forth"; he believes, however, that "a constitutional connection" between *Meyer* and *Carey* "should require something more than this."[50]

With the retreat of the Court in recent years from its earlier intimations of a right to privacy, judicial reliance on *Meyer* has decreased. In recent decisions, the Court has rejected invitations to use *Meyer* and *Pierce* to expand the vistas of personal liberties. In its landmark decision in 1986 upholding Georgia's antisodomy law, for example, the Court explicitly stated that the court of appeals had improperly cited *Meyer* in support of its extension of the right of privacy to protect consensual homosexual sodomy. Although the Court reaffirmed its agreement with the decision in *Meyer,* it declared that *Meyer* did not provide support for the invalidation of the Georgia law. The Court explained, "No connection between family, marriage, or procreation on the one hand and homosexual activity on the other has been demonstrated."[51]

In reaffirming the validity of *Roe* in their opinion for the Court in the more recent *Casey* decision, Justices Sandra Day O'Connor, Anthony M. Kennedy, and David H. Souter cited *Pierce* and *Meyer* in support of their contention that "the Constitution places limits on a State's right to interfere with a person's most basic decisions about family and parenthood."[52] In arguing that *Roe* should be overruled, four justices averred that the "Court in *Roe* reached too far when it analogized the right to abort a fetus to the rights" that were involved in *Pierce* and *Meyer*.[53]

Although the vitality of *Meyer* and *Pierce* has waned in cases in which political liberals have challenged governmental infringement on alleged rights, conservatives continue to find *Meyer* and *Pierce* useful in defending the traditional values that were involved in those cases. The Court relied on *Meyer* and *Pierce,* for example, in its 1972 decision that held that compulsory high school attendance laws violated the religious freedom of Amish families.[54] David M. Smolin has argued that "*Meyer* and its progeny, properly understood, support the destruction, rather then the recognition, of abortion and autonomy rights" insofar as those decisions were based on natural law, embodied in common law, that acknowledged "the primacy of the family in relation to the state."[55]

Barbara Bennett Woodhouse, however, recently has criticized *Meyer* and *Pierce* for aggrandizing private rights at the expense of community values and "constitutionalizing a patriarchal notion of parental rights" that "interrupted the trend of family law moving toward children's rights."[56]

The legacy of the parochial school decisions is therefore constantly changing. Having originally provided a justification for preventing undue state interference with parochial schools, the decisions helped to build a bridge between the old due process and the new due process and anticipated the incorporation of the Bill of Rights into state law. The decisions later were the basis for the reemergence of a constitutional right to privacy. With the ebbing of the privacy doctrine, the decisions retain vitality in the area of parental rights and provide a context for the discussion of recent attempts to make English an official language and to require the use of English in certain public places. Although judicial interpretations of *Meyer* and *Pierce* no doubt will continue to change as the Constitution evolves, *Meyer*'s recognition that "the individual has certain fundamental rights which must be respected" by the state under the Fourteenth Amendment seems likely to endure.

Epilogue

The educational controversies that created so much tension in American life between 1917 and 1927 demonstrate both the fragility and the resiliency of civil liberties in the United States. The proposals and enactments of legislation to interfere with private and parochial education provide a potent reminder that ethnic and cultural animosities are never far from the surface of America's highly heterogeneous society and that majoritarian tyranny arising from those tensions is a constant threat in a democracy. The refusal of voters and legislators to enact more extreme measures, however, is a tribute to the tolerance and self-restraint that has characterized the American polity. Moreover, the Supreme Court's nullification of those measures provides one of the finest examples of how the American judiciary can protect minorities against hostile legislators and individuals. And the prevention of state intrusions on the sanctity of familial relationships in the Court's trilogy of school decisions between 1923 and 1927 provided new and fertile definitions of the scope of the principles of limited government on which the Constitution is based.

The disputes out of which the parochial school cases arose seem in many ways remote and archaic, since the assimilation of German Americans, Lutherans, and Roman Catholics into the mainstream of American life now is virtually complete. Although nearly one-quarter of today's Americans can trace at least part of their ancestry to Germany, a self-consciously German-American community has ceased to exist outside a few remote corners of the United States. In an age when the vestiges of German ethnicity are confined to such innocuous forms as the Oktoberfest, it is easy to forget that German Americans not so very long ago constituted a politically potent and culturally aggressive community that was envied, feared, and resented by many Anglo-Americans.

Although the one-quarter of Americans who are Roman Catholic make up a vital and highly visible community, most Catholics have become so politically, economically, socially, and geographically integrated into American society that they no longer appear distinctive to most Protestants, much less exotic or threatening. The primary distinction between Catholics and Protestants today is religious rather than cultural, and the growth of ecumenicism and secularism has eroded the significance even of this difference. Accordingly, the anxieties of the Protestant majority about the Roman Catholic minority have long since receded, until organized anti-Catholicism has virtually disappeared in all but the most outré of extremist groups. In an age in which nativist anxiety has become concentrated on the growing nonwhite population, most nativist organizations have gone so far as to welcome white Catholics into their fold and some Catholics have responded to the invitation. Similarly, the pietistic Anglo-American Protestants who traditionally were among the most bitter antagonists of the Roman Catholics have found that their Catholic brethren are effective allies in their ongoing struggle against secularism.

Because the cultural antagonisms that led to the assaults on ethnic Americans and their parochial schools after the First World War are largely forgotten, the intensity of the controversies over the rights of parents and parochial schools that culminated in *Meyer, Pierce,* and *Farrington* may be difficult to comprehend fully. Any proposal today for the virtual abolition of private and parochial elementary schools would thoroughly shock prevailing sensibilities, and most Americans probably would be amazed to learn that such legislation was enacted during their own century in one state and seriously considered in at least two others.

Memories of the school controversies also may have faded because the injustices that were perpetrated against ethnic Americans during and after the First World War pale beside the much longer and more egregious history of injustices to African Americans. Moreover, the internment of West Coast Japanese Americans during World War II provides a more recent and more compelling example of racial and ethnic injustice during wartime. And the assaults on ethnic Americans during the First World War era are not remotely comparable to the atrocities later perpetrated in other lands by Nazis and Communists.

But even though ethnic Americans were not killed, displaced, enslaved, or disenfranchised, the indignities that they suffered at the hands of the as-similationists of the late 1910s and early 1920s were acute and often poignant. They are worth recalling for their own sake, for we should honor the memory of those Americans who suffered humiliation and deprivations, however involuntarily, for the sake of their culture and religion.

The history of the school controversies has more than an antiquarian significance, however, since the antagonisms that animated the controversies arose out of human proclivities that will not disappear. As one commentator observed shortly after the Supreme Court handed down its decision in *Pierce*, the issues responsible for the enactment of the Oregon and Nebraska laws would remain "dynamic forces in the life of the community. They are as old as civilization; they probably will survive in one guise or another as long as the race survives."[1] Or, as Albert Camus observed at the end of *The Plague*, "the plague bacillus never dies or disappears for good."[2]

The animosities that led to the assault on ethnic Americans and their parochial schools, however remote and even quaint they may seem today, continue to exist in different forms. Although there is little hostility against Catholics or their schools per se, there is intense controversy over public aid to parochial schools, and anxieties about Roman Catholic political power are not far from the surface of the bitter controversy over abortion. The widespread concern about the growing use of the Spanish language is reminiscent of the fears of earlier generations of Anglo-Americans, who worried that the proliferation of xenophonic aliens would reduce English-speaking persons to strangers in their native land.

The parochial school controversies and other cultural conflicts have been in part the product of blind bigotry, but a careful examination of any clash of cultures is likely to reveal the interplay of complex and often ambiguous forces. Although the movements to interfere with parochial education partly demonstrate the virulence and menace of the new strain of ethnic and religious animosities that swept through the United States during the 1920s, it would be a mistake to dismiss the antiparochial movements as no more than a manifestation of bigotry. As the advocates of parochial education shrewdly perceived, many of the attempts to restrict private and parochial schools were motivated by a reforming impulse that was characteristic of the progressive movement. Like their nineteenth-century counterparts, the reformers of the early twentieth century properly recognized that education was the cornerstone of democracy. Their faith in the public school as the only effective agent of transmitting American ideals, though ultimately misplaced, is not so inexplicable or sinister if put in the context of the early twentieth century rather than measured by the standards of today.

Anglo-Americans of the early twentieth century naturally were suspicious of alternatives to public education, since the principal alternative so often was no education at all. In an age when some states still lacked compulsory education laws and many lacked effective truancy laws, it is not surprising that reformers tended to believe that compulsory public schooling was the only effective means of ensuring that each child received an education. Reformers were particularly resistant to any effort that might weaken the extension of universal public education, for millions of children still remained outside school to loiter in the streets or to toil in factories and on farms. Fears that the parochial schools detracted from the public schools likewise were not unfounded. The high and growing enrollments in parochial schools in rural areas sometimes did threaten the viability of local public schools. Although the more cosmopolitan Anglo-Americans recognized that parochial schools provided an education for children who otherwise might have no education, many other Americans feared that parochial schools warped ethnic children and would contribute to the decline and possibly even the demise of public education. Here again, these apprehensions were not irrational even if they ultimately were groundless.

Americans who had little knowledge or understanding of Continental traditions naturally feared that the transmission of ethnic cultures in parochial schools would perpetuate the attitudes that kept much of Europe mired in poverty and political tyranny and infuse those attitudes into the mainstream of American life. In rural areas in the Middle West in which ethnics were heavily concentrated, Anglo-Americans particularly worried that their way of life was threatened by unassimilated immigrants. They correctly questioned how ethnic children could develop job skills and a patriotic attitude when they attended shabby schools taught by teachers who knew little about American life and failed to learn the English language. Although not all parochial schools suffered from these deficiencies, until the 1920s many were inferior to public schools. The rising standards of the parochial schools, their willingness to teach the common subjects in English, and their acquiescence to inspection by public authorities went far toward eroding support for compulsory public education.

The school controversies illustrate how various components of the nation's constitutional system—including individual citizens, legislators, executive officials, and the courts—may cooperate in ameliorating the antagonisms that arise out of cultural differences. The manner in which such a broadly defined constitutional system helped to resolve the tension between the interests of the states and the special needs of minority groups likewise demonstrates how the system may accommodate both unity and diversity. The same democratic system that at first produced a real threat of majoritarian derogation of the fundamental rights of minorities ultimately operated to protect those rights. Most proponents of Americanization and advocates of the preservation of ethnic culture eventually agreed that democratic values and ethnicity were not mutually exclusive. In most states, voters and legislators were willing to allow parochial schools to teach distinctive cultural and religious beliefs if the schools would conform to the pedagogical standards and political orthodoxy of the public schools. In those states in which the political system was unwilling to make this accommodation, the Supreme Court imposed this balance as a matter of law after weighing the competing interests of the state and the private schools.

The school controversies also illustrate how persecuted or otherwise disadvantaged social groups may try to protect their existing rights or establish new rights. Each minority group that opposed parochial school legislation needed to initiate highly organized and expensive campaigns that enlisted the support of other minority groups and significant segments of the Anglo-American majority. Actively opposing anti–parochial school measures at the legislative, judicial, and electoral levels, the minorities suffered many temporary setbacks but ultimately prevailed.

The success of this political activism demonstrated the folly of the political passivity advocated by many prominent leaders of the German-American and Japanese-American communities, who were unduly loath to offend Anglo-Americans. Parochial school advocates had to take affirmative action to protect their own interests, for they would have waited in vain for the majority to intercede on their behalf. The history of the parochial school struggle shows that activists within a majority group may be all too willing to ignore or impugn the rights of minorities. Passivity almost certainly would have ensured the triumph of hostile legislation in many states. The success of the opposition depended on brave individuals such as Robert T. Meyer, and bold organizations such as the Japanese language schools, who were willing to defy the law and initiate legal challenges despite the reluctance of many members of their communities to act.

While the history of the parochial school struggle demonstrates that minority groups must initiate action to protect their own rights, it also shows the effectiveness of organized campaigns to protect those rights. Although the advocates of parochial education won their ultimate victory in the United States Supreme Court, they attracted a remarkable degree of support at other political levels, persuading a broad spectrum of their fellow citizens of the justice of their cause. The editors of *America,* acknowledging that opposition to compulsory public education was motivated in part by tax considerations, believed that "the people's sense of justice and liberty was the leading factor" in the defeat of the 1920 Michigan initiative.[3] Likewise, they recognized that the defeat of parochial school measures in Michigan and Washington in 1924 "was due largely to our fair-minded non-Catholic fellow-citizens."[4] The stillborn campaigns for compulsory public education in other states were a similar tribute to the majority's sense of fairness and its willingness to be persuaded by parochial school advocates who explained the public benefits of nonpublic education and the significant constitutional dimensions of the struggle against public education. Officials in various states mitigated the harshness of measures affecting parochial education after proponents lobbied for their schools. Martin Graebner correctly discerned that legislators were amenable to the arguments of parochial school advocates, and even the bigoted Governor Harding of Iowa was willing to relax the enforcement of his language edict in response to personal appeals by patriotic clerics. As Theodore Graebner pointed out, the very existence of German-language schools during wartime testified to America's tolerance of diversity.

The sophistication and complexity of the opposition to the campaigns against the parochial schools make it clear that appeals for judicial protection of rights ordinarily will be effective only when public attitudes already have created a social and political environment that is receptive to the vindication of such rights. Although the Supreme Court often has been the agent of profound social change, it never has initiated any great social movement. The decisions in the parochial school cases were possible only because ethnic Americans had successfully convinced a large segment of Anglo-Americans of the salutary character of parochial education. Even so, the willingness of the lower courts to uphold the language laws and the dissents of Justices Holmes and Sutherland on the Supreme Court provide a sharp reminder that the outcome of the *Meyer* case was by no means a foregone conclusion, particularly since the Court previously had demonstrated little inclination to protect human rights against infringement by states. And if *Meyer* had been decided differently, the Court might not have ruled as it did in *Pierce* or *Farrington*. The Court's decisions reflected a growing public acceptance of ethnic Americans, even though these rulings were handed down at a time when nativism seemed to be on the rise. They also reflected a growing public revulsion against governmental intrusion in the personal lives of Americans. But they were not inevitable.

The preservation of the liberties granted by these decisions likewise is not inevitable. Although the Court's declaration that "the individual has certain fundamental rights which must be respected" is likely to endure for as long as America is a free society, the interpretation and form of such rights will depend on persons and institutions that will fight for their rights as courageously as did the opponents of the parochial school laws.

Notes

Introduction

1. *One Hundredth Anniversary, 1873–1973, Zion Evangelical Lutheran Church* (privately published by Zion Church, 1973), pp. 4, 6, 8, 10, 34–38.

2. Ibid., pp. 6, 36.

3. *Zion Lutheran Church Records, 1875–1976,* series 3, vol. 2, *Minutes, 1876–1969* (hereinafter cited as *Minutes*), p. 57 (minutes of meeting of July 7, 1918); author's interview with Clarence Heiden, Hampton, Nebraska, June 27, 1990; author's interview with Raymond Parpart, Hampton, Nebraska, June 27, 1990.

4. *Minutes,* pp. 53–54 (record of the annual meeting, 1918).

5. *Meyer v. Nebraska,* 262 U.S. 390 (1923), *Record* (hereinafter cited as *Record*), pp. 19–20, 33 (testimony of C. F. Brommer), 24–25 (testimony of Raymond Parpart); *Minutes,* p. 78 (minutes of church council meeting of Jan. 5, 1920).

6. Heiden interview.

7. Parpart interview; *Record,* pp. 21–23 (testimony of Raymond Parpart), 25–26 (testimony of Arthur S. Nelson), 29–31 (testimony of Frank E. Edgerton).

8. Arthur F. Mullen, *Western Democrat* (New York: Funk, 1940), p. 218. These and the following quotations from Meyer are based on the recollections of Mullen, Meyer's attorney, nearly two decades after Meyer made the remarks to Mullen. Although Mullen's autobiography places Meyer's statements in quotation marks, the statements probably lack literal accuracy.

9. Heiden interview.

10. Parpart interview; *Record,* p. 30 (testimony of Frank E. Edgerton); *Grand Island Independent,* Jan. 3, 1988.

11. Mullen, *Western Democrat,* p. 218.

12. *Minutes,* pp. 81–82 (minutes of church council meeting of May 30, 1920).

13. "Found Guilty of Teaching German, Gets Fine of $25," *Lincoln Daily Star*, June 30, 1920, p. 9, col. 5.

14. "Minutes of Quarterly Meeting," Oct. 12, 1919, *Minutes*, p. 72.

15. Mullen, *Western Democrat*, p. 218.

16. Parpart interview.

17. Ibid.

18. *Record*, p. 33 (testimony of C. F. Brommer).

Chapter 1

1. David Tyack, Thomas James, and Aaron Benavot, *Law and the Shaping of Public Education, 1785–1954* (Madison: University of Wisconsin Press, 1987), pp. 23–25.

2. Alexis de Tocqueville, *Democracy in America*, vol. 1 (New York: Knopf, 1945), p. 54; Arnold Schrier and Joyce Story, eds., *A Russian Looks at America: The Journey of Aleksandr Borisovich Lakier in 1857* (Chicago: University of Chicago Press, 1979), pp. 34–43, 75–76; James Bryce, *The American Commonwealth* (London: Macmillan, 1891), vol. 1, 2d ed., pp. 443–44, 585, 588; vol. 2, p. 617.

3. 347 U.S. 483 (1954).

4. *Engel v. Vitale*, 370 U.S. 421 (1962); *Abington School District v. Schempp*, 374 U.S. 203 (1963).

5. Lawrence A. Cremin, *American Education: The Colonial Experience, 1607–1783* (New York: Harper & Row, 1970), p. 177.

6. Ibid., pp. 176, 183.

7. Ibid., p. 183.

8. Lloyd P. Jorgenson, *The State and the Non-Public School, 1825–1925* (Columbia: University of Missouri Press, 1987), pp. 4–9.

9. Carl F. Kaestle, *Pillars of the Republic: Common Schools and American Society, 1780–1860* (New York: Hill & Wang, 1983), p. 91.

10. Tyack, James, and Benavot, *Law and the Shaping of Public Education*, p. 28.

11. Oscar Handlin, "Education and the European Immigrant, 1820–1920," in Bernard J. Weiss, ed., *American Education and the European Immigrant: 1840–1940* (Urbana: University of Illinois Press, 1982), p. 8.

12. Tyack, James, and Benavot, *Law and the Shaping of Public Education*, pp. 20–42.

13. Jorgenson, *State and the Non-Public School*, pp. 21–22.

14. Kaestle, *Pillars of the Republic*, p. 79 (quotation) and pp. 75–103 passim.

15. Lawrence A. Cremin, *American Education: The National Experience, 1783–1876* (New York: Harper & Row, 1980), pp. 50–73.

16. Harold A. Buetow, *Of Singular Benefit: The Story of Catholic Education in the United States* (New York: Macmillan, 1970), pp. 1–43; Glen Gabert, *In Hoc Signo? A Brief History of Catholic Parochial Education in America* (Port Washington, New York: Kennikat Press, 1973), pp. 3–10.

17. Daniel F. Reilly, *The School Controversy (1891–1893)* (Washington, D.C.: Catholic University of America Press, 1943), pp. 4–6.

18. Ibid., pp. 12–18, 20–22.

19. Raymond B. Culver, *Horace Mann and Religion in the Massachusetts Public Schools* (New Haven: Yale University Press, 1929), pp. 236–37.

20. F. Michael Perko, "The Building Up of Zion: Religion and Education in Nineteenth-Century Cincinnati," *Cincinnati Historical Society Bulletin* 38 (Summer 1980): 99.

21. Neil G. McCluskey, "America and the Catholic School," in Neil G. McCluskey, *Catholic Education in America: A Documentary History* (New York: Bureau of Publications, Teachers College, Columbia University, 1964), pp. 5–6, 12–13, 19–20; Gabert, *In Hoc Signo?* p. 31; David B. Tyack, *The One Best System: A History of American Urban Education* (Cambridge: Harvard University Press, 1974), pp. 85–86.

22. Gabert, *In Hoc Signo?* pp. 23–24; Perko, "Building Up of Zion," pp. 99–110; Jorgenson, *State and the Non-Public School,* pp. 76–83.

23. Selwyn K. Troen, *The Public and the Schools: Shaping the St. Louis System, 1838–1920* (Columbia: University of Missouri Press, 1975), pp. 42, 44.

24. Ibid., pp. 52–53.

25. Gabert, *In Hoc Signo?* pp. 20, 41.

26. Francis X. Curran, *The Churches and the Schools: American Protestantism and Popular Elementary Education* (Chicago: Loyola University Press, 1954), p. 85; James W. Sanders, *The Education of an Urban Minority: Catholics in Chicago, 1833–1965* (New York: Oxford University Press, 1977), pp. 18–19.

27. See John Higham, *Strangers in the Land: Patterns of American Nativism, 1860–1925,* 2d ed. (New Brunswick, N.J.: Rutgers University Press, 1988), p. 24; Kaestle, *Pillars of the Republic,* p. 95.

28. Carl F. Kaestle, *The Evolution of an Urban School System: New York City, 1750–1850* (Cambridge: Harvard University Press, 1973), pp. 141–42.

29. George M. Stephenson, *A History of American Immigration, 1820–1924* (New York: 1926; repr. Russell & Russell, 1964), p. 101.

30. Handlin, "Education and the European Immigrant," p. 8.

31. John Daniels, *America via the Neighborhood* (New York: Harper & Brothers, 1920), pp. 249–50.

32. Frederick C. Luebke, *Immigrants and Politics: The Germans of Nebraska, 1880–*

1900 (Lincoln: University of Nebraska Press, 1969), p. 46; Kaestle, *Pillars of the Republic,* pp. 163–64.

33. Kaestle, *Evolution of an Urban School System,* p. 153; Tyack, *One Best System,* pp. 84–85; Jorgenson, *State and the Non-Public School,* pp. 66–67.

34. Sanders, *Education of an Urban Minority,* p. 26, quoting *New World,* Aug. 11, 1906, pp. 3, 4.

35. Gabert, *In Hoc Signo?* p. 22; Tyack, *One Best System,* pp. 84–86; Jorgenson, *State and the Non-Public School,* pp. 60–67; Kaestle, *Evolution of an Urban School System,* pp. 153–54.

36. Sanders, *Education of an Urban Minority,* pp. 28–29, 130–32.

37. Ibid., p. 37.

38. Cremin, *American Education: The National Experience,* pp. 166–69; Troen, *Public and the Schools,* pp. 41, 43.

39. Cremin, *American Education: The National Experience,* p. 169.

40. Ibid., pp. 45–47.

41. Lawrence A. Cremin, *American Education: The Metropolitan Experience, 1876–1980* (New York: Harper & Row, 1988), pp. 134–35.

42. Ibid., pp. 128–29, 134.

43. Gabert, *In Hoc Signo?* pp. 48–52.

44. Ibid., pp. 53–54; Buetow, *Of Singular Benefit,* pp. 151–53.

45. Gabert, *In Hoc Signo?* pp. 56–58.

46. McCluskey, *Catholic Education in America,* p. 25; Cremin, *American Education: The Metropolitan Experience,* p. 551.

47. Henry Pratt Fairchild, *Immigration: A World Movement and Its American Significance* (New York: Macmillan, 1913), pp. 269–73.

48. Gabert, *In Hoc Signo?* pp. 60–61; Cremin, *American Education: The Metropolitan Experience,* pp. 130–32.

49. McCluskey, *Catholic Education in America,* pp. 9–11.

50. Lewis J. Sherrill, *Presbyterian Parochial Schools, 1846–1870* (New Haven: Yale University Press, 1932; New York: Arno Press, 1969), pp. 1–6, 46–51, 56–64, 67–68, 73–82, 174–82; Jorgenson, *State and the Non-Public School,* pp. 108–10; Curran, *Churches and the Schools,* pp. 28–36.

51. *Brief Amici Curiae on Behalf of the Domestic and Foreign Missionary Society of the Protestant Episcopal Church, Pierce v. Society of Sisters,* 268 U.S. 510 (1925), pp. 2–3.

52. Walter H. Beck, *Lutheran Elementary Schools in the United States,* 2d ed. (St. Louis: Concordia Publishing House, 1965), p. 10.

53. Ibid., pp. 10 n. 14, 25–48; Gabert, *In Hoc Signo?* pp. 25, 31.

54. The Lutheran Church—Missouri Synod, organized in Missouri in 1847, is a

nationwide denomination that today is the second largest Lutheran body in the United States. It was known as the German Evangelical Lutheran Church of Missouri, Ohio and Other States until 1917. The word "German" was dropped in 1917, and the denomination has been known by its present name since 1947.

55. Beck, *Lutheran Elementary Schools,* pp. 101–18, 175–77. See also August C. Stellhorn, *Schools of the Lutheran Church—Missouri Synod* (St. Louis: Concordia Publishing House, 1963), pp. 116–18, 172–77.

56. James S. Hamre, "Norwegian Immigrants Respond to the Common School: A Case Study of American Values and the Lutheran Tradition," *Church History* 50 (Sept. 1981): 302–15; Frank C. Nelsen, "The School Controversy among Norwegian Immigrants," *Norwegian-American Studies* 26 (1974): 206–19.

57. Nelsen, "School Controversy," p. 217.

58. Beck, *Lutheran Elementary Schools,* pp. 136–43.

59. Hamre, "Norwegian Immigrants," pp. 312–15.

60. Beck, *Lutheran Elementary Schools,* p. 223.

61. Troen, *Public and the Schools,* pp. 55–56.

62. Kathleen Neils Conzen, *Immigrant Milwaukee, 1836–1860: Accommodation and Community in a Frontier City* (Cambridge: Harvard University Press, 1976), pp. 181–82.

63. Hyman B. Grinstein, *The Rise of the Jewish Community of New York, 1654–1860* (Philadelphia: Jewish Publication Society of America, 1945), pp. 228, 234–35, 238, 240; Nathan H. Winter, *Jewish Education in a Pluralist Society: Samson Benderly and Jewish Education in the United States* (New York: New York University Press, 1966), pp. 3–6; Seymour Fromer, "In the Colonial Period," in Judah Pilch, ed., *A History of Jewish Education in America* (New York: National Curriculum Research Institute of the American Association for Jewish Education, 1969), pp. 5–23.

64. Grinstein, *Rise of the Jewish Community,* pp. 244–45; Jeremiah J. Berman, "Jewish Education in New York City, 1860–1900," *YIVO Annual of Jewish Social Studies* 9 (1954): 247–48.

65. Hyman B. Grinstein, "In the Course of the Nineteenth Century," in Pilch, *History of Jewish Education,* pp. 37–38; Berman, "Jewish Education in New York City," pp. 253–60; Stephan F. Brumberg, *Going to America, Going to School: The Jewish Immigrant Public School Encounter in Turn-of-the-Century New York City* (New York: Praeger, 1986), pp. 62–65.

66. Brumberg, *Going to America,* pp. 68–69.

67. Selma Cantor Berrol, *Immigrants at School: New York City, 1898–1914* (New York: Arno Press, 1978), pp. 75–142.

68. Winter, *Jewish Education in a Pluralist Society,* pp. 18, 21, 23–24; Meir Ben-

Horin, "From the Turn of the Century to the Late Thirties," in Pilch, *History of Jewish Education,* pp. 56–59, 68.

69. Berrol, *Immigrants at School,* p. 61; Leonard Dinnerstein, "Education and the Advancement of American Jews," in Weiss, *American Education and the European Immigrant,* pp. 49–50.

70. Ben-Horin, "From the Turn of the Century," p. 83.

71. Ibid., pp. 67–70; Berman, "Jewish Education in New York City," pp. 258–75; Winter, *Jewish Education in a Pluralist Society,* pp. 16–23.

72. Judah Pilch, "From the Early Forties to the Mid-Sixties," in Pilch, *History of Jewish Education,* pp. 121, 142.

73. Tyack, James, and Benavot, *Law and the Shaping of Public Education,* p. 14.

74. Higham, *Strangers in the Land,* pp. 59–60.

75. Tyack, James, and Benavot, *Law and the Shaping of Public Education,* pp. 93–96, 171–73, 124–25, 178.

76. Robert T. Handy, *A Christian America: Protestant Hopes and Historical Realities* (New York: Oxford University Press, 1971), pp. 101–5.

77. Tyack, *One Best System,* pp. 107–8; Frederick C. Luebke, "Legal Restrictions on Foreign Languages in the Great Plains States, 1917–1923," in Paul Schach, ed., *Languages in Conflict* (Lincoln: University of Nebraska Press, 1980), pp. 1–2; Heinz Kloss, "German Language Maintenance Efforts," in Joshua A. Fishman, ed., *Language Loyalty in the United States* (The Hague: Mouton, 1966), p. 235.

78. Kloss, "German Language Maintenance Efforts."

79. Troen, *Public and the Schools,* pp. 67–73.

80. Steven L. Schlossman, "Is There an American Tradition of Bilingual Education? German in the Public Elementary Schools, 1840–1919," *American Journal of Education* 91 (Feb. 1983): 157.

81. Schlossman, "Is There an American Tradition of Bilingual Education?" pp. 145, 150–51, 152–53, 156, 170; Troen, *Public and the Schools,* pp. 60, 61–63, 67.

82. Troen, *Public and the Schools,* pp. 64–65.

83. Ibid., pp. 66, 71.

84. Kloss, "German Language Maintenance Efforts," pp. 236.

85. Fairchild, *Immigration,* pp. 410–11.

86. Luebke, "Legal Restrictions on Foreign Languages," p. 2.

87. Kloss, "German Language Maintenance Efforts," p. 236; Troen, *Public and the Schools,* pp. 75–77.

88. Paul Kleppner, *The Cross of Culture: A Social Analysis of Midwestern Politics, 1850–1900* (New York: Free Press, 1970), p. 78.

89. Perko, "Building Up of Zion," p. 99.

90. *Congressional Record,* 44th Cong., 1st Sess. (Dec. 7, 1875) 4:175.

91. Donald Bruce Johnson, ed., *National Party Platforms, Vol. 1: 1840–1956* (Urbana: University of Illinois, 1978), p. 54.

92. Higham, *Strangers in the Land,* p. 29.

93. Committee on State School Systems, "Compulsory Education," *National Educational Association Journal of Proceedings and Addresses* (1891): 295–96.

94. Jorgenson, *State and the Non-Public School,* pp. 146–58. See also Higham, *Strangers in the Land,* pp. 35–60.

95. Jorgenson, *State and the Non-Public School,* pp. 159–86.

96. Stellhorn, *Schools of the Lutheran Church—Missouri Synod,* pp. 236–38.

97. Charles Shanabruch, "The Repeal of the Edwards Law: A Study of Religion and Ethnicity in Illinois Politics," *Ethnicity* 7 (Sept. 1980): 315–16.

98. *Lutheran Witness,* June 21, 1890, p. 13; *ibid.,* Nov. 21, 1890, p. 92; ibid., Mar. 7, 1891, pp. 145–46; Stellhorn, *Schools of the Lutheran Church—Missouri Synod,* pp. 238–45.

99. Luebke, "Legal Restrictions on Foreign Languages," p. 3.

100. Shanabruch, "Repeal of the Edwards Law," pp. 316–28; Beck, *Lutheran Elementary Schools,* pp. 245–47.

101. Beck, *Lutheran Elementary Schools,* pp. 317–18.

102. J. C. Ruppenthal, "English and Other Languages under American Statutes," *American Law Review* 54 (Jan./Feb. 1920): 65–78.

103. Donald Lewis Zelman, "Oregon's Compulsory Education Bill of 1922" (Master's thesis, University of Oregon, 1964), p. 8.

104. Higham, *Strangers in the Land,* p. 86.

105. Fairchild, *Immigration,* p. 410.

106. Higham, *Strangers in the Land,* pp. 179–83.

107. William P. Shriver, *Immigrant Forces: Factors in the New Democracy* (New York: Methodist Book Concern, 1913), pp. 146–47.

Chapter 2

1. Albert Marrin, *The Last Crusade: The Church of England in the First World War* (Durham, N.C.: Duke University Press, 1974), p. 89.

2. Carl Wittke, *German-Americans and the World War* (Columbus: Ohio State Archeological and Historical Society, 1936), pp. 8–9, 11–21, 26–27, 37–39, 57–58, 97–98, 120–25.

3. See Joseph S. Roucek, "The Germans," in Joseph S. Roucek and Bernard Eisenberg, *America's Ethnic Politics* (Westport, Conn.: Greenwood Press, 1982), p. 162. The prominence of German Americans in socialist and radical labor movements,

however, had prepared the way for hostility toward this ethnic minority. Paul Finkelman, "The War on German Language and Culture, 1917–1925," in Hans Jurgen Schroder, ed., *Confrontation and Cooperation: Germany and the United States in the Era of World War I, 1900–1914* (London: Berg Publishers, 1993), pp. 177–78.

4. Finkelman, "War on German Language," p. 183; James H. Fowler II, "Creating an Atmosphere of Suppression, 1914–1917," *Chronicles of Oklahoma* 59 (Summer 1981): 202–23.

5. David M. Kennedy, *Over Here: The First World War and American Society* (New York: Oxford University Press, 1980), pp. 26, 70.

6. Espionage Act, ch. 30, Section 3, 40 Stat. 217, 219 (1917), repealed by Act of June 25, 1948, ch. 645, Section 21, 62 Stat. 862.

7. Espionage Act, ch. 30, Section 1, 40 Stat. 230, 230 (codified at 18 U.S.C.A. Section 1717a) (1984).

8. Sedition Act, ch. 75, 40 Stat. 553, 553 (1918), repealed by Act of June 25, 1948, ch. 645, Section 21, 62 Stat. 862.

9. Paul L. Murphy, *World War I and the Origin of Civil Liberties in the United States* (New York: Norton, 1979), p. 332.

10. *Masses Publishing Co. v. Patten,* 244 F. 535 (S.D.N.Y. 1917); *Masses Publishing Co. v. Patten,* 246 F. 24 (2d Cir. 1917).

11. James R. Mock and Cedric Larson, *Words That Won the War: The Story of the Committee on Public Information, 1917–1919* (Princeton: Princeton University Press, 1939); Stephen L. Vaughn, *Holding Fast the Inner Lines: Democracy, Nationalism, and the Committee on Public Information* (Chapel Hill: University of North Carolina Press, 1980).

12. Frederick C. Luebke, *Bonds of Loyalty: German Americans and World War I* (De Kalb: Northern Illinois University Press, 1974), pp. 215–16.

13. *New York Times,* July 22, 1918, p. 7, col. 4.

14. John Higham, *Strangers in the Land: Patterns of American Nativism, 1860–1925,* 2d ed. (New Brunswick, N.J.: Rutgers University Press, 1988), pp. 194–95, 206.

15. James Mennell, "The Suppression of Dissent in the Shenango Valley during World War I," *Journal of Erie Studies* 17 (Spring 1988): 48–52.

16. Richard Krickus, *Pursuing the American Dream: White Ethnics and the New Populism* (Bloomington: Indiana University Press, 1976), p. 142.

17. John Bigelow, ed., *The Complete Works of Benjamin Franklin* (New York: G.P. Putnam's and Sons, 1887), vol. 2, p. 233. See also pp. 296–99.

18. Luebke, *Bonds of Loyalty,* pp. 226–27.

19. Higham, *Strangers in the Land,* pp. 201, 215–16, 217, 218.

20. Ted Sturm, "Drafting God: Pittsburgh Methodist Churches and World

War I," *Western Pennsylvania Historical Magazine* 71 (Jan. 1988): 28.

21. Ibid., passim; Clifford H. Scott, "Assimilation in a German-American Community: The Impact of World War I," *Northwest Ohio Quarterly* (Winter 1980): 161–62.

22. Sturm, "Drafting God," pp. 29, 32 (quotation).

23. John F. Piper, Jr., *The American Churches in World War I* (Athens: Ohio University Press, 1985).

24. Marion L. Huffines, "Language Maintenance Efforts among German Immigrants and Their Descendants in the United States," in Frank Trommler and Joseph McVeigh, eds., *America and the Germans, Vol. 1: Immigration, Language, Ethnicity* (Philadelphia: University of Pennsylvania Press, 1985), pp. 246–47.

25. Luebke, *Bonds of Loyalty,* p. 45.

26. Ibid., pp. 35, 38.

27. Robert H. Buchheit, "German Language Shift in the Nebraska District of the Missouri Synod from 1918 to 1950," *Yearbook of German-American Studies* 20 (1985): 141–44.

28. Luebke, *Bonds of Loyalty,* pp. 39–40.

29. *Northwestern Lutheran,* Aug. 7, 1917, p. 115.

30. Luebke, *Bonds of Loyalty,* p. 238.

31. Martin Graebner to Theodore Graebner, Feb. 4, 1918, Theodore Graebner Papers, Concordia Historical Institute (hereinafter cited as CHI), Box 122, Clayton, Missouri.

32. Luebke, *Bonds of Loyalty,* p. 284.

33. Theodore Graebner, *The Lutheran Church vs. Hohenzollernism: Testimony and Proof Bearing on the Relation of the American Lutheran Church to the German Emperor* (St. Louis: Concordia Publishing House, 1918).

34. Theodore Graebner to William L. Stuckert, Sept. 2, 1917, Graebner Papers, CHI, Box 122.

35. Amber Smith, "A Full Measure: The German-Americans in Tracy, California, 1917–1918," *Pacific Historian* 28 (Spring 1984): 53–62; Nancy Derr, "Lowden: A Study of Intolerance in an Iowa Community during the Era of the First World War," *Annals of Iowa* 50 (Summer 1989): 5–15.

36. *Thirteenth Census of the United States Taken in the Year 1910* (Washington, D.C.: Department of the Census, Government Printing Office, 1913), vol. 2, p. 613; vol. 3, pp. 45, 213, 695.

37. Klaus Wust and Norbert Muehlen, *The Story of German Involvement in the Founding and Development of America* (Philadelphia: National Carl Schurz Association, 1976), p. 47.

38. Ibid.; Frederick C. Luebke, "Ethnic Group Settlement on the Great Plains," *Western Historical Quarterly* 8 (Oct. 1977): 413–15; Randall C. Teeuwen, "The Immigration and Early Education of Germans from Russia," *Journal of the American Historical Society of Germans from Russia* 8 (Summer 1985): 52–57.

39. Lafayette Young, "Iowa's Effort to Prevent Americans from Being Made Foreigners," *New York Times,* Aug. 11, 1918, sec. 4, p. 2, col. 1.

40. Buffalo Center Commercial Club to State Council of Defense, Feb. 20, 1918, and Feb. 26, 1918; H. J. Metcalf to F. S. Wright, Feb. 25, 1918, H. J. Metcalf Papers, State Historical Society of Iowa (hereinafter cited as SHSI), Box 7, Iowa City.

41. H. J. Metcalf to V. O. Bell, Nov. 28, 1917, Metcalf Papers, SHSI, Box 6.

42. H. J. Metcalf to M. H. Fogarty, Apr. 23, 1918, Metcalf Papers, SHSI, Box 7.

43. "A Proclamation," Metcalf Papers, SHSI, Box 10.

44. Oscar H. Horn to William L. Harding, June 3, 1918, Graebner Papers, CHI, Box 122; Oscar H. Horn to Theodore Graebner, June 5, 1918, ibid.; Trinity Lutheran Church Board to William L. Harding, May 30, 1918, ibid.

45. "The New Language Order," *Des Moines Register,* July 17, 1918, p. 6, col. 1.

46. "Objects to Language Edict," *Des Moines Register,* July 17, 1918, p. 3, col. 6; "Disobeys Language Edict," *Des Moines Register,* July 30, 1918, p. 10, col. 2.

47. Richard Neitzel to Theodore Graebner, Oct. 2, 1918, Theodore Graebner Papers, CHI, Box 122..

48. J. E. R. Schmidt to Theodore Graebner, Oct. 13, 1918, Graebner Papers, CHI, Box 122.

49. Nancy Derr, "The Babel Proclamation," *The Palimpsest* 60 (July/Aug. 1979): 114.

50. *Des Moines Register,* June 1, 1918, p. 4, col. 1.

51. Ibid., Aug. 1, 1918, p. 4, col. 1.

52. Herbert Pankratz, "The Suppression of Alleged Disloyalty in Kansas during World War I," *Kansas Historical Quarterly* 42 (Autumn 1976): 282.

53. Martin Graebner to Theodore Graebner, Sept. 28, 1918, Graebner Papers, CHI, Box 122.

54. Order No. 4 of the South Dakota Council of Defense, May 25, 1918, Minnesota Commission of Public Safety file, Box F-184, Minnesota Historical Society (hereinafter cited as MHS), St. Paul.

55. Order No. 13 of the South Dakota Council of Defense, July 16, 1918, Public Safety Commission file, MHS.

56. F. C. Gade to Theodore Graebner, Jan. 8, 1919, Graebner Papers, CHI, Box 41.

57. Anna Zellick, "Patriots on the Rampage: Mob Action in Lewistown, 1917–1918," *Montana: The Magazine of Western History* 31 (Winter 1981): 30, 38–41.

58. Oscar Heilman to Theodore Graebner, May 9, 1918, Graebner Papers, CHI, Box 122.

59. "Stopping the Use of German, Information Number 3," Public Safety Commission file, MHS.

60. Arnold H. Grumm to Theodore Graebner, Oct. 19, 1918, Papers, Box 122.

61. Allan Kent Powell, "The German-Speaking Immigrant Experience in Utah," *Utah Historical Quarterly* 52 (Fall 1984): 327.

62. La Vern J. Rippley, "Conflict in the Classroom: Anti-Germanism in Minnesota Schools, 1917–19," *Minnesota History* 47 (Spring 1981): 182.

63. Theodore Graebner to Martin Graebner, Sept. 24, 1918, Graebner Papers, CHI, Box 122; Martin Graebner to Theodore Graebner, May 3, 1918, ibid.

64. Luebke, *Bonds of Loyalty*, pp. 12–13.

65. See Luebke, *Bonds of Loyalty*, pp. 13–14, 209, 234–35, 247; Kennedy, *Over Here*, pp. 87–88; Murphy, *World War I*, p. 125.

66. A. Orthner and D. Niehaus to State Council of Defense, Apr. 22, 1918, Metcalf Papers, SHSI, Box 7.

67. O. M. Burkhardt to Theodore Graebner, June 1, 1918, Graebner Papers, CHI, Box 122.

68. Theodore Graebner to O. Heilman, May 13, 1918, Graebner Papers, CHI, Box 122.

69. H. C. Peterson and Gilbert C. Fite, *Opponents of War, 1917–1918* (Seattle: University of Washington Press, 1968), pp. 202–7; Donald R. Hickey, "The Prager Affair: A Study in Wartime Hysteria," *Journal of the Illinois State Historical Society* 62 (Summer 1969): 117–34; Luebke, *Bonds of Loyalty*, pp. 3–24.

70. Luebke, *Bonds of Loyalty*, p. 15; Luebke, "Foreign Language Restrictions," pp. 9–10.

71. Pankratz, "Suppression of Alleged Disloyalty in Kansas," p. 286; *Fort Wayne Journal-Gazette* (Indiana), Oct. 21, 1918.

72. Theodore Graebner to H. M. Schreiner, Oct. 8, 1918, Graebner Papers, CHI, Box 122; H. M. Schreiner to Theodore Graebner, Oct. 9, 1918, ibid.

73. J. C. Jackson to A. D. Stewart, Feb. 5, 1918, Public Safety Commission file, MHS.

74. E. H. Nicholas to Minnesota Public Safety Commission, Nov. 22, 1917, Public Safety Commission file, MHS.

75. Edmund Larke to Public Safety Commission, Feb. 25, 1918, Public Safety Commission file, MHS.

76. Flora A. Spicer to H. W. Libby, Feb. 5, 1918, Public Safety Commission file, MHS.

77. Anna Lewis to Gov. Burnquist, July 22, 1918, Public Safety Commission file, MHS; H. C. Schwartz to Minnesota Public Safety Commission, May 14, 1918, ibid.; A. J. Schneider to Public Safety Commission, Dec. 9, 1918, ibid.

78. Arthur Madsen to Public Safety Commission, Aug. 4, 1918, Public Safety Commission file, MHS; Anna Lewis to Gov. Burnquist, July 22, 1918, ibid.; F. C. Schwartz to Public Safety Commission, May 14, 1918, ibid.; E. C. Nicholas to Public Safety Commission, Nov. 22, 1917, ibid.; J. C. Jackson to A. D. Stewart, Feb. 5, 1918, ibid.; A. J. Schneider to Public Safety Commission, ibid.; H. S. Rosecrans to H. J. Metcalf, Feb. 22, 1918, Metcalf Papers, SHSI, Box 7.

79. Schwartz to Public Safety Commission.

80. Spicer to Libby (emphasis in original).

81. Martin Graebner to Theodore Graebner, May 17, 1918, Graebner Papers, CHI, Box 122.

82. Ibid.

83. Luebke, *Bonds of Loyalty,* pp. 38–39.

84. Walter H. Beck, *Lutheran Elementary Schools in the United States,* 2d ed. (St. Louis: Concordia Publishing House, 1965), pp. 183–85, 206, 320–21.

85. Theodore Graebner to O. H. Horn, June 8, 1918, Graebner Papers, CHI, Box 122.

86. Ibid.

87. Ibid.

88. Theodore Graebner to H. Grueber, Sept. 27, 1918, Graebner Papers, CHI, Box 122.

89. J. A. Schlichting to Theodore Graebner, Oct. 26, 1918, Graebner Papers, CHI, Box 122.

90. Otto Bock to Theodore Graebner, Mar. 15, 1918, Theodore Graebner Papers, CHI, Box 122.

91. Theodore Graebner to Martin Graebner, Sept. 24, 1918, Graebner Papers, CHI, Box 122; Theodore Graebner to C. Hafner, Apr. 25, 1918, ibid.; Theodore Graebner to F. W. C. Jesse, Jan. 12, 1919, Graebner Papers, CHI, Box 40; Theodore Graebner to H. M. Mohr, Sept. 24, 1918, Graebner Papers, CHI, Box 122; T. Graebner to Grueber.

92. Theodore Graebner to A. G. Dick, Apr. 30, 1918, Graebner Papers, CHI, Box 122.

93. Theodore Graebner to Hafner.

94. Theodore Graebner to H. M. Mohr, Oct. 10, 1918, Graebner Papers, CHI, Box 122; Graebner to August Griesse, Oct. 8, 1918, ibid.

95. F. C. Gade to Theodore Graebner, Nov. 2, 1918, Graebner Papers, CHI, Box 122.

96. Graebner to Mohr.

97. F. E. Traub to Theodore Graebner, June 15, 1918, Graebner Papers, CHI, Box 122; J. A. Schlichting to Theodore Graebner, Dec. 15, 1917, ibid.

98. Carl Gustav Schultz to H. W. Libby, Oct. 31, 1917, Public Safety Commission file, MHS. For a comprehensive analysis of the controversy over the use of German in the Minnesota public schools, see Rippley, "Conflict in the Classroom," pp. 171–83.

99. H. W. Libby to C. G. Schultz, Mar. 28, 1918, Public Safety Commission file, MHS.

100. "Report on Minnesota Parochial and Private Schools," May 7, 1918, Public Safety Commission file, MHS.

101. Carl Gustav Schultz to unidentified correspondent, Sept. 27, 1918, Public Safety Commission file, MHS.

102. O. C. Kreinheder to Theodore Graebner, Oct. 14, 1918, Graebner Papers, CHI, Box 122.

103. V. J. Wotzka to H. W. Libby, May 10, 1918, Public Safety Commission file, MHS.

104. F. F. Plouf to Commission of Public Safety, May 11, 1918, Public Safety Commission file, MHS.

105. T. Graebner to Hafner.

106. E. G. Jehn to Theodore Graebner, Oct. 14, 1918, Graebner Papers, CHI, Box 122.

107. W. R. Miessler to Theodore Graebner, May 8, 1918, Graebner Papers, CHI, Box 122; Theodore Graebner to W. R. Miessler, May 9, 1918, ibid.

108. Theodore Graebner to F. C. Gade, Nov. 11, 1918, Graebner Papers, CHI, Box 122.

109. P. L. Gabbert to Theodore Graebner, Nov. 3, 1918, and Nov. 12, 1918, Graebner Papers, CHI, Box 122.

110. Herman M. Mohr to Theodore Graebner, Oct. 14, 1918, Graebner Papers, CHI, Box 122.

111. F. T. Ruhland to Mr. Rother, Oct. 15, 1918, and copy of letter signed by Thomas Finnigan, Graebner Papers, CHI, Box 122.

112. "Foreign Languages in the Elementary School," *School and Society,* Nov. 17, 1917, p. 583.

113. Wallace Henry Moore, "The Conflict Concerning the German Language and German Propaganda in the Public Secondary Schools of the United States, 1917–1919" (Ph.D. dissertation, Stanford University, 1937), p. 25.

114. *Farmer's Mail and Breeze,* Jan. 5, 1918 (clipping in Graebner Papers, CHI, Box 122).

115. H. Miles Gordy, "The German Language in Our Schools," *Educational Review* 56 (Oct. 1918): 262; "A German Influence," *New York Times,* July 12, 1917, p. 10, col. 7 (letter to the editor from "A Teacher of Modern Languages," Gadsden, Alabama).

116. Caspar F. Goodrich, "Shall We Teach German in Our Public Schools?" *The Outlook,* May 29, 1918, p. 197.

117. Gordy, "German Language in Our Schools," pp. 262–63.

118. *New York Times,* Feb. 25, 1918, p. 4, col. 2.

119. "German in the Schools," *School and Society,* June 1, 1918, p. 645.

120. "Our Awful Loss If We Drop German," *Literary Digest,* July 13, 1918, p. 28; resolutions adopted by the National Society of the Sons of the American Revolution, May 20, 1918, Public Safety Commission file, MHS.

121. Moore, "Conflict Concerning the German Language," pp. 34–38.

122. P. P. Claxton to Robert L. Slagle, Mar. 12, 1918, reprinted in *School and Society,* Mar. 30, 1918, p. 374; "Patriotism and the Study of German," *New Republic,* Mar. 2, 1918, p. 146; *New York Times,* Mar. 20, 1918, p. 5, col. 7. Although Claxton's opinion was not expressly limited to high schools and colleges, Claxton privately told Graebner that his letter was intended to refer only to those institutions. Theodore Graebner to J. A. Schlichting, Oct. 3, 1918, Graebner Papers, CHI, Box 122 (referring to letter to Graebner from Claxton).

123. Lewis Paul Todd, *Wartime Relations of the Federal Government and the Public Schools, 1917–1918* (New York: Teachers College, Columbia University, 1945), pp. 78–79.

124. John Preston Hoskins, "Modern Language Instruction after the War," *School and Society,* Nov. 23, 1918, pp. 603–4 (read before the Modern Language Conference of the National Education Association, Pittsburgh, July 1918).

125. T. W. Todd, "German in Our Public Schools," *Education* 38 (Mar. 1918): 531.

126. Harington Board of Education to Board of Education, Sept. 14, 1917, Public Safety Commission file, MHS.

127. Allen Wilson Porterfield, "The Study of German in the Future," *School and Society,* Sept. 23, 1916, pp. 437–80; Todd, *Wartime Relations,* p. 533.

128. Todd, *Wartime Relations,* p. 532.

129. Hoskins, "Modern Language Instruction," p. 602.

130. Charles H. Handschin, "The Study of German during the War," *School and Society,* Sept. 1, 1917, p. 254.

131. Frederick Tupper, "The Awful German Language," *The Nation,* Sept. 7, 1918, p. 249; Handschin, "Study of German," pp. 255–56; Hoskins, "Modern Language Instruction," p. 604.

132. *New Republic,* Sept. 7, 1918, p. 250.

133. Moore, "Conflict Concerning the German Language," p. 46.

134. Letter from William Jewett Tucker, president emeritus of Dartmouth College, to editor, *New York Times,* June 13, 1918, p. 12, col. 6.

135. Porterfield, "Study of German in the Future," p. 479; Hoskins, "Modern Language Instruction," p. 604; letter to editor from H. W. Puckett of Columbia University, *New York Times,* Sept. 10, 1917, p. 12, col. 4.

136. "American Students Boycotting German," *Literary Digest,* Mar. 30, 1918, pp. 29–31, 44–74.

137. "Foreign Languages in the Elementary School, p. 584.

138. Polk Lafoon to Woodrow Wilson, Oct. 7, 1918, in Arthur S. Link, ed., *The Papers of Woodrow Wilson,* vol. 51 (Princeton: Princeton University Press, 1985), p. 259; Woodrow Wilson to Polk Lafoon, Oct. 10, 1918, ibid., p. 285.

139. Woodrow Wilson to Joseph Patrick Tumulty, c. Apr. 10, 1918, in *Papers of Woodrow Wilson,* vol. 47 (Princeton, 1984), p. 311. Wilson's comment was inspired by a Wyoming professor who had sought Wilson's views concerning the elimination of German-language instruction in high schools and colleges; ibid., n. 1. See also ibid., vol. 48 (Princeton, 1985), p. 192 (May 28, 1918, entry from diary of Josephus Daniels); Woodrow Wilson to George Creel, Feb. 28, 1918, ibid., vol. 46 (Princeton, 1983), p. 491.

140. Wilson to Tumulty, c. Apr. 10, 1918; Woodrow Wilson to Joseph Patrick Tumulty, c. Oct. 12, 1917, ibid., vol. 44 (Princeton, 1983), p. 364.

141. Tupper, "Awful German Language," p. 248.

142. "American Students Boycotting German," pp. 30–31, 44, 46–50, 52, 54–55, 58, 61–64, 66, 70, 72, 74.

143. John Walker Harrington, "German Becoming Dead Tongue Here," *New York Times,* July 14, 1918, sec. 3, p. 4, col. 1.

144. Moore, "Conflict Concerning the German Language," pp. 29, 30.

145. Todd, *Wartime Relations,* p. 72; Moore, "Conflict Concerning the German Language," pp. 29, 70–83, 88–89.

146. Moore, "Conflict Concerning the German Language," pp. 29, 89–90, 91; "Bars the Teaching of German," *New York Times,* Feb. 23, 1918, p. 7, col. 2.

147. *St. Louis Republic,* July 14, 1918 (clipping in Graebner Papers, CHI, Box 122).

148. Todd, *Wartime Relations,* p. 73.

149. Ibid.

150. "The German Language," *School Review* 25 (Oct. 1917): 599.

151. "Teaching German," *School Review* 26 (June 1918): 457–59.

Chapter 3

1. John Higham, *Strangers in the Land: Patterns of American Nativism, 1860–1925,*

2d ed. (New Brunswick, N.J.: Rutgers University Press, 1988), pp. 224, 222.

2. Mrs. Ed Preston to Knute Nelson, Dec. 18, 1918, Commission of Public Safety, Box F-184, Minnesota Historical Society (hereinafter cited as MHS), St. Paul.

3. C. F. Angell to Commission of Public Safety, Jan. 18, 1919, Public Safety Commission file, MHS.

4. G. H. Kiehl to Theodore Graebner, Feb. 6, 1919, Theodore Graebner Papers, Concordia Historical Institute (hereinafter cited as CHI), Box 123, Clayton, Missouri.

5. Emil Ziegler to Theodore Graebner, Mar. 27, 1919, Graebner Papers, CHI, Box 41.

6. Theodore Graebner to F. C. Gade, Nov. 11, 1918, Graebner Papers, CHI, Box 122.

7. Theodore Graebner to O. C. Kreinheder, Oct. 10, 1918, Graebner Papers, CHI, Box 122.

8. *Journal of the National Education Association,* Mar. 1924, p. 77.

9. "The Tongue of America," *New Age,* Mar. 1924, p. 137.

10. "Illiteracy in the United States," *School and Society,* Mar. 30, 1918, pp. 374–75 (reprinting letter from Secretary of the Interior Franklin K. Lane to President Wilson and Sen. Hoke Smith and Rep. William J. Sears, respective chairmen of the Senate and House committees on education).

11. Andrew F. West, "Our Use of English," *American Review of Reviews,* Oct. 1919, p. 394.

12. Henry C. Johnson, "The English Language—Its New Importance and Universality," *National Education Association Journal of Proceedings and Addresses* 57 (1919): 607–8.

13. Earl C. Arnold, "The Elimination of Illiteracy," *Education* 40 (Oct. 1919): 71.

14. "German Opera," *American Legion Weekly,* Oct. 31, 1919, p. 12.

15. "New Fire under the Melting Pot," *American Legion Weekly,* Jan. 30, 1920, p. 10.

16. "A Verdict for God and Country," *American Legion Weekly,* Nov. 21, 1919, pp. 7–8.

17. I. N. Edwards, "The Legal Status of Foreign Languages in the Schools," *Elementary School Journal* 24 (Dec. 1923): 270–78; J. C. Ruppenthal, "English and Other Languages under American Statutes," *American Law Review* 54 (Jan./Feb. 1920): 65–90; *Appendix II to Brief in Behalf of Appellee, Pierce v. Society of Sisters,* 268 U.S. 510 (1925); Note, "Recent Legislation Forbidding Teaching of Foreign Languages in Public Schools," *Minnesota Law Review* 4 (May 1920): 449–51.

18. La. Laws of 1918, Act 114, Sec. 1.

19. *Journal of the House of the Thirty-Eighth General Assembly* (Iowa, 1919), p. 94.

20. Ibid., p. 141; *Journal of the Senate of the Thirty-Eighth General Assembly* (Iowa, 1919), p. 667.

21. George A. W. Vogel to Theodore Graebner, Mar. 12, 1919, Graebner Papers, CHI, Box 41.

22. *Lutheran Witness,* Mar. 18, 1919, pp. 87–88.

23. *Journal of the House,* pp. 898–900; *Journal of the Senate,* pp. 1571–72.

24. Richard Kretzschmar to O. S. Harrison, Feb. 26, 1919, Graebner Papers, CHI, Box 41.

25. Theodore Graebner to O. S. Harrison et al., Mar. 1, 1919, Graebner Papers, CHI, Box 41.

26. *The Republic,* Apr. 15, 1919 (clipping in Graebner Papers, CHI, Box 41).

27. Martin Graebner to Theodore Graebner, Feb. 19, 1919, Graebner Papers, CHI, Box 41.

28. Ziegler to Theodore Graebner.

29. Martin Graebner to Theodore Graebner (emphasis in original).

30. Warren Harding to Theodore Horst, Jan. 23, 1920, Graebner Papers, CHI, Box 41.

31. Percy E. Davidson, "German Language Legislation and the Spirit of American Education," *School and Society,* Mar. 13, 1920, pp. 301–10.

32. Paul Finkelman, "The War on German Language and Culture, 1917–1925," in Hans Jurgen Schroder, ed., *Confrontation and Cooperation: Germany and the United States in the Era of World War I, 1900–1914* (London: Berg Publishers, 1993), p. 189.

33. Max Loeb, "Compulsory English for Foreign-Born," *The Survey,* July 13, 1918, pp. 426–27.

34. Thomas H. Briggs, "A National Program for Secondary Education," *School and Society,* Mar. 11, 1918, pp. 301–6.

35. "Illiteracy in the United States," *School and Society,* Mar. 30, 1918, pp. 374–75.

36. "Our National Association: Its Battle for a Department of Education," *Journal of the National Education Association,* Mar. 1924, pp. 77–78.

37. S. 4987, 65th Cong., 2d Sess. (1918); H.R. 7 and S. 1017, 67th Cong., 1st Sess. (1921); S. 1337 and H.R. 3923, 68th Cong., 1st Sess. (1923); S. 1584 and H.R. 7, 70th Cong., 1st Sess. (1927).

38. "Child Labor and the Smith-Towner Bill," *New Age,* June 1921, pp. 261–62.

39. *Hearings before the Comm. on Education and Labor, U.S. Senate, on S.* 1337, 68th Cong., 1st Sess. (1924) (hereinafter cited as *Hearings*), pp. 54, 57, 299–300; "Progress on the Education Bill," *Journal of the National Education Association,* May 1924, pp. 187–89.

40. "Grand Commander's Message," *New Age,* Jan. 1924, p. 4; "Let There Be a Department of Education!" ibid., Feb. 1921, pp. 86–87.

41. James Hamilton Hoar to William E. Borah, Jan. 9, 1924, Borah Papers, Box 168, Manuscript Division, Library of Congress.

42. *Educational Record* 2 (Apr. 1921): 58, 60.

43. *Hearings,* pp. 170–85.

44. *School and Society,* Feb. 17, 1921, p. 181; "A Federal Department of Education," *Constitutional Review* 12 (Oct. 1928): 223.

45. Henry St. George Tucker, "Judge Story's Position on the So-Called General Welfare Clause," *American Bar Association Journal,* July 1927, p. 367; *Constitutional Review* 11 (Oct. 1927): 251–52; "Federal Department of Education," p. 226.

46. J. Frederick Wenchel, "A Great Menace," *Lutheran Witness,* Mar. 29, 1921, pp. 99–100; "Present Status of the Sterling-Towner Bill," ibid., Dec. 18, 1923, pp. 405–6; A. C. Stellhorn, "The Sterling-Towner Bill," *Lutheran School Journal,* Dec. 1921, pp. 363–65; Paul L. Blakely, "Juggling for the Smith-Towner Bill," *America,* Feb. 5, 1921, pp. 378–80; "The Bolshevist Smith-Towner Bill," ibid., Jan. 28, 1922, p. 357; "The Masons and Federal Education," ibid., Mar. 11, 1922, p. 497; "The N.E.A., the Masons, and Federal Schools," ibid., June 30, 1923, p. 254.

47. "Federal Department of Education," p. 225.

48. James H. Ryan, "The Sterling-Reed Bill—A Criticism," *Catholic Educational Review* 22 (June 1924): 353.

49. *Hearings,* pp. 106–16.

50. Ibid., pp. 116–19.

51. "The Towner-Sterling Bill," *Legislative Comm. Series No.* 3 (Washington, D.C.: National Education Association, Sept. 1922).

52. *Seattle Times,* Jan. 24, 1923, p. 1.

53. *The New Menace* (Bronson, Missouri), May 13, 1922, in MSS 308 (microfilm) (Papers of Benjamin W. Alcott), Oregon Historical Society (hereinafter cited as OHS), Portland.

54. *The Protestant,* Feb. 1923, p. 1; ibid., Jan. 1923, p. 2; J. F. Noll, "Parochial Schools in Peril," *America,* Nov. 11, 1922.

55. See David H. Bennett, *The Party of Fear: From Nativist Movements to the New Right in American History* (Chapel Hill: University of North Carolina Press, 1988), pp. 208–37.

56. "The Supreme Council," *New Age,* July 1920, pp. 322–23.

57. "More Concerning the Public Schools," *New Age,* Aug. 1920, p. 355.

58. Edward C. Day, "Right of the Child to an Education in the Public School," *New Age,* June 1923, p. 325.

59. Walter B. Jernigan, "Public Schools in Florida," *New Age,* Jan. 1923, p. 16.

60. Paul E. Miller, "Catholicism, the Public School, and Freemasonry," *New Age,* Jan. 1922, pp. 39–40.

61. "More Concerning the Public Schools," *New Age,* Aug. 1920, p. 355.

62. Henry G. Tardy, "Some Fundamental Reasons for Our Public Schools," *New Age,* June 1922, pp. 341–42.

63. "Concerning the Public Schools," *New Age,* Mar. 1920, p. 114; "Education—the Bed-Rock of Democracy," *New Age,* Feb. 1920, p. 70.

64. "For a National University," *New Age,* Mar. 1923, p. 180; "A National University," ibid., Sept. 1920, p. 407; John C. Vivian, "A Prospectus of a National University," ibid., Nov. 1920, pp. 483–84.

65. Gladys C. West, "How the Towner-Sterling Bill Will Benefit Education," *New Age,* Sept. 1923, pp. 547–50; "Education," ibid., pp. 538–40; "Federal Aid to Education," ibid., pp. 668–70; Daniel A. Reed, "The Education Bill," ibid., Jan. 1924, pp. 27–28; "What Is the Education Bill?" ibid., pp. 28–30; "More About the Smith-Towner Bill," ibid., June 1921, pp. 258–59; "The Towner-Sterling Bill," ibid., Sept. 1921, pp. 405–06; "The Towner-Sterling Bill," ibid., Sept. 1922, pp. 565–66.

66. "Grand Commander's Message," p. 4.

67. "Child Labor and Illiteracy," *New Age,* Oct. 1923, pp. 604–5; "Child Labor and the Smith-Towner Bill."

68. "What Is Being Done to Americanize the Foreign-Born," *New Age,* Oct. 1923, pp. 607–8; "Immigration and Americanization," ibid., Jan. 1921, pp. 19–20.

69. "The Problem of Americanization," *New Age,* July 1923, pp. 410–411.

70. Charles P. Sweeney, "Oregon and Liberty," *America,* Sept. 30, 1922, p. 558.

71. "The Next Move in Oregon," *America,* May 3, 1924, p. 64.

72. "A Defeat for Americanism," *America,* Nov. 18, 1922, p. 110.

73. Charles N. Lischka, "The Coming Kulturkampf," *America,* Jan. 12, 1924, p. 313.

74 Mark O. Shriver, Jr., "How Catholics Can Help Their Schools," *America,* Aug. 30, 1924, p. 482.

75. James H. Ryan, "Masons and Education," *America,* Nov. 4, 1922, p. 57.

76. "The Catholic School and Democracy," *America,* Jan. 21, 1922, p. 329.

Chapter 4

1. According to the 1910 census, 4.8 percent of the residents of Nebraska were born in Germany—nearly twice the national average. Both parents of some 7.9 percent of native-born Americans in the state were born in Germany. Approximately 4 percent of the state's population was Austrian-born or had Austrian parents. *Thirteenth Census of the United States Taken in the Year* 1910, vol. 1, pp. 184, 781; vol. 3, p. 50. The 1910 census probably more accurately records the German-American population at the time of the First World War than does the 1920 census, because many German Americans in 1920 may have denied their German birth or ancestry.

2. *Report of the State Council of Defense of Nebraska, Nineteen Hundred Eighteen,* Nebraska State Historical Society (hereinafter cited as NSHS), Record Group (RG) 23, Box 25.

3. *Lincoln Daily Star,* June 26, 1917, p. 6, col. 1.

4. Ibid., June 27, 1917, p. 6, col. 1.

5. Ibid., July 11, 1917, p. 1, col. 6.

6. Ibid., May 9, 1917, p. 5, col. 3.

7. Ibid., July 13, 1917, p. 7, col. 3.

8. Ibid., July 12, 1917, p. 6, col. 1.

9. Ibid., July 17, 1918, p. 1, col. 7; July 18, 1917, p. 5, col. 1.

10. *Minutes of Sixth Meeting,* State Council of Defense, July 24, 1917, NSHS, RG 23, Box 1.

11. Ibid.

12. *Lincoln Daily Star,* Aug. 18, 1917, p. 1, col. 1.

13. Ibid., Aug. 2, 1917, p. 6.

14. Ibid., Sept. 4, 1917, p. 2, col. 4.

15. Ibid., May 12, 1917, p. 5, col. 1; Aug. 8, 1917, p. 4, col. 3; Aug. 20, 1917, p. 6, col. 1; Aug. 23, 1917, p. 7, col. 1; Oct. 12, 1917, p. 6, col. 1; Oct. 22, 1917, p. 6, col. 1; Oct. 31, 1917, p. 6, col. 1.

16. Ibid., Aug. 19, 1917, p. 1, col. 6.

17. J. E. Vacha, "When Wagner Was Verboten: The Campaign against German Music in World War I," *New York History* 64 (Apr. 1983): 171–88; Alan Howard Levy, "The American Symphony at War: German-American Musicians and Federal Authorities during World War I," *Mid-America* 71 (Jan. 1989): 5–13.

18. *Lincoln Daily Star,* Sept. 6, 1917, p. 7; Oct. 22, 1917, p. 6, col. 1.

19. Ibid., Aug. 23, 1917, p. 7.

20. Ibid., Nov. 14, 1917, p. 1, col. 3.

21. Sarka Hrbkova to Mary Oakley, Mar. 14, 1918, NSHS, RG 23, Box 31.

22. Ibid.

23. *Minutes of the Fourteenth Meeting,* State Council of Defense, Nov. 13, 1917, NSHS, RG 23, Box 1.

24. *Report on German Private Schools in Nebraska* (undated), NSHS, RG 23, Box 31.

25. *Lincoln Daily Star,* Dec. 13, 1917, p. 1, col. 7.

26. George Weller and J. Link to the State Council of Defense, Dec. 8, 1917, NSHS, RG 23, Box 31.

27. Ibid.

28. *Minutes of the Sixteenth Meeting,* State Council of Defense, NSHS, Nov. 27, 1917, RG 23, Box 1.

29. *Laws of Nebraska,* 1913, ch. 31, p. 107.

30. *State ex. rel. Thayer v. School District,* 99 Neb. 338, 156 N.W. 641 (1916).

31. James E. Potter, "Barkley vs. Pool: Woman Suffrage and the Nebraska Referendum Law," *Nebraska History* 69 (Spring 1988): 12.

32. Orville H. Zabel, *God and Caesar in Nebraska: A Study of the Legal Relationship of Church and State, 1854–1954* (Lincoln: University of Nebraska Press, 1955), pp. 139–40.

33. *Lincoln Daily Star,* May 12, 1917, p. 5, col. 1.

34. Ibid., Nov. 9, 1917, p. 3, col. 1.

35. Ibid., Sept. 21, 1917, p. 7, col. 1; Oct. 2, 1917, p. 6, col. 1; Oct. 7, 1917, p. 4, col. 1; Oct. 20, 1917, p. 7, col. 2; Nov. 27, 1917, p. 6, col. 1; Sept. 20, 1918, p. 6, col. 1.

36. Ibid., Oct. 7, 1917, p. 4, col. 1; Sept. 21, 1917, p. 7, col. 1.

37. Ibid., Dec. 1, 1917, p. 1, col. 3.

38. Ibid., Sept. 28, 1917, p. 1, col. 6; Nov. 29, 1917, p. 1, col. 5.

39. Ibid., Mar. 1, 1918, p. 1, col. 6.

40. Undated report of unnamed committee, NSHS, RG 23, Box 31.

41. Statement by Nebraska State Council of Defense, Dec. 11, 1917, NSHS, RG 23, Box 31.

42. *Report on German Private Schools in Nebraska,* p. 2.

43. *Evening State Journal and News,* Dec. 12, 1917, p. 6, col. 1.

44. *Lincoln Daily Star,* Nov. 19, 1917, p. 4, col. 4.

45. Mary Miller to Sarka Hbrkova, Dec. 14, 1917, NSHS, RG 23, Box 27.

46. Katherine Langer to Sarka Hrbkova, Nov. 17, 1917, NSHS, RG 23, Box 31.

47. Archie M. Smith to R. L. Metcalfe, Nov. 20, 1917, NSHS, RG 23, Box 31.

48. Jack W. Rodgers, "The Foreign Language Issue in Nebraska, 1918–23," *Nebraska History* (Mar. 1958): 8.

49. George Coupland to L. A. Turner, May 14, 1918, NSHS, RG 23, Box 14.

50. *Lincoln Daily Star,* Dec. 13, 1917, p. 1, col. 7.

51. Ibid., Dec. 31, 1917, p. 11, col. 2.

52. Johannes Lehmann to George Coupland, Apr. 26, 1918, NSHS, RG 23, Box 14.

53. Undated letter addressed to ministers of the Lutheran Iowa Synod, Western District, signed by Johannes Lehmann, O. Kloeckner, and G. P. Krebs, NSHS, RG 23, Box 14.

54. *Lincoln Daily Star,* Jan. 1, 1918, p. 6, col. 1.

55. J. M. Weidenschilling to Theodore Graebner, Apr. 13, 1918, Theodore Graebner Papers, Concordia Historical Institute (hereinafter cited as CHI), Box 122, Clayton, Missouri.

56. *Scottsbluff Telegram,* Jan. 9, 1918; Otto F. Arndt to Theodore Graebner, Jan. 9, 1918, Graebner Papers, CHI, Box 122.

57. *Lincoln Daily Star,* Jan. 22, 1918, p. 1, col. 5.

58. Ibid., Feb. 4, 1918, p. 1, col. 6.

59. Sarka Hbrkova to C. V. Svoboda, Feb. 8, 1918, NSHS, RG 23, Box 31.

60. Sarka Hrbkova to J. W. Ostry, Jan. 17, 1918, NSHS, RG 23, Box 27.

61. Hrbkova to Oakley.

62. F. X. Korte to George Coupland, May 7, 1918, and May 14, 1918, NSHS, RG 23, Box 14; George Coupland to F. X. Korte, May 9, 1918, and May 16, 1918, ibid.

63. Robert N. Manley, "Language, Loyalty, and Liberty: The Nebraska State Council of Defense and the Lutheran Churches, 1917–1918," *Concordia Historical Institute Quarterly* 27 (Apr. 1964): 12.

64. Walter H. Beck, *Lutheran Elementary Schools in the United States,* 2d ed. (St. Louis: Concordia Publishing House, 1965), pp. 336–37.

65. *Lincoln Daily Star,* Dec. 1, 1917, p. 1, col. 3.

66. *Laws of Nebraska,* 1918, ch. 5, p. 38 (36th Special Session); Manley, "Language, Loyalty, and Liberty," p. 13.

67. *Lincoln Daily Star,* May 15, 1918, p. 6, col. 1.

68. Ibid., Apr. 30, 1918, p. 4, col. 3.

69. George Coupland to Rev. Listman, June 6, 1918, NSHS, RG 23, Box 14.

70. R. G. Brown to State Council of Defense, Oct. 14, 1918, NSHS, RG 23, Box 15; George Coupland to Brown, Oct. 15, 1918, ibid.; Homer W. Gray to State Council of Defense, Oct. 15, 1918, ibid.; Coupland to William Noerenberg, Oct. 17, 1918, ibid.; Noerenberg to Council, Oct. 18, 1918, ibid.; Coupland to Noerenberg, Oct. 19, 1918, ibid.

71. Bohus Novotvy to Sarka B. Hrbkova, July 8, 1918, NSHS, RG 23, Box 31.

72. R. W. Rasmussen to State Council of Defense, May 4, 1918, NSHS, RG 23, Box 14.

73. C. A. Longquist to Woodrow Wilson, July 27, 1918, NSHS, RG 23, Box 12; Arthur H. Fleming, Chief of State Councils Section, Council of National Defense, to Longquist, Aug. 9, 1918, ibid.; Fleming to Nebraska State Council of Defense, Aug. 9, 1918, ibid.; Robert M. Joyce to Longquist, Aug. 13, 1918, ibid.; Longquist to Joyce, Aug. 14, 1918, ibid.; Joyce to Longquist, Aug. 24, 1918, ibid.; Longquist to Joyce, Sept. 2, 1918, ibid.; Joyce to Longquist, Sept. 5, 1918, ibid.

74. Henry C. Richmond to G. G. Eisenhart, June 17, 1918, NSHS, RG 23, Box 14; Henry C. Richmond to chairmen of county councils of defense, July 15, 1918, ibid., Box 31; press release from State Council of Defense to Nebraska editors, Aug. 3, 1918, ibid., Box 15.

75. Richmond to council chairmen.

76. George Coupland to L. A. Turner, May 14, 1918, NSHS, RG 23, Box 14; press release dated Aug. 3, 1918.

77. Richmond to Eisenhart.

78. Proclamation sent by Nebraska State Council of Defense to County Chairmen, June 10, 1918, NSHS, RG 23, Box 15; *Lincoln Daily Star,* June 8, 1918, p. 1, col. 1.

79. *Lincoln Daily Star,* Aug. 28, 1918, p. 5, col. 3.

80. "Why the German Language Should Be Abolished in America: Sermon Preached at the Congregational Church, Leigh, Nebraska, Sunday, June 30th 1918, by the Pastor, Rev. L. A. Turner," NSHS, RG 23, Box 25.

81. Sarka Hrbkova to R. L. Metcalfe, July 12, 1918, NSHS, RG 23, Box 14.

82. W. J. Furse to Nebraska State Council of Defense, June 26, 1918, NSHS, RG 23, Box 14.

83. Richmond to council chairmen; press release dated Aug. 3, 1918.

84. *Lincoln Daily Star,* Aug. 27, 1918, p. 3, col. 1.

85. *Report of the Attorney General of the State of Nebraska, 1917–18* (Lincoln: Attorney General's Office), pp. 220–21.

86. Ibid., June 22, 1918, p. 1, col. 3.

87. George Coupland to D. W. Livingston, Nov. 30, 1918, NSHS, RG 23, Box 14.

88. *Lincoln Daily Star,* Sept. 24, 1918, p. 1, col. 3.

89. Writ from Cedar County Council of Defense to Ferd. Schnuettgen, May 31, 1918, and reply from Schnuettgen, NSHS, RG 23, Box 12.

90. *Lincoln Daily Star,* Dec. 17, 1918, p. 1, col. 7.

91. Ibid., Sept. 17, 1918, p. 4, col. 3; Sept. 22, 1918, p. 4, col. 2.

92. Ibid., Oct. 29, 1918, p. 1, col. 3.

93. Ibid., Sept. 28, 1918, p. 8, col. 1.

94. Ibid., Sept. 29, 1918, p. 3, col. 3.

95. Ibid., Nov. 3, 1918, p. 7, col. 1.

96. Frederick C. Luebke, *Bonds of Loyalty: German Americans and the First World War* (DeKalb: Northern Illinois University Press, 1974), p. 299; *Lincoln Daily Star,* Nov. 12, 1918, p. 9, col. 4.

97. Mrs. A. A. McKenzie to State Council of Defense, Dec. 4, 1918, NSHS, RG 23, Box 15.

98. D. W. Livingston to George Coupland, Nov. 29, 1918, NSHS, RG 23, Box 15.

99. *Lincoln Daily Star,* Dec. 17, 1918, p. 1, col. 7.

100. F. W. C. Jesse to Theodore Graebner, Jan. 12, 1919, Graebner Papers, CHI, Box 40.

101. Coupland to Livingston.

102. *Lincoln Daily Star,* Jan. 2, 1919, p. 3, col. 1.

103. *Evening State Journal,* Jan. 9, 1919, p. 11, col. 1.

104. George Coupland to Perry Reed, Dec. 21, 1918, NSHS, RG 23, Box 15; *Lincoln*

Daily Star, Nov. 19, 1918, p. 6, col. 1; Dec. 14, 1918, p. 4, col. 1; Dec. 18, 1918, p. 6, col. 1.

105. *Evening State Journal,* Jan. 7, 1919, p. 1, col. 2; *Lincoln Daily Star,* Jan. 7, 1919, p. 7, col. 3.

106. R. E. Dale, "Back to Normal," *Nebraska History* 38 (Sept. 1957): 179–82.

107. Ibid., pp. 203–4; Orville D. Menard, "Tom Denison, the Omaha Bee, and the 1919 Omaha Race Riot," *Nebraska History* 68 (Winter 1987): 152; Louise F. Rickard, "The Politics of Reform in Omaha, 1918–1921," *Nebraska History* 53 (Winter 1972): 437–39.

108. Michael W. Schuyler, "The Ku Klux Klan in Nebraska, 1920–1930," *Nebraska History* 66 (Summer 1985): 234–35. Although the Atlanta headquarters of the Klan claimed in 1924 that 45,000 Nebraskans were members, this number probably is inflated. Klan membership probably was not proportionately higher in Nebraska than it was in other midwestern states, and its political influence there was weaker than in many of those states.

109. *House Journal,* 37th Session, Jan. 9, 1919, pp. 81–82, 94.

110. Jesse to Graebner.

111. Ibid.

112. *Evening State Journal,* Jan. 23, 1919, p. 11, col. 3.

113. *Lincoln Daily Star,* Jan. 14, 1919, p. 4, col. 1; Jan. 14, 1919, p. 9, col. 4; Jan. 15, 1919, p. 8, col. 3; *Daily Evening Journal,* Jan. 18, 1919, p. 1, col. 1.

114. *House Journal,* Feb. 25, 1919, pp. 14–16; *Evening State Journal,* Feb. 25, 1919, p. 1, col. 3.

115. "Shall the Parochial Schools Be Abolished in Nebraska?" pamphlet in Records of Department of Education, United States Catholic Council, Drawer 218, Department of Archives and Manuscripts, Catholic University of America.

116. Arthur F. Mullen, *Western Democrat* (New York: Funk, 1940), pp. 212–13; *Evening State Journal,* Mar. 19, 1919, p. 3, col. 4; Mar. 20, 1919, p. 13, col. 1; Mar. 26, 1919, p. 1, col. 3.

117. Laws of Nebraska, 1919, ch. 155, pp. 346–51.

118. *Evening State Journal,* Mar. 25, 1919, p. 3, col. 1, quoting *True Voice,* Mar. 21, 1919.

119. *Evening State Journal,* Feb. 11, 1919, p. 5, col. 4.

120. *Lincoln Daily Star,* Jan. 17, 1919, p. 2, col. 3; Jan. 24, 1919, p. 10, col. 2.

121. *Daily Evening Journal,* Jan. 31, 1919, p. 2, col. 2.

122. *Laws of Nebraska,* 1919, ch. 249, p. 1019.

123. *Senate Journal,* 37th Session, 1919, p. 1047; *House Journal,* 1919, p. 1008.

124. *House Journal,* pp. 1006–7; *Senate Journal,* p. 1047.

125. *House Journal,* p. 1008–9.

126. *Laws of Nebraska,* 1919, ch. 234, p. 991; ch. 133, p. 309; ch. 171, p. 383; ch. 250, p. 1020; ch. 248, p. 1018.

127. Burton W. Folsom, Jr., "Tinkerers, Tipplers, and Traitors: Ethnicity and Democratic Reform in Nebraska during the Progressive Era," *Pacific History Review* 50 (Feb. 1981): 67–75.

128. Burton W. Folsom, Jr., "Immigrant Voters and the Nonpartisan League in Nebraska, 1917–1920," *Great Plains Quarterly* 1 (Summer 1981): 161.

Chapter 5

1. Martin Graebner to Theodore Graebner, Apr. 7, 1919, Theodore Graebner Papers, Concordia Historical Institute (hereinafter cited as CHI), Clayton, Missouri.

2. *Report of the Attorney General of the State of Nebraska, 1919–20* (Lincoln: Attorney General's Office), pp. 228–30; E. Eckhardt to Theodore Graebner, May 4, 1919, Graebner Papers, CHI, Box 40.

3. C. F. Brommer to Theodore Graebner, May 14, 1919, Graebner Papers, CHI, Box 40.

4. Ibid.

5. Martin Graebner to Theodore Graebner.

6. Theodore Graebner to H. Brueggemann, May 27, 1920, Graebner Papers, CHI, Box 40.

7. Martin Graebner to Theodore Graebner.

8. Ibid.

9. Theodore Graebner to C. F. Brommer, June 6, 1919, Graebner Papers, CHI, Box 40.

10. Brommer to Graebner.

11. C. F. Brommer to Theodore Graebner, June 18, 1919, Graebner Papers, CHI, Box 123.

12. Arthur F. Mullen, unpublished history of the language laws, pp. 4–5, Arthur F. Mullen Papers, Creighton University, Omaha, Nebraska.

13. The original plaintiffs in the lawsuit were the Missouri Synod and the predominantly Polish Roman Catholic parish of St. Francis in South Omaha. Intervenors in the lawsuit included John Siedlik (a parishioner at St. Francis), three mainly Bohemian Roman Catholic churches in Omaha, the boards of education of two Bohemian schools in South Omaha, and more than one dozen Lutheran parishes. See *Brief of St. Wenceslaus' Church of Omaha [et al.], Intervening Plaintiffs; Brief of John Siedlik, Intervenor; Brief on Behalf of Intervenors.*

14. *Nebraska District of Evangelical Lutheran Synod of Missouri, Etc., et al. v. Samuel R. McKelvie, et al[.], Appellees* (No. 21153); *Brief of Appellants,* pp. 14–25.

15. Ibid., pp. 3–4, 7–8 (reciting Plaintiff's Petition for Relief).

16. Ibid., pp. 8–9 (reciting Plaintiff's Petition for Relief), 18–19, 25–29.

17. *Barron ex. rel. Tiernan v. Mayor and City Council of Baltimore,* 32 U.S. (7 Pet.) 243 (1833).

18. *Permoli v. Municipality No. 1 of the City of New Orleans,* 44 U.S. (3 How.) 589, 609 (1845).

19. See, e.g., *Patterson v. Colorado,* 205 U.S. 454 (1907).

20. *Brief of Appellees, Samuel R. McKelvie and Clarence A. Davis* (No. 21153), pp. 5–6, 11–12.

21. "Arguments in Foreign Tongue Case Are Heard," *Lincoln Daily Star,* Nov. 17, 1919, p. 11, col. 8.

22. *Nebraska District of Evangelical Lutheran Synod of Missouri, Ohio and Other States et al. v. McKelvie,* 175 N.W. 531 (Neb. 1919).

23. *House Journal,* 37th Session, 1919, pp. 1006–1107, Nebraska State Historical Society, Record Group 56, Box 191.

24. *Brief of Appellant, Meyer v. State* (No. 21924), p. 76.

25. 175 N.W. 536.

26. *Nebraska District Messenger,* Apr. 1920 (clipping in Graebner Papers, CHI, Box 40).

27. Brommer to Graebner, June 18, 1919.

28. *Lincoln Daily Star,* Dec. 8, 1919, p. 2, col. 4.

29. *Proceedings of the Nebraska Constitutional Convention,* 1919–1920, vol. 1, pp. LXVII-LXVIII, 133.

30. *Proceedings of the Nebraska Constitutional Convention,* pp. 434, 623, 717, 793, 835; *Lincoln Daily Star,* Feb. 6, 1920, p. 7, col. 2.

31. *Proceedings,* p. 962.

32. Ibid., p. 450.

33. Ibid., p. 953.

34. Ibid., vol. 2, p. 2647.

35. Ibid., pp. 1302, 1305.

36. Ibid., pp. 1300–1301.

37. Ibid., pp. 1293–1301.

38. I. L. Albert and C. E. Sandall to C. F. Brommer, June 20, 1920, C. F. Brommer Papers, CHI.

39. *Lincoln Daily Star,* Dec. 27, 1919, p. 4, col. 1.

40. Ibid., July 1, 1920, p. 6, col. 1.

41. Albert and Sandall to Brommer.

42. *Brief of Appellant, Meyer v. State,* pp. 16–17, 48–70, 70–73, 34–45, 76–77, 31, 32, 45–47.

43. *Brief of Defendant in Error, Meyer v. State,* pp. 11, 10–11, 12–15, 16–17.

44. C. F. Brommer to Theodore Graebner, Feb. 19, 1921, Graebner Papers, CHI, Box 40.

45. Ibid.

46. Walter H. Beck, *Lutheran Elementary Schools in the United States,* 2d ed. (St. Louis: Concordia Publishing House, 1965), p. 332.

47. *Laws of Nebraska,* 1921, ch. 61, pp. 244–45.

48. Ibid., p. 244.

49. Brommer to Graebner, Feb. 19, 1921.

50. *Brief of Joseph T. Votava, Amicus Curiae,* p. 16 (quoting Omaha *World-Herald,* Oct. 30, 1921).

51. *Record, Evangelical Lutheran Synod et al. v. McKelvie et al.* (No. 22424), pp. 20, 28, 54, 39–40, 23, 30, 32, 34, 41, 27, 24–25.

52. *Brief of Appellees,* pp. 17–18, 27–28, 30–34, 5–6, 21, 10–14, 21–30, 10–11, 22, 25, 27–28.

53. *Brief of Appellants,* pp. 31, 31–35, 66, 67–68.

54. *Brief of the American Legion, Department of Nebraska, as Amicus Curiae,* p. 25.

55. *Meyer v. State,* 187 N.W. 100 (Neb. 1922).

56. *Memorandum Opinion Denying Motion for Rehearing, Meyer v. State.* In his motion for a rehearing, Meyer argued that the court had unduly emphasized the issue of religious liberty and that it had failed to address the question of whether the statute violated the Fourteenth Amendment by extending the scope of the police power. Meyer reiterated his previous Fourteenth Amendment arguments and also argued that the statute violated parental rights. *Brief of Plaintiff in Error on Motion for Rehearing, Meyer v. State,* passim, pp. 4–5.

57. *Nebraska District of Evangelical Lutheran Synod of Missouri, Ohio and Other States v. McKelvie,* 108 Neb. 448, 187 N.W. 927, 929 (Neb. 1922).

58. 187 N.W. at 930 (Morrissey, J., dissenting).

59. *Meyer v. State,* 187 N.W. at 104 (Letton, J., dissenting).

60. *Appellant's Abstract of Record, Bartels v. State,* pp. 2–10.

61. *Bartels v. State,* 191 Iowa 1060, 1064–65 (1921); *Appellant's Brief and Argument, Bartels v. State,* pp. 11–12, 37–51, 19–21, 41–42, 54–59; *Appellant's Reply Brief and Argument,* pp. 2–8, 13–14.

62. *Appellee's Brief and Argument, Bartels v. State,* pp. 7–9, 30, 23–24.

63. Ibid., pp. 69, 52, 52–53, 53–60.

64. *Bartels v. State,* 191 Iowa 1060, 1073, 181 N.W. 508 (1921).

65. Ibid., 1069–70.

66. Ibid., 1074, 1073, 1069–70, 1071–72, 1063–64, 1072.

67. Ibid., pp. 1075, 1076, 1076–77, 1083.

68. *Brief on Behalf of Plaintiffs in Error, Bohning v. Ohio,* 262 U.S. 404 (1923) (Nos. 561 and 562), pp. 15–16 (quoting *Ohio Senate Journal* 108 [1919]: 1238).

69. "Religious German Catechism Schools—Not Violation of Amended Senate Bill No. 137," in *Opinions of the Attorney-General of Ohio for the Period from January 13, 1919, to January 1, 1920,* vol. 2, pp. 1043–46 (quotation from p. 1045).

70. Carl M. Zorn to Theodore Graebner, Aug. 30, 1919, Theodore Graebner Papers, CHI, Box 41.

71. Theodore Graebner to Carl M. Zorn, Sept. 2, 1919, Theodore Graebner Papers, CHI, Box 41.

72. *Record, Bohning v. Ohio,* pp. 14–17, 5–6.

73. *Brief on Behalf of Plaintiffs in Error,* pp. 13–15.

74. Ibid., pp. 13, 17–18.

75. Ibid., p. 13.

76. *Bohning v. State* and *Pohl v. State,* 102 Ohio St. 474, 475, 476–77.

77. *Lutheran Witness,* Nov. 9, 1920, p. 362.

Chapter 6

1. Although some Nebraska Lutherans opposed an appeal to the Supreme Court, Pastor C. F. Brommer and Arthur F. Mullen persuaded church leaders to support the continuation of the fight against the language law. Robert T. Meyer to Arthur F. Mullen, Apr. 29, 1938, Mullen Papers, Creighton University, Omaha, Nebraska.

2. *Brief of August Bartels, Plaintiff in Error, Bartels v. Iowa,* 262 U.S. 404 (1923) (No. 134) (hereinafter cited as *Brief of Bartels*), p. 18; *Brief and Argument for Plaintiff in Error, Meyer v. Nebraska,* 262 U.S. 390 (No. 325) (hereinafter cited as *"Brief of Meyer"*), pp. 14–15; *Brief of Evangelical Lutheran Church of Missouri, Ohio and Other States, Nebraska District of Evangelical Lutheran Synod v. McKelvie,* 262 U.S. 404 (1923) (No. 440) (hereinafter cited as *Brief of Missouri Synod*), p. 46; *Brief on Behalf of Plaintiffs in Error, Bohning v. Ohio* and *Pohl v. Ohio,* 262 U.S. 404 (1923) (nos. 561 and 562) (hereinafter cited as *Brief of Bohning and Pohl*), p. 21; *Oral Argument of Arthur F. Mullen, in Behalf of Plaintiffs-in-Error, Meyer v. Nebraska,* 262 U.S. 404 (1923) (No. 325) (hereinafter cited as *Mullen Argument*), p. 10.

3. *Brief of Missouri Synod,* p. 46; *Brief of Meyer,* p. 15; *Brief of Bartels,* pp. 15, 21–23, 26, 38.

4. *Brief of Bohning and Pohl,* pp. 18–20.

5. *Brief of Missouri Synod,* p. 48.

6. *Brief of Meyer,* p. 16.

7. *Brief of Bartels*, pp. 13–14, 30, 24, 15; *Brief of Bohning and Pohl*, pp. 27–28, 23, 25; *Brief of Missouri Synod*, pp. 20, 24, 61–63, 23, 47, 38, 39–44.

8. *Brief of Bohning and Pohl*, pp. 27–28; *Brief of Bartels*, pp. 13–14; *Brief of Missouri Synod*, p. 61; *Mullen Argument*, p. 12.

9. *Brief of Bohning and Pohl*, pp. 24–25; *Brief of Bartels*, p. 30; *Brief of Missouri Synod*, pp. 23, 47 (quotation).

10. *Brief of Bartels*, pp. 15, 38–39.

11. *Brief of Missouri Synod*, p. 38.

12. *Mullen Argument*, pp. 12, 16; Arthur F. Mullen, *Western Democrat* (New York: Funk, 1940), pp. 222–23.

13. *Brief of Bartels*, pp. 14, 30, 31–33; *Brief of Meyer*, pp. 7–9; *Brief of Missouri Synod*, pp. 39–44, 57–61; *Mullen Argument*, p. 9.

14. *Brief of Meyer*, p. 18; *Brief of Bartels*, p. 39; *Brief of Missouri Synod*, pp. 25, 49–50, 51; *Mullen Argument*, p. 6; *Brief of Bohning and Pohl*, pp. 29–30.

15. *Brief on Behalf of Defendants in Error, Bohning v. Ohio* and *Pohl v. Ohio*, 262 U.S. 404 (1923) (Nos. 561 and 562) (hereinafter cited as *Brief of Ohio*), p. 6; *Brief and Argument of State of Nebraska, Defendant in Error* (hereinafter cited as *Brief of Nebraska in Meyer*), pp. 12–13; *Brief and Argument of Nebraska, Nebraska District of Evangelical Lutheran Synod v. McKelvie*, 262 U.S. 404 (1923) (No. 440) (hereinfter cited as *Brief of Nebraska in McKelvie*), pp. 14–41; *Brief of the State of Iowa, Defendant in Error, Bartels v. Iowa*, 262 U.S. 404 (1923) (No. 134) (hereinafter cited as *Brief of Iowa*), pp. 5, 10–14.

16. *Brief of Nebraska in Meyer*, pp. 12–13.

17. *Brief of Nebraska in McKelvie*, pp. 14–15.

18. *Brief of Ohio*, p. 6.

19. *Brief of Iowa*, pp. 10–11.

20. *Brief of Nebraska in McKelvie*, pp. 68, 16.

21. *Brief of Nebraska in Meyer*, p. 15.

22. *Brief of Iowa*, p. 12.

23. *Brief of Nebraska*, pp. 44–45.

24. *Brief of Iowa*, p. 7.

25. *Brief of Ohio*, p. 6.

26. *Brief of Nebraska in McKelvie*, p. 66; *Brief of Iowa*, pp. 5–6; *Brief of Nebraska in Meyer*, pp. 37–39.

27. *Brief of Nebraska in Meyer*, p. 45; *Brief of Nebraska in McKelvie*, pp. 49–50; *Brief of Iowa*, p. 9.

28. *Mullen Argument*, pp. 5–10, 14, quotation from pp. 7–8; Mullen, *Western Democrat*, pp. 225–28.

29. Arthur F. Mullen to F. X. McMenany, Mar. 17, 1923, Records of the United

States Catholic Conference, Box 9, Department of Archives and Manuscripts, Catholic University of America (hereinafter cited as USCC Archives).

30. *Schenck v. United States,* 249 U.S. 47 (1919); *Frohwerk v. United States,* 249 U.S. 204 (1919); *Debs v. United States,* 249 U.S. 211 (1919); *Abrams v. United States,* 250 U.S. 616 (1919).

31. *Schaefer v. United States,* 251 U.S. 466 (1920); *Pierce v. United States,* 252 U.S. 239 (1920).

32. 254 U.S. 325 (1921).

33. W. H. Taft to G. H. Grosvenor, July 12, 1912, cited in Henry F. Pringle, *The Life and Times of William Howard Taft, Vol. 2* (Hamden, Conn.: Archon Books, 1964), p. 834.

34. Robert Michaelson, "Common School, Common Religion? A Case Study in Church-State Relations, Cincinnati, 1869–70," *Church History* 38 (1969): 208–9; Michael Perko, "The Building Up of Zion: Religion and Education in Nineteenth-Century Cincinnati," *Cincinnati Historical Society Bulletin* (1980), 106–7; Lloyd P. Jorgenson, *The State and the Non-Public School, 1825–1925* (Columbia: University of Missouri Press, 1987), pp. 119–20. On appeal, the Ohio Supreme Court unanimously reversed the trial court's decision.

35. William Howard Taft to Luther M. Kuhns, Nov. 12, 1912, William Howard Taft Papers, Series 8, Reel 515, Manuscript Division, Library of Congress (hereinafter cited as LC).

36. William Howard Taft to Francis Pieper, Nov. 2, 1912, Taft Papers, Series 8, Reel 515, LC.

37. 254 U.S. 335–36.

38. David Burner, "Edward Terry Sanford," in Leon Friedman and Fred L. Israel, eds., *The Justices of the United States Supreme Court, 1789–1969: Their Lives and Major Opinions,* vol. 3 (New York: Chelsea House, 1969), p. 2203.

39. George F. Milton, Jr., "Sanford—Neither Radical nor Reactionary," *The Outlook,* Feb. 14, 1923, p. 299.

40. James F. Watts, Jr., "Joseph McKenna," in Friedman and Israel, *Justices of the United States Supreme Court,* vol. 3, pp. 1719–20.

41. Pierce Butler to William Howard Taft, Nov. 9, 1922, Taft Papers, Series 3, Reel 247, LC.

42. Theodore Buenger, "Memorandum in Regard to Pierce Butler," Jan. 1, 1923, Theodore Graebner Papers, Box 41, Concordia Historical Institute, Clayton, Missouri.

43. David Burner, "Pierce Butler," in Friedman and Israel, *Justices of the United States Supreme Court,* vol. 3, p. 2183.

44. David J. Danelski, *A Supreme Court Justice Is Appointed* (Westport, Conn.: Greenwood, 1964), pp. 4–5, 16–17, 19, 54, 56–63, 100–107; John T. Hubell, "A Question of Academic Freedom: The William A. Schaper Case, " *Midwest Quarterly* 17 (Winter 1976): iii–21.

45. *Berger v. United States,* 255 U.S. 22, 43–44 (1921).

46. Stephen Tyree Early, Jr., "James Clark McReynolds and the Judicial Process" (Ph.D. dissertation, University of Virginia, 1954), pp. 30–31, 36.

47. David Burner, "George Sutherland," in Friedman and Israel, *Justices of the United States Supreme Court,* vol. 3, p. 2134.

48. *Meyer v. Nebraska,* 262 U.S. 390 (1923); *Bartels v. Iowa, Bohning v. Ohio, Pohl v. Ohio, Nebraska District of Evangelical Lutheran Synod of Missouri, Ohio and Other States, et al. v. McKelvie, et al.,* 262 U.S. 404 (1923).

49. Arthur F. Mullen to John J. Burke, June 14, 1923, USCC Archives, Box 9.

50. 262 U.S. at 402, 400.

51. 262 U.S. at 399.

52. 262 U.S. at 400.

53. 262 U.S. at 401, 402.

54. 262 U.S. at 401.

55. 262 U.S. at 403.

56. 262 U.S. at 402.

57. William Howard Taft to George Fox, July 31, 1923, Taft Papers, Series 3, Reel 255, LC. See also Taft to Mrs. Bellamy Storer, June 27, 1923, ibid.

58. William Howard Taft to Helen Manning, June 11, 1923, Taft Papers, Reel 255, Series 3, LC.

59. 262 U.S. 412–13.

60. Mullen, *Western Democrat,* p. 224–25. As Barbara Bennett Woodhouse has pointed out, the Court's opinion also appears to have been influenced by an amicus brief submitted by William D. Guthrie, a prominent New York attorney, ardent political conservative, and devout Roman Catholic. Barbara Bennett Woodhouse, "'Who Owns the Child?' *Meyer* and *Pierce* and the Child as Property," *William and Mary Law Review* 33 (Summer 1992): 1077–80, citing *Brief of Amicus Curiae* (coauthored by William D. Guthrie and Bernard Hershkopf), *Meyer v. Nebraska,* 262 U.S. 390 (1923). Guthrie's brief did not take any position on the validity of the language laws, but it warned that the recently enacted Oregon law requiring compulsory public education embodied the communistic and Platonic doctrines of public usurpation of parental authority. Guthrie urged the Court to refrain from making any statement concerning the state's power to monopolize public education until it had an opportunity to consider the constitutionality of the Oregon law. According

to Woodhouse, Guthrie intended to "contain any damage" from a ruling in favor of the language laws, and his brief "may actually have helped turn the current of the Justices' sympathies, so that the widely supported language laws, instead of sweeping along public school laws, were themselves swept away on a tide of antipathy toward abolition of private education." Woodhouse, "Who Owns the Child?" p. 1080.

61. 250 U.S. at 630.

62. Fred Rodell, *Nine Men: A Political History of the Supreme Court from 1790–1955* (New York: Random House, 1955), p. 205.

63. *Buck v. Bell*, 274 U.S. 200 (1927).

64. *Bailey v. Alabama*, 219 U.S. 219 (1911).

65. Oliver Wendell Holmes to Harold Laski, Apr. 20, 1917, in *Holmes-Laski Letters: The Correspondence of Mr. Justice Holmes and Harold J. Laski, 1916–1935, Vol. 1: 1916–1935*, (Cambridge: Harvard University Press, 1953) p. 80. Cf. ibid., Apr. 12, 1917, p. 78.

66. *Transcript of Proceedings, Nebraska District v. Evangelical Lutheran Synod, et al., District Court of Dodge County, September 1, 1921.*

67. Mullen to Burke.

Chapter 7

1. Robert Lacey, *Ford: The Men and the Machine* (Boston: Little, Brown, 1986), pp. 205–17; Anne Jardim, *The First Henry Ford: A Study in Personality and Business Leadership* (Cambridge: MIT Press, 1970), pp. 139–47, 150–53.

2. Theodore Andres to Theodore Graebner, Nov. 19, 1918, Theodore Graebner Papers, Concordia Historical Institute (hereinafter cited as CHI), Box 122, Clayton, Missouri.

3. H. Grueber to Theodore Graebner, Oct. 2, 1918, Graebner Papers, CHI, Box 122.

4. *Oregon School Cases: A Complete Record* (Baltimore: Belvedere Press, 1925), p. 830.

5. Timothy Mark Pies, "The Parochial School Campaigns in Michigan, 1920–1924: The Lutheran and Catholic Involvement," *Catholic Historical Review* 72 (Apr. 1986): 223.

6. Thomas Francis Lewis, "A Study of Attempts to Abolish Private and Parochial Education by Constitutional Amendment in 1920 and 1924" (Master's thesis, University of Detroit, 1952), p. 7.

7. Frank B. Woodford, *Alex J. Groesbeck: Portrait of a Public Man* (Detroit: Wayne State University Press, 1962), p. 224.

8. Pies, "Parochial School Campaigns," p. 224; Grueber to Graebner.

9. *Hamilton v. Vaughan,* 170 N.W. 554–55 (1919); *Hamilton v. Vaughan,* 172 N.W. 619 (1919).

10. Letter dated Jan. 26, 1920, from Wayne County Civic Association to Michigan voters, Graebner Papers, CHI, Box 40.

11. *Religious Bodies: 1926, Volume 1, Summary and Detailed Tables* (Washington, D.C.: U.S. Government Printing Office, 1930), pp. 196–98. Approximately 21 percent were Roman Catholic and 5 percent Lutheran. Of the Lutherans, nearly half were communicants of the Missouri Synod and a substantial part of the remainder likewise were members of synods that maintained a system of parochial schools.

12. Donald W. Disbrow, *Schools for an Urban Society* (Lansing: Michigan Historical Commission, 1968), p. 93.

13. John Frederick Stach, "A History of the Lutheran Schools of the Missouri Synod in Michigan, 1845–1940" (Ph.D. dissertation, University of Michigan, 1940), pp. 147–49.

14. *Lutheran Witness,* Nov. 23, 1920, p. 380.

15. Lewis, "Attempts to Abolish Private and Parochial Education," p. 17; Pies, "Parochial School Campaigns," p. 226.

16. Lewis, "Attempts to Abolish Private and Parochial Education," p. 17; Pies, "Parochial School Campaigns," p. 226–27.

17. Edward D. Kelly to James Cardinal Gibbons, May 6, 1920, Records of the United States Catholic Conference (hereinafter cited as USCC), Box 9, Department of Archives and Manuscripts, Catholic University of America, Washington, D.C.

18. Thomas J. Shelley, "The Oregon School Case and the National Catholic Welfare Conference," *Catholic Historical Review* 75 (July 1989): 439–40.

19. *The Proposed School Amendment to the Constitution of Michigan: Reasons Why It Should Not Pass,* p. 6 (pamphlet in Graebner Papers, CHI, Box 40).

20. *Grand Rapids Herald,* Apr. 5, 1920 (clipping in Graebner Papers, CHI, Box 40).

21. *Detroit Journal,* Oct. 7, 1920 (clipping in Graebner Papers, CHI, Box 40).

22. James Hamilton, "Michigan School Amendment," *New Age,* Oct. 1920, p. 459.

23. Thomas Elton Brown, "Patriotism or Religion? Compulsory Public Education and Michigan's Roman Catholic Church, 1920–1924," *Michigan History* 64 (July/Aug. 1980): 40.

24. Lewis, "Attempts to Abolish Private and Parochial Education, pp. 65–70.

25. Brown, "Patriotism or Religion?" p. 37.

26. Ibid., p. 38.

27. *Reasons Why,* p. 7.

28. Ibid.

29. Disbrow, *Schools for an Urban Society,* pp. 87–88.

30. *Reasons Why,* p. 7.

31. Brown, "Patriotism or Religion?" p. 40.

32. Pies, "Parochial School Campaigns," pp. 229–30.

33. Lewis, "Attempts to Abolish Private and Parochial Education," p. 57.

34. Pies, "Parochial School Campaigns," pp. 229–30.

35. Lewis, "Attempts to Abolish Private and Parochial Education," pp. 56, 60, 62, 63; Stach, "History of the Lutheran Schools," p. 149.

36. F. A. Hertwig to Theodore Graebner, May 26, 1921, Graebner Papers, CHI, Box 40; Theodore Graebner to F. A. Hertwig, June 5, 1921, ibid.

37. John Fahning to Theodore Graebner, Dec. 22, 1920, Graebner Papers, CHI, Box 40; Theodore Graebner to John Fahning, Dec. 27, 1920, ibid.

38. Lewis, "Attempts to Abolish Private and Parochial Education," pp. 31–34; Woodford, *Alex J. Groesbeck,* pp. 33, 111.

39. *Hamilton v. Vaughan,* 179 N.W. 553 (1920).

40. Ibid., pp. 557–59.

41. Lewis, "Attempts to Abolish Private and Parochial Education," pp. 64–65.

42. Rudolph H. C. Meyer to Theodore Graebner, Nov. 4, 1920, Graebner Papers, CHI, Box 40.

43. *America,* Nov. 13, 1920, pp. 86–87.

44. Lewis, "Attempts to Abolish Private and Parochial Education," p. 74; Pies, "Parochial School Campaigns," p. 231; Brown, "Patriotism or Religion?" p. 41.

45. *School Review,* Jan. 1923, p. 2; Brown, "Patriotism or Religion?" p. 41.

46. Disbrow, *Schools for an Urban Society,* p. 89.

47. Grueber to Graebner.

48. Henry Frincke, "The Michigan Law for the Supervision of Private, Denominational, and Parochial Schools," *Lutheran School Journal* 56 (June 1921): 185–86; Disbrow, *Schools for an Urban Society,* p. 89.

49. Stach, "History of the Lutheran Schools," pp. 152–54.

50. R. H. C. Meyer to Theodore Graebner, Mar. 3, 1923, Graebner Papers, CHI, Box 40.

51. Stach, "History of the Lutheran Schools," pp. 155–59.

52. Ibid., pp. 154–55.

53. Theodore Graebner, "An Impossible Amendment and an Anti-Social Petition," published by the Lutheran Schools Committee, in Lutheran Schools Committee file, Graebner Papers, CHI, Box 40.

54. Letter from Lutheran Campaign Committee to pastors and teachers of the Michigan District of the Missouri Synod, Sept. 26, 1921, Graebner Papers, CHI, Box 40.

55. *Hamilton v. Deland*, 221 Mich. 541, 191 N.W. 829 (1923). Under Michigan law, a petition for an initiative was required to have one-tenth as many names as there were votes in the preceding gubernatorial election. Proponents of the school measure collected only 59,648 of the requisite 105,853 signatures before the filing date for the 1922 election. They later collected another 8,519 signatures and attempted after the November 1922 election to place the initiative on the ballot for the spring 1923 election. Since 583,670 persons voted for governor in the 1922 election, only 58,367 signatures were needed to place an initiative on the 1923 ballot. The supreme court upheld the secretary of state's rejection of signatures gathered before the 1922 filing date.

56. *Lutheran Witness,* Mar. 13, 1923, p. 87; John C. Baur to district leaders of the Lutheran Schools Committee, Sept. 23, 1922, Graebner Papers, CHI, Box 40.

57. Baur to district leaders.

58. Timothy Mark Pies and Beth Ann Klemp, "Outlaw Parochial Education?" *Concordia Historical Institute Quarterly* 61 (Winter 1988): 165.

59. Disbrow, *Schools for an Urban Society,* p. 88.

60. Arthur H. Bone, ed., *Oregon Cattleman/Governor/Congressman: Memoirs and Times of Walter M. Pierce* (Portland: Oregon Historical Society, 1981), p. 162.

61. Brown, "Patriotism or Religion," pp. 41–42.

62. Lewis, "Attempts to Abolish Private and Parochial Education," pp. 74–78, 80, 83.

63. Ibid., pp. 78–81; *Free Schools Bulletin,* Feb. 1924, p. 1, in Graebner Papers, CHI, Box 40.

64. *Hamilton v. Deland,* 227 Mich. III, 198 N.W. 843 (1924).

65. Ibid., at 198 N.W. 843–47.

66. Pies and Klemp, "Outlaw Parochial Education?" p. 167.

67. Lewis, "Attempts to Abolish Private and Parochial Education," pp. 84–93; Pies, "Parochial School Campaigns," p. 234.

68. Paul J. Nussbaum to John J. Burke, May 23, 1924, USCC Records, Box 9.

69. "Report of School Defense Committee, 1924," p. 1, Theodore Graebner Papers, CHI, Box 40.

70. "The Truth about the School Amendment," p. 5, MSS 646 (Lutheran Schools Committee), Folder 42, Oregon Historical Society (hereinafter cited as OHS), Portland.

71. "Truth about the School Amendment," p. 6; *Detroit Free Press,* Sept. 22, 1924 (editorial). The Roman Catholic pamphlet estimated that the cost of new buildings would be "well over" $70 million, while the *Free Press* estimated that the initial cost would be $171 million, the current value of parochial schools in Michigan. Since the public schools would not have needed to duplicate parochial school facilities completely, the Roman Catholic figure seems more realistic.

72. *Detroit Free Press,* Sept. 22, 1924 (editorial).

73. "Truth about the School Amendment," p. 9.

74. "Let Common Sense Prevail" (publication of the Lutheran Schools Committee), pp. 3–6, MSS 646, Folder 42, OHS.

75. Pies, "Parochial School Campaigns," p. 236; "Report of School Defense Committee," p. 2.

76. "Report of School Defense Committee," p. 2.

77. *A Pamphlet Containing Copies of All Measures . . . to be Submitted to the Legal Voters . . . on November 3, 1924* (Olympia, Wash.: Frank M. Lamborn, Public Printer, 1924), pp. 3–4.

78. "Bill Is Misnamed" (editorial), *Tacoma Daily Ledger,* Oct. 29, 1924, p. 5, col. 1; "School Bill Defeat Seen," *Seattle Post-Intelligencer,* Nov. 2, 1924, p. 14, col. 5; "School Bill Opposes Principles—Chadwick," ibid., Oct. 28, 1924, p. 6, col. 2; "School Bill Assailed at Mass Meeting," ibid., Sept. 25, 1924, p. 1, col. 5.

79. "Bishop Raps School Bill," *Seattle Post-Intelligencer,* Oct. 14, 1924, p. 6, col. 6; "Church Issues Call for Fight on School Bill," ibid., Oct. 2, 1924, p. 3, col. 5.

80. John J. Burke to Augustin F. Schinner, Jan. 31, 1924, USCC Records, Box 9.

81. William P. O'Connell to J. H. Ryan, Sept. 25, 1924, USCC Records, Box 9; J. H. Ryan to William P. O'Connell, Sept. 30, 1924, ibid.

82. "School Debate Packs Forum," *Spokesman Review* (Spokane), Nov. 3, 1924, p. 6, col. 3.

83. "Demos Hear Debate over School Bill," *Seattle Post-Intelligencer,* Nov. 2, 1924, p. 16, col. 1.

84. "Crowds Cheer School Debate," *Spokesman Review* Oct. 31, 1924, p. 12, col. 1; "Miss Hurn Hits School Measure," ibid., Oct. 22, 1924, p. 6, col. 1.

85. "School Debate Packs Forum."

86. "School Bill Flayed at Young Men's G.O.P. Meet," *Seattle Post-Intelligencer,* Oct. 31, 1924, p. 6, col. 2; "Defeat Initiative 49 and Save State from Strife over Schools," ibid., Oct. 29, 1924, p. M-18, col. 1; "Coyle Backs Fight against School Bill," ibid., Oct. 19, 1924, p. 2, col. 3; "Attack School Bill," *Seattle Daily Times,* Oct. 30, 1924, p. 8, col. 5; "Defeat of School Bill Seen," ibid., Nov. 2, 1924, p. 8, col. 5.

87. "School Bill Attacked," *Seattle Daily Times,* Oct. 20, 1924, p. 10, col. 3.

88. "Pastor Scores School Bill as Un-American," *Seattle Post-Intelligencer,* Sept. 22, 1924, p. 5, col. 1.

89. "Smash This Un-American Bill" (editorial), *Seattle Daily Times,* Nov. 2, 1924, p. 6, col. 1.

90. "Defeat Initiative 49"; "Bill Is Misnamed."

91. "School Bill Opposes Principles—Chadwick."

92. William P. O'Connell to James H. Ryan, Oct. 4, 1924, USCC Records, Box 9; "Coyle Backs Fight"; "School Act Has Chamber Foes," *Spokesman Review,* Oct. 23, 1924, p. 6, col. 6; "Defeat of School Bill Seen"; "Attack School Bill."

93. "School Bill Scored by Nicholas Murray Butler," *Seattle Post-Intelligencer,* Oct. 31, 1924, p. 6, col. 2.

94. O'Connell to Ryan.

95. *Abstract of Votes Polled in the State of Washington at the General Election Held November 4, 1924* (undated pamphlet published by J. Grant Hinkle, secretary of state).

Chapter 8

1. David B. Tyack, "The Perils of Pluralism: The Background of the Pierce Case," *American Historical Review* 74 (1968): 75–76. In 1922, barely 12,000 Oregon schoolchildren attended private schools. Of these, more than 7,000 attended Roman Catholic grade schools, 750 were enrolled in Adventist institutions, and 450 went to Lutheran schools. Most of the remainder attended nondenominational schools. *Oregon Voter,* Sept. 16, 1922, p. 16.

2. *Religious Bodies: 1926, Volume 1, Summary and Detailed Tables* (Washington, D.C.: U.S. Government Printing Office, 1930), p. 240.

3. Edwin V. O'Hara, "The Oregon School Law," *Catholic Educational Association Bulletin* 20 (Nov. 1923): 497.

4. Lawrence J. Saalfeld, *Forces of Prejudice in Oregon, 1920–1925* (Portland, Ore.: Archdiocesan Historical Commission, 1984), pp. 61–62; Priscilla F. Knuth, "Nativism in Oregon" (Master's thesis, Reed College, 1947), pp. 127–30, MSS 33, Oregon Historical Society (hereinafter cited as OHS), Portland.

5. Donald Lewis Zelman, "Oregon's Compulsory Education Bill of 1922" (Master's thesis, University of Oregon, 1964), p. 37.

6. James D. Ziegler, "Epilogue to Progessivism: Oregon, 1920–1924" (Master's thesis, University of Oregon, 1958), pp. 43–44; Arthur H. Bone, ed., *Oregon Cattleman/Governor/Congressman: Memoirs and Times of Walter M. Pierce* (Portland: Oregon Historical Society, 1981), p. 160.

7. 1919 Session Laws, p. 34, ch. 19, sec. 1.

8. Saalfeld, *Forces of Prejudice,* p. 63.

9. Zelman, "Oregon's Compulsory Education Bill," p. 40.

10. Bone, *Oregon Cattleman,* p. 160.

11. Saalfeld, *Forces of Prejudice,* pp. 2–3; Tyack, "Perils of Pluralism," p. 75.

12. Eckard Vance Toy, "The Ku Klux Klan in Oregon: Its Character and Program" (Master's thesis, University of Oregon, 1959), p. 33.

13. David A. Horowitz, "Social Morality and Personal Revitalization: Oregon's Ku Klux Klan in the 1920s," *Oregon Historical Quarterly* 90 (Winter 1989): 369, 378–79.

14. A. B. McCain, ed., *The Oregon School Fight: A True and Complete History* (Portland, Ore.: A.B. McCain, 1924), pp. 21–22.

15. See James D. Barnett, *The Operation of the Initiative, Referendum, and Recall in Oregon* (New York: Macmillan, 1915).

16. Alan L. Gallagher, "The Oregon Compulsory School Bill of 1922: A Re-Evaluation" (Master's thesis, Corpus Christi State University, 1984), p. 10.

17. Bone, *Oregon Cattleman*, p. 162.

18. Ibid., p. 161; *Oregon School Cases: A Complete Record* (Baltimore: Belvedere Press, 1925), p. 733.

19. Saalfeld, *Forces of Prejudice*, pp. 67–68.

20. Bone, *Oregon Cattleman*, pp. 63–64.

21. Ibid., pp. 163–64, 5–6, 10–21.

22. Saalfeld, *Forces of Prejudice*, p. 73; Bone, *Oregon Cattleman*, pp. 164, 169.

23. Bone, *Oregon Cattleman*, pp. 209–11; Malcolm Clark, Jr., "The Bigot Disclosed: Ninety Years of Nativism," *Oregon Historical Quarterly* 75 (June 1974): 167–71.

24. Minutes of meetings of Ku Klux Klan in La Grande, Oregon, Nov. 21, 1922; Mar. 13, 1923; and Apr. 17, 1923; MSS 2604, OHS. As Alan Gallagher has suggested, however, the LaGrande records are not conclusive: Pierce might have called himself a Klansman when he addressed the Klan even though he did not actually join. Gallagher, "Oregon Compulsory School Bill," p. 94 n. 47. Similarly, the Klansman who introduced Pierce might have been overeager to claim him as a member.

25. Lloyd P. Jorgenson, *The State and the Non-Public School, 1825–1925* (Columbia: University of Missouri Press, 1988), p. 208.

26. Tyack, "Perils of Pluralism," pp. 77–78; Jorgenson, *State and the Non-Public School,* p. 208.

27. David Tyack, Thomas James, and Aaron Benavot, *Law and the Shaping of Public Education, 1785–1954* (Madison: University of Wisconsin Press, 1984), p. 180; *The Scribe,* Nov. 3, 1922, p. 3; J. P. Kavanagh to John Burke, Dec. 15, 1923, Records of the United States Catholic Council (hereinafter cited as USCC), Box 14, Department of Archives and Manuscripts, Catholic University of America, Washington, D.C.

28. Tyack, "Perils of Pluralism," p. 77.

29. Gallagher, "Oregon Compulsory School Bill," p. 35.

30. Jorgenson, *State and the Non-Public School,* p. 206.

31. Tyack, "Perils of Pluralism," p. 82; Gallagher, "Oregon Compulsory School Bill," p. 66; "The Public School Bill," *Oregon Teachers Monthly,* Oct. 1922, p. 12 (editorial).

32. *Oregon School Cases,* p. 733.

33. "Public School Bill," p. 12.

34. Tyack, "Perils of Pluralism," p. 80; Tyack, James, and Benavot, *Law and the Shaping of Public Education,* p. 178.

35. *Oregon School Cases,* p. 733.

36. *New Age,* Oct. 1922, p. 603.

37. "Compulsory Education," *Oregon Teachers Monthly,* Nov. 1922, p. 6.

38. O'Hara, "Oregon School Law," p. 499.

39. Justin McGrath to John J. Burke, Nov. 11, 1922, USCC, Box 14.

40. Zelman, "Oregon's Compulsory Education Bill," pp. 12–14.

41. Robert W. Bruere, "The Supreme Court on Educational Freedom," *The Survey* 54 (July 1, 1925): 379.

42. George Estes, *The Old Cedar School* (privately published by Luther I. Powell, Portland, Ore., 1922).

43. Tyack, "Perils of Pluralism," p. 80.

44. *Old Cedar School,* pp. 13, 16–18, 24–26.

45. Ibid., pp. 20, 7.

46. "School Competition," *Oregon Voter,* Aug. 19, 1922, p. 5.

47. "Twenty-four Reasons—Why You Should Vote Official Ballot 315, 'No,' the School Monopoly Bill, Misnamed 'Compulsory Education Bill,' at the November Election" (pamphlet prepared by Dudley G. Wooten, executive director of the Catholic Civic Rights Association of Oregon), Lutheran Schools Committee, MSS 646, Folder 42, OHS.

48. *The Scribe,* Oct. 27, 1922, p. 3.

49. "School Competition."

50. "Twenty Reasons Why the Proposed Anti–Parochial School Amendment Is Wrong" (prepared by Oregon Religious Liberty Association of Portland Oregon), in Lutheran Schools Committee File, MSS 646, Folder 42, OHS.

51. "Twenty-four Reasons," p. 10.

52. "Cost for 4,862 More Kids," *Oregon Voter,* Sept. 9, 1922, p. 4.

53. "Twenty-four Reasons," p. 4.

54. Bone, *Oregon Cattleman,* pp. 164–66, 176.

55. Dean Collins, "School Bills, School Bills," *Oregon Voter,* Sept. 30, 1922, p. 8.

56. Thomas J. Shelley, "The Oregon School Case and the National Catholic Welfare Conference," *Catholic Historical Review* 75 (July 1989): 441.

57. Alexander Christie to John J. Burke, undated letter with notation of mailing on July 13, 1922, USCC Records, Box 14.

58. John J. Burke to Alexander Christie, July 30, 1922, USCC Records; Shelley, "Oregon School Case," pp. 442–43.

59. Saalfeld, *Forces of Prejudice,* p. 73.

60. Bone, *Oregon Cattleman,* p. 166.

61. Ibid., p. 166.

62. *Oregon Voter,* Oct. 7, 1922, p. 15.

63. *The Scribe,* Nov. 3, 1922, p. 3.

64. Saalfeld, *Forces of Prejudice,* p. 75.

65. Tyack, James, and Benavot, *Law and the Shaping of Public Education,* p. 184.

66. Stephen A. Lowell to Lutheran Schools Committee, Oct. 10, 1922, and attached letter to editor, Lutheran Schools Committee file, MSS 646, Folder 42, OHS.

67. *Official Abstract of Votes, 1902–1928, 1930–1948* (Division of Elections, Office of the Secretary of State), State of Oregon.

68. Tyack, "Perils of Pluralism," p. 91.

69. Rudolph Messerli to F. Pfotenhauer, Nov. 10, 1922, Lutheran Schools Committee file, MSS 646, Folder 29, OHS.

70. "The School Law," *Oregon Voter,* Nov. 11, 1922, p. 6 (editorial).

71. *Literary Digest,* Nov. 25, 1922, p. 13.

72. O'Hara, "Oregon School Law," p. 500.

73. "The Oregon Bill" (editorial), *Journal of Education* 96 (Dec. 14, 1922): 592.

74. Dudley G. Wooten, *Remember Oregon* (Denver, Colo.: American Publishing Society, c. 1923), p. 15.

75. "The School Bill," *The Scribe,* Oct. 27, 1922, p. 3 (editorial).

76. O'Hara, "Oregon School Law," p. 500; Wooten, *Remember Oregon,* p. 15.

77. Bone, *Oregon Cattleman,* pp. 190–92; Zelman, "Oregon's Compulsory Education Bill, " pp. 61–62.

78. Minutes of meeting of Ku Klux Klan in La Grande, Oregon, Jan. 26, 1923, MSS 2604, OHS.

79. "School Law," p. 6.

80. Messerli to Pfotenhauer.

81. Memorandum from Justin McGrath to John J. Burke, Apr. 18, 1925, USCC Archives, Box 14.

82. John J. Burke to William D. Guthrie, Apr. 20, 1925, USCC Records, Box 14.

83. Alexander Christie to Edward D. Hanna, undated letter, USCC Records, Box 14.

84. Circular letter to bishops from NCWC Administrative Committee, Jan. 27, 1923, USCC Records, Box 14; Christie to Hanna; Shelley, "Oregon School Case," pp. 440–44.

85. Michael Slattery to John J. Burke, Nov. 9, 1922, USCC Records, Box 14.

86. P. J. Hanley to Peter J. Muldoon, June 29, 1925, USCC Records, Box 14.

87. For widely varying evaluations of Guthrie's career, see George Martin, *Causes and Conflicts: The Centennial History of the Association of the Bar of the City of New York* (New York: Houghton Mifflin, 1970), pp. 218–21; and Clement E. Vose, *Constitutional Change: Amendment Politics and Supreme Court Litigation since 1900* (Lexington, Mass.: Heath, 1972), pp. 155–57.

88. Archbishop of San Francisco to Peter Cardinal Gasparri, Feb. 28, 1925, USCC Records, Box 14.

89. Arthur F. Mullen to James H. Ryan, Apr. 1, 1924, Arthur F. Mullen Papers, Creighton University (hereinafter cited as CU), Omaha, Nebraska; Mullen to Mark Sullivan, June 19, 1925, ibid.; Mullen to William D. Guthrie, June 2, 1925, ibid.; Guthrie to Mullen, July 1, 1925, ibid.; Mullen to Guthrie, July 14, 1925, ibid.; Guthrie to Mullen, July 22, 1925, ibid.; Mullen to Nelson Collins, June 10, 1925, ibid.; Mullen to Francis P. Matthews, Apr. 13, 1937, ibid.; Mullen, "The Truth about the Foreign Language Cases!" (typed manuscript), ibid.

90. Shelley, "Oregon School Case," p. 450.

91. *Brief on Behalf of Appellee,* submitted by J. P. Kavanagh et al. (hereinafter cited as *Kavanaugh Brief*), pp. 15–24, 33–44; *Brief on Behalf of the Appellee,* submitted by William D. Guthrie and Bernard Hershkopf (hereinafter cited as *Guthrie Brief*), pp. 86–89.

92. William D. Guthrie to J. P. Kavanagh, Jan. 2, 1924, USCC Records, Box 14.

93. William D. Guthrie to John J. Burke, Jan. 5, 1923, USCC Records, Box 14.

94. William D. Guthrie to John J. Burke, Jan. 4, 1924, USCC Records, Box 14.

95. "'Private Schools and the Fourteenth Amendment,'" *National Catholic Welfare Conference Bulletin* 6 (Dec. 1924): 14. After the district court ruled in favor of the schools, Mullen tried to persuade the Missouri Synod to have a Lutheran parent and parochial school teacher intervene in the action. But A. C. Stellhorn, executive secretary of the Missouri Synod's School Board, deferred to the "good judgment" of the Oregon attorneys and expressed confidence that the Supreme Court would affirm the district court decision even in the absence of intervention by noncorporate parties. Arthur T. Mullen to A. C. Stellhorn, Apr. 1, 1924, Mullen Papers, CU; Stellhorn to Mullen, Apr. 8, 1924, ibid.

96. *Transcript of Record, Pierce v. The Society of Sisters of the Holy Names of Jesus and Mary* (No. 583), pp. 2–9.

97. McCain, *Oregon School Fight,* pp. 86, 88, 98–99, 100, 103, 131, 127, 129, 89, 94, 126, 128–29 (quotations from pp. 127, 129).

98. Ibid., pp. 113, 119, 111, 115, 63, 106–8 (quotations from pp. 114, 111, 115).

99. *Society of the Sisters of the Holy Names of Jesus and Mary v. Pierce, et al.*, 296 F. 928, 931–38 (quotation from 936–37) (D. Ore. 1924).

100. 296 F. Supp. 928, 931–38 (quotations from 937–38).

101. *Literary Digest*, Apr. 26, 1924, pp. 33–34.

102. *Oregon Voter*, Apr. 5, 1924, p. 35.

103. "The Fight for the Catholic School," *America*, Aug. 2, 1924, p. 378.

104. Willis S. Moore to Wallace McCamant, Apr. 8, 1924, Attorney General Case Files, Box II, Oregon State Archives, Eugene; McCamant to Moore, Apr. 1, 1924, and Apr. 9, 1924, ibid.; McCamant to Isaac H. Van Winkle, June 4, 1924, ibid.; George E. Chamberlain to Van Winkle, Jan. 10, 1925, ibid.

105. Justin McGrath to John J. Burke, June 3, 1924, USCC Records, Box 14.

106. *Appendix I (revised) to Brief on Behalf of Appellee, Pierce v. Society of Sisters*, p. 53.

107. *Brief of Appellant, the Governor of the State of Oregon* (hereinafter cited as *Governor's Brief*), pp. 39–40, 46, 61, 72.

108. *Brief of Appellant, Isaac H. Van Winkle* (hereinafter cited as *Attorney General's Brief*), p. 72.

109. Ibid., p. 22.

110. *Oregon School Cases*, p. 646.

111. *Governor's Brief*, p. 37.

112. *Attorney General's Brief*, pp. 73, 78.

113. Ibid., pp. 22, 71.

114. *Supplement to Brief of Appellant, the Governor of Oregon*, pp. 8–10.

115. *Governor's Brief*, pp. 28–29.

116. *Governor's Brief*, pp. 49–50, 43–44; *Attorney General's Brief*, p. 48.

117. *Governor's Brief*, pp. 30–33, 53; *Attorney General's Brief*, pp. 22–23, 28.

118. *Brief of Appellee, Hill Military Academy* (hereinafter cited as *Hill Academy Brief*), p. 18; *Kavanaugh Brief*, p. 53.

119. *Hill Academy Brief*, pp. 23–25, 44; *Kavanaugh Brief*, pp. 55–56, 61; *Brief for American Jewish Committee*, p. 12; *Oral Argument of Mr. Guthrie on Behalf of Appellee in Support of Decision of United States District Court Holding Unconstitutional and Void the Compulsory Public School Law of that State under Initiative Petition, November 7, 1922* (hereinafter cited as *Guthrie Argument*), p. 17.

120. *Guthrie Brief*, pp. 58, 81, 86 (quotation); *Oral Argument of Mr. Kavanaugh on Behalf of Appellee* (included under cover of *Guthrie Argument;* hereinafter cited as *Kavanaugh Argument*), p. 33; *Brief for American Jewish Committee*, p. 8.

121. *Guthrie Brief*, p. 86; *Kavanaugh Brief*, pp. 93–94; *Guthrie Argument*, p. 16; *Kavanaugh Argument*, p. 34.

122. *Hill Academy Brief,* pp. 16, 12.

123. *Guthrie Brief,* pp. 74, 86; *Brief for American Jewish Committee,* p. 7; *Guthrie Argument,* p. 26.

124. *Lochner v. New York,* 198 U.S. 45 (1905).

125. *Hill Academy Brief,* pp. 13–15; *Kavanaugh Brief,* p. 29; *Guthrie Brief,* pp. 48–50.

126. *Guthrie Brief,* pp. 3–4, 6–7 (quotations), 11; *Brief Amicus Curiae on Behalf of the Domestic and Foreign Missionary Society of the Protestant Episcopal Church* (hereinafter cited as *Episcopal Brief*), p. 3; *Hill Academy Brief,* p. 48.

127. *Guthrie Argument,* p. 19; *Brief for American Jewish Committee,* p. 9; *Kavanagh Brief,* pp. 33, 35 (quotation), 44 (quotation).

128. *Kavanaugh Brief,* pp. 63–68; *Guthrie Brief,* p. 68; *Guthrie Argument,* p. 27.

129. *Literary Digest,* Apr. 18, 1925, p. 32.

130. *Kavanaugh Brief,* pp. 58–59; *Guthrie Brief,* p. 23 (quotation); *Brief for American Jewish Committee,* p. 7; *Episcopal Brief,* pp. 4–9 (quotation from p. 5).

131. William D. Guthrie to John J. Burke, Oct. 22, 1923, USCC Records, Box 14.

132. William D. Guthrie to James Hugh Ryan, Feb. 20, 1925, USCC Records, Box 14.

133. *Brief on Behalf of Appellee, I (Guthrie Brief),* pp. 87–89; *Brief on Behalf of Appellee, II (Kavanaugh Brief),* pp. 68–83.

134. John J. Burke to Thomas F. O'Mara, Mar. 25, 1925, USCC Records, Box 14.

135. *Oregon School Cases,* pp. 453–54.

136. *Pierce, Governor of Oregon, et al. v. Society of Sisters, Pierce, Governor of Oregon, et al. v. Hill Military Academy,* 268 U.S. 510, 531 (1922).

137. 268 U.S. 510, 534.

138. 268 U.S. 510, 535.

139. Arthur F. Mullen to Nelson Collins, June 10, 1925, Mullen Papers, CU.

140. Arthur F. Mullen to Francis P. Matthews, Apr. 13, 1937, Mullen Papers, CU.

141. William D. Guthrie, "The Oregon School Law," *Columbia,* June 1924, p. 5; Guthrie to Mullen, July 1, 1925.

142. *Literary Digest,* June 13, 1925, pp. 7–8.

143. "Oregon School Law Invalid" (editorial), *Journal of Education* 101 (June 4, 1925): 652; Bruere, "Supreme Court on Educational Freedom," p. 380.

144. William D. Guthrie to John J. Burke, Mar. 18, 1925, USCC Records, Box 14.

145. John J. Burke to Thomas F. O'Mara, June 10, 1925, USCC Archives, Box 14; Burke to J. P. Kavanaugh, June 10, 1925, ibid.

146. Thomas F. O'Mara to John J. Burke, July 1, 1925, USCC Records, Box 14.

147. "The Supreme Court Speaks," *America,* June 13, 1925, p. 208.

Chapter 9

1. Sandra E. Wagner-Seavey, "The Effect of World War I on the German Community in Hawaii," *Hawaiian Journal of History* 14 (1980): 109–34.

2. Frank F. Chuman, *The Bamboo People: The Law and Japanese-Americans* (Del Mar, Calif.: Publisher's, 1976), pp. 33–36, 46–51, 75, 76–80.

3. *Ozawa v. United States,* 260 U.S. 178 (1922).

4. *Farrington v. Tokushige,* 273 U.S. 283, 290–91 (1927).

5. Koichi Glenn Harada, "A Survey of the Japanese Language Schools in Hawaii" (Master's thesis, University of Hawaii, 1934), pp. 51–52, 34, 44, 77–78.

6. John N. Hawkins, "Politics, Education, and Language Policy: The Case of Japanese Language Schools in Hawaii," *Amerasia* 5 (1978): 47.

7. "Foreign Language Schools in Hawaii," *New Age,* July 1920, pp. 309–10.

8. Hawkins, "Japanese Language Schools," p. 46.

9. *A Survey of Education in Hawaii* (1920), p. 134.

10. "New Way to Kill Foreign Schools," *Honolulu Star-Bulletin,* Nov. 12, 1920, p. 1, col. 8; "Holstein Urges Quick Action on Foreign Schools," ibid., Nov. 16, 1920, p. 1, col. 4; "Move on in House to Kill Schools," ibid., Nov. 19, 1920, p. 1, col. 4; "Senate Committee in Favor of Adoption of Foreign Language Bill," *Pacific Commercial Advertiser,* Nov. 19, 1920, p. 1, col. 4 (quotation).

11. "Senate Is Urged to Pass Language Schools Law Now," *Honolulu Star-Bulletin,* Nov. 18, 1920, p. 1, col. 2 (quotation); "Moderation or Radicalism?" (editorial), ibid., Nov. 20, 1920, p. 6, col. 2; "Regulate Language Schools, Not Abolish Them, Is Final Decision of Commerce Body," ibid., Nov. 16, 1920, p. 6, col. 3.

12. "Foreign Schools To Be Regulated," *Honolulu Star-Bulletin,* Nov. 23, 1920, p. 1, col. 1.

13. *A Brief Survey of the Foreign Language School Question* (Honolulu: 1923) (no author identified), pp. 1–3; "A Statement by the Japanese Committee in Regard to the Curtailment of the First Grades" (Appendix A), ibid., pp. 7–8; "Petition Presented by the Attorney for the Japanese Society of Hawaii" (Appendix I), ibid., pp. 18–19; "Petition by the Directors of the Japanese Society" (Appendix H), ibid., pp. 14–16.

14. "A Statement by American Members of the Joint Committee on Revision of Japanese Language School Text Books" (Appendix B), in *Brief Survey,* pp. 8–9.

15. "Letter to the Chairman of Committee on Welfare Work from the Joint Committee" (Appendix F), in *Brief Survey,* pp. 12–13; "Reply from the Chairman of the Committee on Welfare Work" (Appendix G), ibid., pp. 13–14.

16. "Petition by the Directors of the Japanese Society."

17. "Petition Presented by the Attorney for the Japanese Society of Hawaii" (Appendix I), in *Brief Survey,* pp. 16–24 (quotations from p. 24).

18. Ibid.

19. "Statement by the Governor" (Appendix J), in *Brief Survey*.

20. "Statement by the Department," in *Brief Survey*.

21. "Only One Sound Policy," *Honolulu Star-Bulletin,* Nov. 20, 1922, p. 6, col. 1.

22. "Petition Presented by the Attorney," p. 23.

23. Ibid., p. 5; "Statement Disapproving the Test Suit by the Japanese" (Appendix K), in *Brief Survey*, p. 27.

24. "Temporary Injunction as Modified by Judge Banks" (Appendix M), in *Brief Survey,* pp. 32–33.

25. "Opinion Expressed by Judge Banks of the Circuit Court in His Decision in the Test Suit" (Appendix L), in *Brief Survey,* pp. 27–32.

26. *Farrington v. Tokushige,* 11 F.2d 710–15 (1926).

27. *Petitioners' Brief, Farrington v. Tokushige,* pp. 2, 3–5, 11–13; *Petition for Writ of Certiorari and Brief in Support Thereof, Farrington v. Tokushige,* pp. 9–10.

28. *Petitioners' Brief,* pp. 8–9, 23–24, 39; *Petition for Writ of Certiorari,* p. 19.

29. *Petitioners' Brief,* pp. 19–23; *Petition for Writ of Certiorari,* pp. 15–22.

30. *Respondents' Brief, Farrington v. Tokushige,* pp. 51–54, 55; *Brief of Respondents, Farrington v. Tokushige* (on motion for writ of certiorari), pp. 7, 8, 4–5.

31. *Respondents' Brief,* pp. 56–57, 64; *Brief of Respondents,* pp. 9–10.

32. *Farrington v. Tokushige,* 273 U.S. 284 (1927).

33. 273 U.S. at 298, 299.

34. *Honolulu Advertiser,* Feb. 23, 1927, p. 12, col. 1.

35. Harada, "Survey of the Japanese Language Schools," pp. 73, 84.

Chapter 10

1. Author's interviews with Raymond Parpart and Clarence Heiden, Hampton, Nebraska, June 27, 1990; *One Hundredth Anniversary, 1873–1973, Zion Evangelical Lutheran Church* (privately published by Zion Church, 1973), pp. 8, 36.

2. Robert T. Meyer to Arthur F. Mullen, Apr. 29, 1938, Mullen Papers, Creighton University, Omaha, Nebraska.

3. Parpart interview.

4. 261 U.S. 525 (1923). Although the law made explicit reference to the relationship between wages and the health and morals of women, the Court held that the statute deprived women of the right to work for any wages that they wished to accept. Taft, Sanford, and Holmes dissented, and Brandeis recused himself from deliberation.

5. Klaus H. Heberle, "From Gitlow to Near: Judicial 'Amendment' by Absent-Minded Incrementalism," *Journal of Politics* 34 (1972): 465; Charles Warren, "The

New 'Liberty' under the Fourteenth Amendment," *Harvard Law Review* 39 (1926): 454; Comment, "The Supreme Court's Attitude toward Liberty of Contract and Freedom of Speech," *Yale Law Journal* 41 (1931): 269; Leo Pfeffer, *This Honorable Court* (Boston: Beacon Press, 1965), pp. 283–84.

6. Papers of Louis D. Brandeis, Harvard Law School Library, Part 2, Reel 33 (notebook entitled "Chatham," p. 19). The same reel contains a Library of Congress transcript of the conversation. This transcript has some errors, particularly the use of the phrase "Right to appeal" rather than "Right to speech" at the head of the list of protected freedoms.

7. Frankfurter explains in his notes on the conversation that "there may be some aspects of property that are fundamental—but not regard as fundamental specific limitations upon it. Whereas right to your education & to utter speech is fundamental *except* clear and present danger." Ibid., p. 20.

8. 268 U.S. 652, 666 (1925).

9. See Heberle, "From Gitlow to Near.".

10. *Prudential Life Insurance Co. v. Cheek,* 259 U.S. 530, 542–43 (1922).

11. *Gilbert v. Minnesota,* 254 U.S. 325, 332, 343 (1921).

12. Mark DeWolfe Howe, *The Garden and the Wilderness: Religion and Government in American Constitutional History* (Chicago: University of Chicago Press, 1965), p. 122.

13. "Islam and the Oregon Public School Law, " *American Bar Association Journal* 12 (Nov. 1926): 753–57.

14. Carl Zollmann, "Parental Rights and the Fourteenth Amendment," *Marquette Law Review* 8 (1923): 57–58.

15. Although the appellees in the second *McKelvie* case had stated in their brief to the Nebraska Supreme Court that the Norval Act violated their right to free speech under the federal and Nebraska constitutions, the appellees did not elucidate this point. *Brief of Appellees, Nebraska District of Evangelical Lutheran Synod v. McKelvie,* 262 U.S. 404 (1923), pp. 5–6. The state pointed out to the Nebraska Supreme Court that the First Amendment's guarantee of free speech acted only as a limitation on the powers of Congress. *Brief of Appellants, McKelvie,* 262 U.S. 404, p. 66. The state argued that the Nebraska constitution's guarantee of freedom of speech could not be construed "to authorize profanity or a foreign language." Ibid., pp. 66–67.

16. Stephen Arons, "The Separation of Church and State: *Pierce* Reconsidered," *Harvard Educational Review* 46 (Feb. 1976): 96–97.

17. *Griswold v. Connecticut,* 381 U.S. 479 (1965).

18. *Tinker v. Des Moines Independent Community School District,* 393 U.S. 506 (1969).

19. Philip Bobbitt, *Constitutional Fate: Theory of the Constitution* (New York: Oxford University Press, 1982), pp. 239–40.

20. Arthur F. Mullen, *Western Democrat* (New York: Funk, 1940), p. 226.

21. See e.g., John Hart Ely, *Democracy and Distrust: A Theory of Judicial Review* (Cambridge: Harvard University Press, 1980), pp. 14–21; Robert H. Bork, *The Tempting of America: The Political Seduction of the Law* (New York: Free Press, 1990), p. 225; *Planned Parenthood of Southeastern Pennsylvania v. Casey*, 112 S.Ct. 2883 (1992) (Justice Antonin Scalia, concurring in part and dissenting in part).

22. Howe, *Garden and the Wilderness*, p. 124.

23. Mullen, *Western Democrat*, pp. 224–25.

24. These cases included *Bailey v. Drexel Furniture Co.*, 259 U.S. 20 (1922) (invalidating the second federal child labor law); *Duplex Printing Press Co. v. Deering*, 254 U.S. 443 (1921) (applying the antitrust laws to certain labor union activities); *United Mine Workers v. Coronado Coal Co.*, 259 U.S. 344 (1922) (sustaining antitrust action against a labor union for property damages incurred during a strike); *Truax v. Corrigan*, 257 U.S. 312 (1921) (invalidating an Arizona statute that restricted the use of injunctions against striking employees); and *Eisner v. Macomber*, 252 U.S. 189 (1920) (excluding stock dividends from income subject to taxation).

25. The full text of Sen. La Follette's address was published in *Congressional Record*, 67th Cong., 2d Sess. (June 21, 1922), 62:9076–82.

26. S. 4483, 67th Cong., 4th Sess. (1923).

27. William G. Ross, *A Muted Fury: Populists, Progressives, and Labor Unions Confront the Courts, 1890–1937* (Princeton: Princeton University Press, 1994), pp. 227–32, 234–41.

28. "Address of the Chief Justice Taft," *American Bar Association Journal* 9 (June 1923): 348–52 (quotation from 352); *New York Times*, May 31, 1923, p. 14, col. 8.

29. William Howard Taft to Caspar S. Yost, Sept. 11, 1924, Taft Papers, Series 3, Reel 267, Manuscript Division, Library of Congress; Taft to Calvin Coolidge, Sept. 16, 1924, ibid.

30. La Follette Family Papers, Manuscript Division, Library of Congress, Series B, Box 228 (Detroit speech, Oct. 9, 1924, p. 9; Chicago speech, Oct. 11, 1924, pp. 12–13; Omaha speech, Oct. 20, 1924, p. 24).

31. Mark Sullivan, "Looking Back on La Follette," *World's Work*, Jan. 1925, p. 331; *New Republic* (editorial), Nov. 5, 1924, p. 235; Kenneth C. MacKay, *The Progressive Movement of 1924* (New York: Columbia University Press, 1947), p. 160. For a fuller discussion of attempts during the 1920s to curb the judiciary's power and the role of the Court issue in the 1924 presidential campaign, see Ross, *Muted Fury*, chaps. 9, 10, 11, and 12.

32. See Joseph Alsop and Turner Catledge, *The 168 Days* (1937; reprint, New York: DeCapo Press, 1973), p. 73. Opposition, however, was not at all monolithic. See James J. Kenneally, "Catholicism and the Supreme Court Reorganization Proposal of 1937," *Journal of Church and State* 25 (Autumn 1983): 469–89.

33. Leo J. Hoban to W. E. Borah, Mar. 16, 1937, W. E. Borah Papers, Box 483, Manuscript Division, Library of Congress.

34. "Freedom of Contract" (editorial), *The Survey,* June 15, 1923, p. 317.

35. *The Survey* (editorial), Apr. 15, 1925, p. 77.

36. Felix Frankfurter, "Can the Supreme Court Guarantee Toleration?" (unsigned editorial), *New Republic,* June 17, 1925, pp. 85–87, reprinted in Philip B. Kurland, ed., *Felix Frankfurter on the Supreme Court: Extrajudicial Essays on the Court and the Constitution* (Cambridge: Harvard University Press, 1970), pp. 174–78.

37. "The Downfall of the Oregon Law," *America,* June 16, 1923, p. 207; John Wiltbye, "Is the Oregon Law Dead?" *America,* June 23, 1923, pp. 237–38.

38. See William J. Brennan, Jr., "State Constitutions and the Protection of Individual Rights," *Harvard Law Review* 90 (Jan. 1977): 489–504.

39. Kenneth B. O'Brien, Jr., "Education, Americanization, and the Supreme Court: The 1920's," *American Quarterly* 13 (1961): 165–66.

40. Cf. Paul L. Murphy, *The Constitution in Crisis Times, 1918–1969* (New York: Harper & Row, 1972), pp. 83–84.

41. 268 U.S. 652, 666 n. 9.

42. See e.g., *Washington ex rel. Seattle Trust Co. v. Roberge,* 278 U.S. 116, 121–23 (1928) (invalidating a zoning ordinance provision making the right to maintain a home for aged persons within a particular district dependent on the consent of owners of two-thirds of the property within four hundred feet of the proposed building); *Louis K. Liggett Co. v. Baldridge,* 278 U.S. 105, 113–14 (1928) (invalidating a Pennsylvania statute that required all owners of stock in a corporation operating a pharmacy to be registered pharmacists); *Weaver v. Palmer Bros Co.,* 270 U.S. 402, 415 (1926) (invalidating a Pennsylvania statute prohibiting the use of reclaimed wool in the manufacture of bedding to prevent deception); *Yu Cong Eng v. Trinidad,* 271 U.S. 25, 526 (1926) (invalidating a Philippine statute requiring Chinese merchants to keep their books in English or Spanish); *Charles Wolff Packing Co. v. Court of Industrial Relations,* 262 U.S. 522, 544 (1923) (invalidating a Kansas statute authorizing an administrative board to fix the hours of labor in industries related to food, clothing, and fuel when a labor and management dispute threatened production).

43. *United States v. Carolene Products Co.,* 304 U.S. 144, 152 n. 4 (1938).

44. Laurence H. Tribe, *American Constitutional Law,* 2d ed. (Mineola, N.Y.: Foundation Press, 1988), pp. 1318–19.

45. *Griswold v. Connecticut,* 381 U.S. 479 (1965).

46. 381 U.S. 482–83.

47. *Carey v. Population Services,* 431 U.S. 678, 684–85 (1977).

48. *Thornburgh v. American College of Obstetricians and Gynecologists,* 476 U.S. 747, 772 (1986).

49. 476 U.S. 792.

50. John Hart Ely, "The Supreme Court 1977 Term, Foreword: On Discovering Fundamental Values," *Harvard Law Review* 92 (Nov. 1978): 5, 11 n. 40.

51. *Bowers v. Hardwick,* 478 U.S. 186, 190–91 (1986).

52. *Planned Parenthood of Southeastern Pennsylvania v. Casey,* 112 S. Ct. 2791, 2806 (1992).

53. Ibid., p. 2860 (Chief Justice William H. Rehnquist and Justices Byron R. White, Antonin Scalia, and Clarence Thomas concurring in part and dissenting in part).

54. *Wisconsin v. Yoder,* 406 U.S. 205, 213–14 (1972).

55. David M. Smolin, "The Jurisprudence of Privacy in a Splintered Supreme Court," *Marquette Law Review* 75 (Summer 1992): 1064, 1052. Like the four justices in *Casey,* Smolin believes that *Roe* and similar decisions have removed *Meyer* and *Pierce* from their original moorings, which supported conservative values.

56. Barbara Bennett Woodhouse, "'Who Owns the Child?' *Meyer* and *Pierce* and the Child as Property," *William and Mary Law Review* 33 (Summer 1992): 996–1001, 1112–22, and passim.

Epilogue

1. Robert W. Bruere, "The Supreme Court on Educational Freedom," *The Survey* 54 (July 1, 1925): 381.

2. Albert Camus, *The Plague* (New York: Modern Library, 1948), p. 278.

3. "The Battle for Freedom in Michigan," *America,* Aug. 5, 1922, p. 369.

4. "Michigan's Battle for Freedom," *America,* Nov. 22, 1924, p. 141.

A Note on the Sources

Primary Sources

Several collections of documents were invaluable. The Theodore Graebner Papers at the Concordia Historical Institute in Clayton, Missouri, provide rich and abundant insights into the suppression of German language and culture during the First World War, the enactment of legal restrictions on the use of foreign languages after the war, and the judicial challenges to the language laws. Graebner acted as a sort of clearing-house for information about the travails of the German-American Lutheran communities throughout the United States. As editor of the *Lutheran Witness* and a prominent scholar, he naturally conducted a far-flung correspondence, and he also voluntarily collected information for the Bureau of Investigation about the harassment of German Americans. Previously neglected in studies of the language disputes, the Graebner correspondence is extensive and includes frank and confidential discussions about such controversial subjects as the loyalty of German Americans, the condition of parochial schools, and the practical difficulties of asserting constitutional rights in the face of mob violence and official coercion. The Graebner Papers also provide a unique source of legislative history about the enactment of statutes that restricted the use of foreign languages, since many correspondents informed Graebner about the details of the legislative processes in various states. The Concordia Historical Institute also holds a small and largely insignificant collection of the papers of Pastor C. F. Brommer.

The files of the United States Catholic Conference at the Catholic University of America in Washington, D.C., provide important insights into the Roman Catholic challenge to Oregon's compulsory public education law. In particular, the correspondence of National Catholic Welfare Conference officials and attorneys explores the scope and contour of Catholic fears about the menace to parochial education and offers a detailed explanation of the church's litigation strategy. These collections became available to scholars only recently. Thomas J. Shelley used them effectively in "The Oregon School Case and the National Catholic Welfare Conference," *Catholic Historical Review* 75 (July 1989): 439–57. Future students of the *Pierce* will ignore the Catholic University collections at their peril.

The Arthur F. Mullen Papers at Creighton University in Omaha yield little information about Mullen's work on the *Meyer* case that was not provided in his autobiography, *Western Democrat* (New York: Funk, 1940). The files contain various drafts of that book, copies of briefs and other official papers related to *Meyer* that are available at the Nebraska State Historical Society, correspondence, and drafts of various memoranda and articles in which Mullen attempted to glorify his role in the case. The only gem in the collection is a 1938 letter to Mullen in which Robert T. Meyer discussed the background and significance of *Meyer*.

The Council of Defense files at the Nebraska State Historical Society in Lincoln provide extensive documentation of the council's role in investigating and harassing German Americans. The files include minutes of council meetings, press releases, correspondence to and from persons who had run afoul of the council, and letters to and from persons who questioned the loyalty of their German-American neighbors. The Historical Society also has records of the legislative history of the enactment of the Siman and Norval acts which provide more information than one usually is able to obtain about state statutes of such a distant time.

The Nebraska State Historical Society also houses microfilms of the congregational records of the Zion Lutheran Church. The minutes, which alternatively were kept by Robert T. Meyer and Carl Firnhaber, the teacher at Zion's North School, are handwritten in the old German schrift. Although they are difficult to read and often cryptic, they nevertheless provide a few useful tidbits about the background of the *Meyer* case. The originals are available at the Zion Lutheran Church in Hampton, Nebraska.

The records of the Iowa State Council of National Defense are contained in the papers of H. J. Metcalf, who served as secretary of the council. These papers, located in the State Historical Society of Iowa, Iowa City, are much less numerous than are the records of the Nebraska Council of Defense, but they nevertheless provide useful insights into the widespread anti-German animus that led to the repression of the German language in Iowa.

The files of the Commission of Public Safety at the Minnesota Historical Society in St. Paul provide extensive documentation about the controversy over the use of the German language in this heavily German state.

The Oregon Historical Society in Portland holds only one significant set of primary materials concerning the Oregon school law, a useful file collected by the Lutheran Schools Committee. The file also includes documents concerning the Michigan school initiatives. In addition, the library has a copy of the *Old Cedar School*, the remarkable Ku Klux Klan tract in support of the Oregon law; a collection of theses and dissertations concerning the school law; and various contemporary Oregon periodicals. The Oregon State Archives in Eugene have a file of correspondence concerning the tangled negotiations for the selection of the state's counsel in the *Pierce* case.

Secondary Sources

Several periodicals were particularly useful in preparing this book. The *Lincoln Daily Star* and *Evening State Journal* provide extensive information about the growing anti-German animus in wartime Nebraska, and the *Des Moines Register* offers similar information for Iowa. The Jesuit periodical *America* has a wealth of information and commentary about attacks on the parochial schools, and the Masonic publication *New Age* offers significant insights into the psychology and strategies of the proponents of compulsory public education.

The historical antecedents of the educational controversies that are the subject of this book are ably presented in Lloyd P. Jorgenson, *The State and the Non-Public School, 1825–1925* (Columbia: University of Missouri Press, 1987). Carl F. Kaestle, *Pillars of the Republic: Common Schools and American Society, 1780–1860* (New York: Hill & Wang, 1983), also provides useful information and valuable insights. For an understanding of the history of American nativism, John Higham's trenchant *Strangers in the Land: Patterns of American Nativism, 1860–1925*, 2d ed. (New Brunswick, N.J.: Rutgers University Press, 1988), originally published in 1955, remains indispensable. Also useful is David H. Bennett, *The Party of Fear: From Nativist Movements to the New Right in American History* (Chapel Hill: University of North Carolina Press, 1988).

The attacks on German Americans and their culture during the First World War are comprehensively explored and analyzed in Frederick C. Luebke, *Bonds of Loyalty: German Americans and World War I* (DeKalb: Northern Illinois University Press, 1974). Luebke, the dean of historians of German America, has authored other works that were useful in the preparation of this book, especially "Legal Restrictions on Foreign Languages in the Great Plains States, 1917–1923," in Paul Schach, ed., *Languages in Conflict* (Lincoln: University of Nebraska Press, 1980). David M. Kennedy, *Over Here: The First World War and American Society* (New York: Oxford University Press, 1980), and Stephen L. Vaughn, *Holding Fast the Inner Lines: Democracy, Nationalism, and the Committee on Public Information* (Chapel Hill: University of North

Carolina Press, 1980), say little about hostility toward German Americans but provide useful analyses and accounts of the psychology and logistics of the war effort. Paul L. Murphy, *World War I and the Origin of Civil Liberties in the United States* (New York: Norton, 1979), helps to place the language laws in the broader context of the suppression of rights during the war and the judicial expansion of the right of free speech after the war. Nancy Derr, "The Babel Proclamation," *Palimpsest* 60 (July/Aug. 1979): 99–115, provides a fine account of the anti-German hysteria in Iowa, the state in which the *Bartels* case arose.

The *Meyer* case itself has received remarkably little attention from historians and legal scholars. Several short studies of the general background of case appeared more than two decades ago, particularly Robert N. Manley, "Language, Loyalty, and Liberty: The Nebraska State Council of Defense and the Lutheran Churches, 1917–1918," *Concordia Historical Institute Quarterly* 27 (Apr. 1964): 1–16; Thomas O'Brien Hanley, "A Western Democrat's Quarrel with the Language Laws," *Nebraska History* 50 (Summer 1969): 151–71; and Jack W. Rodgers, "The Foreign Language Issue in Nebraska, 1918–23," *Nebraska History* 39 (Mar. 1958): 1–22. My article, "A Judicial Janus: Meyer v. Nebraska in Historical Perspective," *University of Cincinnati Law Review* 57 (1988): 125–204, was the first detailed study of *Meyer* and its companion cases. While this book was in progress, Barbara Bennett Woodhouse published an important article, "'Who Owns the Child?' *Meyer* and *Pierce* and the Child as Property," *William and Mary Law Review* 33 (Summer 1992): 995–1122, which helps to place *Meyer* and *Pierce* in a broad historical and legal context and offers fresh insights into their significance.

In contrast to the language laws, the Michigan campaigns for compulsory public education have received considerable scholarly attention. Three recent articles provide useful information and analysis: Timothy Mark Pies, "The Parochial School Campaigns in Michigan, 1920–1924: The Lutheran and Catholic Involvement," *Catholic Historical Review* 72 (Apr. 1986): 222–38; Thomas Elton Brown, "Patriotism or Religion? Compulsory Public Education and Michigan's Roman Catholic Church, 1920–1924," *Michigan History* 64 (July/Aug. 1980): 38–42; and Timothy Mark Pies and Beth Ann Klemp, "Outlaw Parochial Education?," *Concordia Historical Institute Quarterly* 61 (Winter 1988): 161–71. Also useful is Thomas Francis Lewis, "A Study of Attempts to Abolish Private and Parochial Education by Constitutional Amendment in 1920 and 1924" (Master's thesis, University of Detroit, 1952).

The Oregon law has produced an abundance of studies, although Woodhouse's article is the only major attempt to connect the compulsory public education law to the language laws. The classic study of *Pierce* is David B. Tyack, "The Perils of Pluralism: The Background of the Pierce Case," *American Historical Review* 74 (1968): 74–

98. Lloyd P. Jorgenson has made useful contributions in a chapter in *The State and the Non-Public School* and in "The Oregon School Law of 1922: Passage and Sequel," 54 *Catholic Historical Review* (1968): 455–66. Also informative are M. Paul Holsinger, "The Oregon School Bill Controversy, 1922–1925," *Pacific Historical Review* 37 (1968): 327–41; David A. Horowitz, "Social Morality and Personal Revitalization: Oregon's Ku Klux Klan in the 1920s," *Oregon Historical Quarterly* 90 (Winter 1989): 365–84; and Malcolm Clark, Jr., "The Bigot Disclosed: Ninety Years of Nativism," *Oregon Historical Quarterly* 75 (June 1974): 108–90. Thomas J. Shelley, "The Oregon School Case and the National Catholic Welfare Conference," *Catholic Historical Review* 75 (July 1989): 439–57, draws on the recently available archives at Catholic University to provide valuable insights into the coordination of Roman Catholic opposition to the Oregon law. The law also has been the subject of a multitude of dissertations and theses, some of the more useful of which are cited in the notes.

There has been no major study of the Hawaiian statutes and cases. Available secondary sources are cited in the notes.

Index